IN
LOVE,
IN
SORROW

IN LOVE, IN SORROW

The Complete

Correspondence of

Charles Olson and

Edward Dahlberg

Edited, with an Introduction by,

PAUL CHRISTENSEN

PARAGON HOUSE ■ New York

First edition, 1990
Published in the United States by
Paragon House
90 Fifth Avenue
New York, NY 10011

Designed by Irving Perkins Associates

Manufactured in the United States of America

Library of Congress Cataloging-in-Publication Data

Olson, Charles, 1910–1970.
    In love, in sorrow : the complete correspondence of Charles Olson
and Edward Dahlberg / edited with an introduction by Paul
Christensen.
        p.   cm.
    ISBN 1-55778-202-4
    1. Olson, Charles, 1910–1970—Correspondence. 2. Dahlberg,
Edward, 1900–1977—Correspondence. 3. Poets, American—20th
century—Correspondence. 4. Authors, American—20th century—
Correspondence. I. Dahlberg, Edward, 1900–1977. II. Christensen,
Paul, 1943–   . III. Title.
PS3529.L655Z484   1990
811'.54—dc20
[B]   89-39244
                                                          CIP

INTRODUCTION

When Charles Olson first met Edward Dahlberg, it was not without its ironies and foreshadowings, like the beginning of a long, leisurely nineteenth-century novel. Olson was a tall, gangling twenty-five-year-old academic, an English instructor at Clark University in Worcester, Massachusetts, who had heard that Dahlberg was spending some time in Gloucester, where Olson worked in the summers as a letter carrier. He had read Dahlberg's first novel, *Bottom Dogs* (1929), and had decided to call upon him the Sunday evening of August 9, 1936. It was eight o'clock when Olson knocked and had his name sent up to Dahlberg's room. In the front parlor two local painters were having their weekly social as a player piano tinkled away off-key. Olson bided his time while he waited for Dahlberg to appear, but Dahlberg remained in his room. A little after midnight, Dahlberg was informed that his visitor was still waiting on the front porch, and he rushed down to apologize and to welcome him in. For four hours the two men sat engaged in an excited discussion about Melville and Shakespeare, as Olson related the information he had gleaned from studying Melville's notes and marginalia in his edition of the plays. When Olson left the boardinghouse, Dahlberg was vividly impressed with Olson, whom he valued from the start as his protégé and confidant.

Dahlberg had come to Gloucester, a small summer resort and fishing village on the coast of Cape Ann, to get away from the dog days in New York and to rethink his direction as a writer. The year before he had been turned down for a Guggenheim fellowship to work on a new novel, but now he was started on a book of essays in which he intended to attack not only the contemporary state of fiction but his own novels as well. As John Cech notes in his study of their relationship, *Charles Olson and Edward Dahlberg: A Portrait of a Friendship* (1982), hearing from Olson of Melville's use of Shakespeare prompted the main thesis of Dahlberg's critical essays in *Can These Bones Live* (1941): too many American writers shunned the great tradition of Western classics in their obsession to be original.

Dahlberg's conversations with Olson that summer shook him out of his literary malaise into a productive new career as critic, first of American literature, and soon after of American culture and civilization. The key to his insights turned on the premise that a writer's strengths lay in his or her grasp of the past, with its store of insights and perfected forms ready for use in new writing. America's desire to be separate from the past and from the Old

World had, Dahlberg believed, provoked the mediocre literature of experiment and so-called technical innovation he frankly despised. And though he believed there was need for a core of tradition in contemporary literature, Dahlberg rejected Anglo-American writing as a provincial and derivative result of drawing from only one small area of Christian culture to the exclusion of all the rest of European and classical art. All of America's mistakes as a culture and a society could be laid at the threshold of its refusal to remember the ancient past or to model its ideals upon what had already been nobly achieved.

The lanky, six-foot-seven Olson who had come to call on Dahlberg was also at a crossroads in his life. He had decided to return to graduate school to study with F. O. Matthiessen at Harvard, rather than continue teaching at Clark University. His father, Karl Olson, had died the year before, and though he was on his own now, his only goal that summer was to continue to work on the Melville papers, an interest that had earlier won him an Olin Fellowship to Yale through the poet Wilbert Snow, his professor at Wesleyan University. Olson seemed riddled with doubts; a brief experience as a Gloucester fisherman on the *Doris M. Hawes* had told him that he was not cut out for a life at sea, and now, as a summer letter carrier, he was following briefly in his father's footsteps, though he had not been all that close to his father. Indeed, his father's death had left him with some unresolved conflicts in their relationship that would later surface in his poems and the few short stories he attempted. Walking into Dahlberg's life that August evening may have given him a new sense of career as well as a mentor who, after a few hours of engrossing talk about literature, was only too willing to play a fatherly role in his life.

A friendship formed in that initial, late-night meeting in East Gloucester; each seemed to fulfill a need in the other. No sooner was Olson enrolled at Harvard to begin doctoral work than he began receiving a patter of letters of fatherly advice and counsel from Dahlberg. The first postcard of this correspondence shows Dahlberg's concern for Olson's health, and gives a gentle nudge to "start work on the Melville book," along with the warning that "inaction spawns inferiority." Here in gist are some of the central themes of Dahlberg's letters to his protégé: the paternal goading and cajoling he tirelessly expressed throughout their twenty-year friendship, and an impatience with Olson's fitful energies and occasional lapses into utter lassitude. "I believe in you," he tells Olson, an endorsement and encouragement he generously lavished on his friend many times over the years. The strength of the relationship was mainly psychological, rooted in the roles they filled for each other as father and son. But where this relation served well to sustain the two men emotionally, it concealed and frustrated their growing intellectual differences, and inhibited Olson from dealing openly with his objections to Dahlberg's views, until it was too late to come to a renewed understanding.

The relationship suffered three important shocks before it ended in 1955 in bitterness and vituperation. The first came in 1940, when Olson had completed the first drafts of his "Melville" book, the version that Dahlberg found too derivative of his own style and too green as critical discourse. The reader will get a taste of Dahlberg's critical methods with Olson from the letter of July 16, 1940, the only such letter of editorial advice that survives from this stage of their friendship. Olson had been staying in Dahlberg's apartment on his visits from Gloucester, where he now lived with his mother. The decision to move to New York in February 1940 precipitated a bitter confrontation with Dahlberg when Olson insisted on putting their friendship on a less intimate footing, to give Olson more room to develop his own direction as a writer. Dahlberg perceived this move as a slight and broke off the relationship altogether; hence, the first long break in the correspondence after Dahlberg's letter of August 1, 1940.

Seven years later, Dahlberg renews the correspondence (April 9, 1947) on hearing of the publication of Olson's *Call Me Ishmael*, on which he offers hearty congratulations. But no sooner was there a thaw than Olson procrastinated in responding, and Dahlberg gives his friend a verbal thrashing in return. In actuality, Olson was reluctant to reply, perhaps dreading the resumption of what may have seemed to him a confining, demanding relationship. Dahlberg warmed slowly and eventually the friendship was resumed—amid a few spats—until their crisis over a review of *The Flea of Sodom* in 1950 erupted and deeply wounded both men.

The letters that go beyond August 1950 lose the intensity, camaraderie, and warmth of earlier correspondence, as Dahlberg reluctantly gives up his hold upon Olson and begins treating him as an equal, a literary colleague on whom to make few or no claims; gradually the friendship withered for lack of any nurturing interests. By 1950, however, both writers had formed close new friends with whom to share their intimacies about writing and publishing. Though Olson accepted the final break between them, and ceased to mention Dahlberg thereafter, Dahlberg continued to brood upon the friendship with increasing bitterness, considering its end one of the great betrayals of his emotionally chaotic life. Dahlberg's deep affection for Olson had come to be fused with memories of his parents and his anguished childhood, the stuff of his fiction and memoirs. The loss of Olson became associated with the pain of other emotional losses: the breakup of the family in 1907, and again in 1912, when he began a five-year residence in the Jewish Orphan Asylum in

Cleveland; his mother Lizzie's death in 1946, just prior to renewing his friendship with Olson; later, with the loss of his two sons, Geoffrey and Joel, when he separated from his wife Winifred. The theme running through all these (and other lesser) crises in Dahlberg's life is loss, isolation, the broken thread of family or friendship. Olson was not spared Dahlberg's profound bitterness because he stood for a history of anguished losses—and Dahlberg preferred to think it was not only Olson's fault that their friendship had failed, but that it was his malevolent nature to have wanted it to.

There was little Olson could do to rebut the growing stream of accusations that characterize Dahlberg's letters after their renewed friendship in 1947. Almost everyone who writes about Dahlberg observes—with some discomfort—that he was a difficult, demanding individual, suspicious of even his closest friends, most of whom he had grievously insulted one time or another over the course of their relations. Even Sir Herbert Read, who had replaced Olson as his closest friend, came under the glare of Dahlberg's ire, as Charles deFanti writes in his biography of Dahlberg, *The Wages of Expectation* (1978), an unflattering portrait of a man grimly tortured by his emotional hunger, and intemperately vengeful and abusive when he thought others misused him. When Read, his last champion and collaborator in literary affairs, was the victim of Dahlberg's wrathful assaults, Read responded in exasperation, "What is my role in this exchange of letters? To be *advocatus diaboli* and to find some few virtues, some extenuating circumstances, to throw into the scales you have so heavily weighted in your wrath?" (*Truth Is More Sacred*, p. 57). Though their friendship survived through Read's lingering illness and death, deFanti notes flatly that "Dahlberg reacted with only mild interest when notified of his old friend's passing" (p. 233).

But Olson was, in some respects, guilty of little lapses in obligation, and showed at times a maddening disregard for the punctilios of friendship so keenly observed by Dahlberg. Weeks would pass before Olson would jot a hastily scribbled note or brief reply to Dahlberg's decorously crafted epistles, those "missives" he lavished such care in writing to impress his protégé. Olson would occasionally rise to sustained eloquence or intellectual brilliance in replies, or avidly engage Dahlberg on new topics of interest, but no sooner did the correspondence warm with luminous exchanges than Olson would become mired in activities at Black Mountain College or lapse into one of his debilitating moods at home in Washington. Dahlberg wanted their letters to sizzle and galvanize their relationship, to be a dialogue between poets instead of the sometimes drably practical, erratic exchanges that characterize stretches of their correspondence.

For Olson's part, he much preferred playing the role of master with other correspondents—in particular, Cid Corman, editor of *Origin*, and with Robert Creeley, who edited the Divers Press in Majorca and later joined Olson at Black Mountain. In those letters, Olson was freer to speak his mind, to indulge in verbal pyrotechnics and even, at times, some bullying tactics he had learned—perhaps—from feeling the lash of Dahlberg, and earlier, of Ezra Pound. Had Dahlberg read a little more subtly into the subtext of Olson's *Call Me Ishmael*, he might have discerned an identification with Ishmael that would have told him a little of Olson's frustrations with the surrogate fathers, the Ahabs, in his life. Ishmael, like the mythological son Enceladus, had his utmost ordeal in attempting to overthrow the parent to become a man himself. Olson lived those harrowing challenges in his effort to outdo Pound at the long poem, and to out-master Dahlberg. Letting go of his obligations with Dahlberg from time to time allowed Olson to experience the freedom he required in that relationship; but the reader will notice that Dahlberg chose those very opportunities to rein in his errant pupil, often with a verbal birching that would leave Olson either apologetic or apoplectic.

Dahlberg has no comment on Olson's fascination with battlefields, fallen armies, the remains of conflict still vivid at the Civil War sites he visited in Virginia on the weekends in July 1950. But even here the theme of the frustrated son is just below the surface—the horror of youths rushing to their deaths under paternal officers. The death of youth haunted Olson throughout his work, in such poems as "There Was a Youth Whose Name Was Thomas Granger," executed for the charge of bestiality in early New England; to the young sailor of the *Maximus* poems, who played toreador to a young bull-calf and died gored in a pasture at Dogtown, behind Gloucester. Soldiers, sailors, Ishmael, the pattern is of a son who can only reach manhood through the ordeal of facing death. The father stood as the impediment to that goal, sometimes as the enemy to be vanquished.

A month before visiting the Virginia battlefields Olson wrote one of his most formidable poems in the projective mode, "In Cold Hell, In Thicket," where a figure stands gripped by fear and indecision as he relives the terror of history around him in a snow-covered battlefield, struggling to summon the will to move on in his own embattled, confused life. Even in "I, Mencius," Olson is a son and protégé, angrily rebuking a pitiless father, Ezra Pound, in language he would use again in his defenses against Dahlberg's cruel attacks over a review he had failed to write for *The Flea of Sodom*. As an apprentice to the art of writing, Olson felt he served cruel masters.

These letters are the drama of two American writers locked in a struggle over their views of contemporary society and culture that eventually dragged everything else of importance between them into its irreconcilable conflict. Before it is over, the reader inexorably becomes a member of the jury on whom the burden of reaching a verdict finally rests. Edward Dahlberg will strike many as a relentlessly demanding and self-pitying nag who took undue advantage of his role as mentor, father-surrogate, and counselor to Charles Olson to exact from him the last ounce of loyalty and devotion; there are times when Dahlberg's ploys and stratagems wear thin from repetition. At such moments, it is not hard to sympathize with a reluctant, much put-upon Olson, who comes away from some of their quarrels the more reasonable of the two defendants. But these letters will have an insidious hold upon the scrupulous reader who will want to weigh evenly the testimony of each man that it was the other who was betrayer, finagler, opportunist, reneger on the duties of friendship, or of literature. Is Olson altogether blameless when he tries to explain his inability to furnish a review for Dahlberg's *The Flea of Sodom?* Are his explanations entirely candid, or was he holding back from fear of associating himself with a book that denounced the liberal establishment in New York? This is Dahlberg's charge against Olson, and there is point to his accusation—which Olson inadequately addresses.

But the grim dispute over an unfulfilled promise is hardly the point of literary significance in these letters, even though the story of that dispute occupies almost the entire body of the correspondence from 1948 to well after their bitter falling out late in the fall of 1950. What really matters here is that both writers were moving toward writing their best work, agonizing over their principles and methods of writing as the melodrama of their suffering friendship unfolds. Each looked to the other for support as they doggedly pursued separate goals and visions in their writing. Their harsh verbal feuds unleash everything from insults and personal attacks to brilliant critiques of each other's strengths and weaknesses, as they grappled with some of the key issues defining postmodernism and with the major themes of post–World War II literature.

Both writers were in profound agreement in their diagnosis of what ailed American literature in the postwar era: the Anglo-American tradition itself, with its overtones of colonial dependency on the mother country in manners, customs, race, and class hierarchies. Such faults had been the topic of American writers ever since the American Renaissance; but the crisis of that tradition and its strong cultural bonds was brought to a head by World War II, which concluded the European struggle for imperial expansion. That left England in tatters and America as a new world power, with a choice whether to continue identifying itself racially and culturally with Britain, or with establishing some new and independent character in the world—as a force of world culture and of the world's races.

To know what was at stake in that choice, one had to go back and examine the ideology of the American Renaissance itself, when the national vision was first articulated. This is where Dahlberg and Olson both converge and depart from one another: in Olson's *Call Me Ishmael* (1947), whose early versions and drafts Dahlberg had had a hand in, Melville's portrait of Ahab as a Western hero is taken apart to expose the long history of alienation behind his aggressions against nature. Ahab's egocentricity stands for the anthropocentric nature of the West and its relentless imperialism, whereas Ishmael, the lone survivor and heir to Western life after the "fall," emerges as the new hero, a "figure of outward" whose intelligence turns away from self and back to the world. Ishmael marked the end of an epoch of human alienation that began with the migrations out of Mesopotamia and culminated in the humanistic cultures of Western Europe, of which America was a distant offshoot. Ahab was the destructive measure of Western idealism, its Lear-like protagonist, raging against a world he had come to regard as abstract and inert.

Dahlberg was a watchful and patient mentor of Olson as he ground through the early writing on this study of Melville. In 1938, when Olson published the essay "Lear and *Moby-Dick*" as part of that study, Dahlberg was jubilant. Here at last was a solid connection between a New World writer and the genius of the Old. Dahlberg had put behind him the early naturalistic novels he had been publishing since 1929. In his first, *Bottom Dogs*, D. H. Lawrence wrote in a foreword that here was a portrait of "psychic disintegration" set in America, of "cold wills functioning with a minimum of consciousness . . . brutally and deliberately unaware." There followed a second version of his autobiography in *From Flushing to Calvary* (1932), covering the early years in Kansas City and the move to Brooklyn with his mother. Both books established Dahlberg's identity as a Midwestern naturalist of the stripe of Dreiser and Sherwood Anderson, and put him squarely in the Socialist camp during the Roosevelt years. After a visit to Berlin in 1933, where Dahlberg witnessed the Reichstag Fire and was mauled in the street by anti-Semites, he rushed home to write *Those Who Perish* (1934), perhaps the first Nazi protest novel written in America. But there were lingering preoccupations with violence and "psychic disintegration" that ran all through these books, and Lawrence's foreword to *Bottom Dogs* came to haunt him as an indictment of his early canon. Looking back on those years in a letter to Allen Tate in 1962, Dahlberg remarked that "I resolved as early as '34 to be a man of letters, and to be an eremite to do so." By the time Olson met Dahlberg in the summer of 1936, he was struggling to redirect himself into a second career as a "man of letters."

It was *this* Dahlberg who labored so attentively over Olson's first efforts at criticism, perhaps as much to engage himself in the analysis of American literature as to foster the success of another writer ten years his junior. Dahlberg had started writing a new novel he called "Bitch Goddess," but quit and published only a small portion of it in the magazine *Signature*. It was the end of Dahlberg's fiction writing. The new Dahlberg emerged in his own critical study, originally entitled *Can These Bones Live;* it bears the marks of his collaboration with Olson on the ur-*Call Me Ishmael*, the version that Dahlberg denounced as too imitative and derivative of his own writing. Already the complexities of a literary relationship are bound up in the circumstances of these two books: the one aborted, put aside for five years, rewritten in blind haste over a few months in 1945, and published in 1947, the other formed partly out of the experience of Olson's struggle and early failure to complete a study on the same subject, but which Olson apparently had gone over with his own editorial pencil, as he later remarks in a letter to Dahlberg.

But *Can These Bones Live* has an importance apart from anything having to do with Olson. It is the work of a writer who had so thoroughly renounced his former self that in this new work he emerges reborn, an Ishmael himself. Dahlberg reconstructs not from Melville's epic but from the Genesis story of Hagar and Abraham, the tale of a mother and her son driven out of the father's house and left to wander the earth. Dahlberg's various retellings of his own life in the novels now found its mythical key in the persona of Ishmael, a wanderer in the deserts of America. Dahlberg had connected the Ishmael story directly to himself, and found a subtle, telling equivalent between the wide wastes of the Pacific in which Ishmael wandered with Ahab and the "macadam meadows" of America's cities, where Dahlberg had wandered with his mother. Against these contemporary wastelands Dahlberg would later contrast the lush, pastoral, pre-industrial "plains of Mamre" where Abraham, his mythical father, dwelled 4,000 years before.

Dahlberg's survey of the American Renaissance takes up where Lawrence's *Studies in Classical American Literature* (1923) and Williams' *In the American Grain* (1925) leave off. Dahlberg's book takes an even loftier perspective (merging that of Henry Adams with Randolph Bourne) by arguing that in America the last shreds of pagan faith and sensuality had perished, leaving behind the dregs of religion in Puritanism and the destructive illusion of an all-powerful State. Only two writers emerge as brave souls, Thoreau and

Randolph Bourne, who had courageously rejected the notion of the State and, in Bourne's case, exposed the aridity of a Christian faith shorn of its Hebraic (Mediterranean) roots. Dahlberg expands on Adams' perception of America as a masculine culture by pointing out the utter absence of sensual females in American writing. The pithy, gnomic prose used here was to be Dahlberg's Old Testament lyric mode thereafter—a style of highly wrought, sometimes archaic speech that grew not by paragraphs, themes, or topical links but by gists of perception butted together in brief mosaic-like structures. Such prose, composed of an eccentric, autodidact's vocabulary of obsolete, ornate, allusive terms, and a syntax arising from biblical prose, seems clumsy and pretentious at first, a rube American grandiloquence. But its oracular rhythms and its pithy aphoristic statements build the impression of a very hardheaded, stern-thinking outsider, someone out on the social borders even in matters of style and learning, as well as vision.

This was the persona Dahlberg unleashed on Olson, a bardic, salt-cured tongue out of the rich, Mediterranean past. It must have seemed at times to Olson that he conversed with a man behind a fabulous mask, a dark prophet's face that discouraged the slangy, informal rebuttals that were Olson's forte. Playing his role to the hilt in these letters, Dahlberg will upbraid Olson for his use of vernacular, redirecting, perhaps, Lawrence's invective at the low style in which *Bottom Dogs* had been written. But Dahlberg's rebirth as prophetic eremite had two important advantages: however shambling the prose may seem, there is distinct authority in its sonorous pronouncements, a language craftily intended to arouse that residue of scriptural authority in the American reader's mind. For Olson, as for us, reading such prose can run a chill of reluctance up the spine at the thought of disagreement, though we may chafe plenty at Dahlberg's sweeping condemnations.

The other advantage is the impersonal role of such a voice, half myth, half generalized consciousness, with which to revile the New Testament civilizations beyond the Pillars of Hercules. Dahlberg's concoction of voices—from Herodotus, Ezekiel, and Homer to Blake, Dreiser, and Bourne—forms the sort of prophetic persona found in the century's long poems, from Pound's Homeric eyewitness to Eliot's Tiresias, or Williams' Paterson. Dahlberg's prose, superficially archaic, is rich in structures that would soon become essential postmodern conventions, a sweeping revision of Western history, a rejection of received canons, an outcast heroic persona who anticipates the protean intelligence at the center of Olson's first successful poem, "The Kingfishers," and the mythopoeic voice of his *Maximus* sequence. Though he loudly defended traditional forms against the disintegrative tendencies of modern writing, Dahlberg goes deep into the orders of traditional prose to wring a peculiarly original rhetoric to fit the temper of his own outraged persona. When Dahlberg applies his cudgels to other men's dilutions and reconstitutions, we must remember that he does so in his own highly manufactured role and with a prose he had welded together from the detritus of libraries and secondhand bookstores.

Can These Bones Live spreads out around the strict topical focus of Olson's Call Me Ishmael, filling in, shading, giving background and wide vista to what Olson was laboring to articulate narrowly about Melville. Dahlberg extrapolated from the conditions in one novel the temperament of moral, sensual, and religious squeamishness that ran all through American writing. He was one-upping his protégé in this book, but he was keenly aware in doing so that it was Olson who first saw the possibilities of decoding an American myth in Moby-Dick and of laying out a large social criticism on the basis of it. So it can be said his protégé Olson made possible Dahlberg's own rebirth as writer. The sheer exuberance and sharp-tongued debate that pour out of Can These Bones Live is a declaration of renewed energies; Dahlberg was venting old grievances from his days as a young Socialist in the New York of the thirties—the "angry decade"—but between breaths he assailed the very circles of the Left in which he once thrived. He was now reborn politically as well; like others of his generation, he had swung wide to the right and was anxious to renounce his leftist sympathies and the utopian social visions Stalinism had long since discredited:

> Not since Thoreau has any American save Randolph Bourne shown such lucid anger against the mummery of the State. The State myth continues, nourished by doctrine, gospel, and leaders. Pragmatism, socialism, trade unionism, and communist statutes lead to state idealism. What hope is there in this slavish, self-cozening instrumentalism? Is there a Gideon here with pitchers and trumpets to rout Philistia? The State, the Tower of Babel, which Johovah destroyed by confounding the tongues that there might be diverse races, is the logarithmic "classless society" of one speech, one culture, one international Babel-Fatherland in which ideals shall be shibboleths, and the spirit the flag of Bread. It is this abject herd craving for universal unity which is, as Dostoevski wrote in "The Grand Inquisitor," the chief misery of mankind.

What Dahlberg had finally decided, in unwitting corroboration of Eliot's similar views in "The Idea of a Christian Society" (1939), is that a large nation cannot escape from the curse of the State, where human fulfillment perishes in political abstractions and the individual vanishes into the ranks of functionaries. In drawing that sum, however, he had already sown the seed of discord between himself and Olson. If human society were ungovernable through the power and agencies of a state system, there remained but one alternative to social renewal in the industrial West: a return to the values of ancient Mediterranean civilizations, the polytheistic religions and small city-state societies of early Greece. That meant a blanket condemnation of all the tendencies of thought and art going forward rather than backward historically. Dahlberg's position as a social critic was that modernity itself had to be destroyed by means of historical and esthetic critique. Hence, adopting an archaic mode of prose as his voice was more than a mask or a pretense, but an elemental function of his social views. The way forward was to retrench to an early model of Western life, the pre-Christian era of tiny human settlements largely self-governing and supported by pastoral economies.

Meanwhile Olson was enrolled in Harvard's graduate American Studies program, newly established under the influences of Frederick Jackson Turner's "scientific history," which brought together various disciplines from the humanities and the sciences in its broad approach to the study of American civilization. Olson was surrounded by an array of diverse but congruent perspectives on the formation of American identity and expression, an experience which gave him his peculiar stamp as a critic and theorist in literature. By merging diverse approaches to a phenomenon of cultural life, in which he drew on such fields as the physical sciences, geography, Carl Sauer's biophysical historiography, anthropology, and economics to pursue a literary question, Olson escaped the narrowly subjective procedures of routine literary analysis. At Harvard, he was learning how to analyze human behavior and expression from a boldly empirical perspective, which in turn led him to formulate the sort of revisionist critical approach to Melville that attracted Dahlberg's interest as well.

Germinating in him during those Harvard seminars was also the lesson that human history had a shape, a contour not unlike the cycles of Vico's historicism. Prior to the restless millennia of human migration was an epoch of stable human settlements dotting the Mesopotamian delta, where all the rudiments of mythology and archaic vision were originally conceived and fed into the rich culture of Sumerian civilization. After that, however, as he wrote in his essay "The Gate and The Center," a "bowl went smash," and the intense cultural activity of this era ended in a human diaspora that eventually spread out to the rest of the world. Human migration ended the patient vigil on nature of primordial society and began an era of anthropocentric civilizations culminating in the abstract cultures of Athens and Rome, imperial civilizations whose main interest was in their own advancement and conquest of nature. The Americans were "the last first people" of migratory history, the last to enter a new territory that brought voyaging humanity back to the beginning of its trek; the far shores of America were the cradles of Asia. Thus Melville's epic took account of a profound juncture of human history by narrating the death of its last heroic traveller. But where Dahlberg all along maintained that the discovery of the New World was a tragic error, Olson assumed from the start that the New World was in fact the place where the archaic vision would be restored.

The courses at Harvard suggested to Olson, at least in germ, that the new sciences of man were actually the revival of archaic mythology, as the ecumenical approach to history reconstructed the myriad terms of relation of a mystical bond between the human being and nature, the vision of which had been lost during the long epoch of migration. The present frontiers of thought pushed against the realms of myth, but—and here is the rub between Dahlberg and Olson—thought could not grow by renouncing its own inexorable movement forward, as Dahlberg seemed to insist; it lived upon its own experience, which required that one engage the now in all of its force and meaning in order to wrest from it its hidden truth. And the real was not accessible through the abstractions and aloof logical analyses of orthodox discourse; its truths were revealed through close, sympathetic observation and intuition, acts of mind that depended upon a metaphysic wholly different from the kind nurtured in the migratory conditions of Western thought. The study of nature demanded both vigilance and humility, virtues of the archaic mind that long predated the era of Semitic cultures forming Dahlberg's utopia.

Dahlberg was, we must assume, unaware of these fundamentals of Olson's poetics. He knew little about the issues of contemporary science, and far less about the debates then raging in philosophical channels over the nature of language, reason, and phenomenological awareness, from which Olson was deriving some of his esthetic arguments. Cerebral as these issues may be, they come down to some very practical, and amusing, results when reading these letters. It will be noted—with few exceptions—that Dahlberg's letters are tidy, fastidious as to grammar and punctuation, and eloquently formal in tone. Dahlberg's esthetic did not engage the fundamentals of expression itself as the basis on which to reconstitute vision or thought. Dahlberg was mainly concerned with the spiritual and moral condition of American society, and with a contrasting set of social and cultural ideals from Hebraic, Greek, and occasionally Roman literature by which to counter the degradation of con-temporary life.

Olson's letters respond with increasing deformality of structure as his interest in the philosophy of language deepened. Olson's prose begins to resemble the sprawling forms of his projective poems, the strategies of which he was exuberantly displaying to Dahlberg without comment. He tacitly announced his theories of language and poetic strategy by demonstrating them in his indented and sprawling paragraphs, his underhanging lines of prose, and all the other typographical flourishes he indulged in his correspondence with Dahlberg—and even more so in his letters to Cid Corman, Creeley, and others of his immediate circle in these same years. Dahlberg's only response to these graphic performances is to occasionally compose a letter in lower case, a convention he observed for a few months and quietly dropped.

With hindsight, we may read these letters and find even in their stylistic minutiae subtle, unacknowledged differences that would plague their friendship and finally erupt into open dispute. It was Dahlberg's habit to argue deductively, from generalities to specific cases; but Olson's concern with scientific method and with a quasi-scientific poetry of experience, led him to scrupulously study texts for their particulars, in order to demonstrate the experiential primacy of imaginative works. Olson applied his Ockham's razor to the areas of emotion and to subjectivizing tendencies of lyric discourse, the very passions of literature that were of chief concern to Dahlberg. Dahlberg sometimes felt that Olson's thinking was bloodless and academic, and avoided "the logic of the heart" on which his own arguments moved. Toward the end of their friendship, Olson no longer concealed his dislike for Dahlberg's generalities and categorical judgments, saying at one point, "I would woo you fr all generalization ('saturday nov 11 50')," defining generality as the source of moralizing in art—i.e., the reduction of experience to universals. The textures of prose of both correspondents confirm their fundamental differences as thinkers: Dahlberg's tendency toward lush, sensuous lyrical speech, fraught with judgments, opinions, sweeping condemnations, or wildly emotional praise; Olson's cooler, more precise vocabulary, an analytical prose that moves carefully from context to context while maintaining a subtle distance from the matter being discussed—a tendency which infuriated Dahlberg when it was his own writing or character under scrutiny.

With *The Flea of Sodom*, the friendship between Dahlberg and Olson reached a final impasse. It was Dahlberg's frequent contention that Olson approved of, enthusiastically praised, and supported the text from the outset. Indeed, there is much to corroborate this view. Beginning with Olson's telegram of August 1948, calling the manuscript of the *Flea* a "delight," and "beautiful," Olson follows up with a long letter dated Monday, September 20, 1948, in which he jubilantly refers to the work as the "Book of Edverbs, the

Mount of Dahl." He quotes profusely from the first part, "The Flea of Sodom," and begins a curious process of "reviewing" the work for Dahlberg's eyes only. In those letters where Olson puts the text under his elaborate scrutiny, he was looking for instances where experience remained unaltered as it entered the form of a sentence, paragraph, or the larger units of argument in the essay. In these early deliberations over Dahlberg, Olson was formulating the rough beginnings of his "Projective Verse" essay, where he vigorously argued against "closed" or *a priori* structures, where content is subsumed to design and intent, and those open forms where content accumulates and determines its own shape and internal relations. There were numerous instances of parables, aphorisms, pithy condensations of language, but there were also long spates of abstract generality, and try as he could, Olson could not systematically differentiate the two modes of writing and find his principle. Olson's letters documented a slightly muddled enthusiasm, the picture of an adoring disciple who finds both what he admires and what he tacitly, and politely, abhors.

"I am in love with FLEA," Olson wrote, in part obliged to say so, in part moved and fascinated by the densities and brilliant curiosities of this style of parable, allegory, lyric concision compressed into Dahlberg's new work. Olson slowly involved himself at another level of the book's life by offering to send the manuscript to various New York publishers. In part this was repayment for similar duties Dahlberg had performed on behalf of Olson's essay "Lear and *Moby-Dick*" in *Twice-A-Year,* where Dahlberg had served as coeditor with Dorothy Norman, and again, for Dahlberg's work in soliciting recommendations for Olson's first Guggenheim award. Olson was eager to undertake these duties—of seeking publishers, and ultimately, of attempting to have the book printed at Black Mountain College, as part of his obligation in the friendship. By a curious coincidence, however, Dahlberg's other friend, Herbert Read, would soon intervene and rescue the book, and then take over altogether in writing a foreword, catalog copy, and collaborating many times thereafter on literary projects with Dahlberg. What caused the demise of one friendship now cemented another.

The slow buildup of tensions as the conflict grew in complexity is part of the dread (and pleasure) of reading these letters. Dahlberg is not a man of patience, but one to nurse a grudge to a point where he can no longer restrain his rage, regardless of the consequences. This is the steady drumbeat of the letters from July 1950 on. Olson has asked Harvey Breit for space to review the *Flea* in the *Times,* but he informs Dahlberg of this fact limply, without enthusiasm or conviction. No sooner has he said this than he proceeds to offer a "review" in private once again in his letters of August 1 and 2, 1950.

No doubt Dahlberg both appreciated the evidence of Olson's enthusiasms, but could detect a sinister nuance in the letters as well—that Olson was lavishing praise in the wrong place. As he will later tell Olson angrily, there are many reviewers who praise authors privately and then damn them publicly. "I do earnestly wish, Charles, you would write a critique on THE FLEA," he tells him on August 15, 1950, "let me too not be without that food from Sidon, Damascus, or Gihon, without which we cannot be fabulous." The letter goes on to speak indirectly of treachery between friends, though lightly, remarking at one point, "after you have composed a perfect quatrain, may you then admit that a friend buries his friend with the same myrtle, cypress, and Plutonian spade and implements as his enemies."

By August 28, Olson is keenly aware of the dangerous ground they now enter on the matter of the "critique" or "review." "You have me very troubled," he tells Dahlberg, complaining that a "review" would be a "usurpation of my forces and my senses." Olson proceeds to harden his position against the review, though always couching his demurrals in paragraphs that indicate he will go through with it, nonetheless. He will call on Harvey Breit "and get the thing . . . settled directly between us," using language a suspicious, overly sensitive Dahlberg would know to parse into its reluctant, concealed denials. In these tense moments new roles emerge between the men: a quiet, profound aloofness of authority in Dahlberg, so like Ahab's before his cringing crew, and a quietly resolved Ishmael, or a Billy Budd, or a Bartleby, hardening his resistance to this demanding parent/god. Dahlberg had glimpsed a side of Olson's nature that few had seen; perhaps Olson's own father was the only other, when, upon leaving for a postal union meeting just prior to his death, he had asked his son Charles, then twenty-four years of age, for use of his newer, larger suitcase for the trip. Olson remembers refusing his father this small request, which may have been the simple gesture that forever estranged them. The polite, indirect appeals by Dahlberg would soon end, and be replaced by demands, and finally imprecations and explosions of wrath.

But what had Olson seen in *The Flea* that made him draw back and withhold publishing even a brief review? Some of the things he clearly liked in Dahlberg he also found, in greater degree, in Creeley's short stories; not long after this feud he wrote a very favorable note of introduction to their appearance in the *New Directions Annual* XIII (1951). Creely's was the essence of a new mode of writing, and the act of saying so by way of a short "review" was uncomplicated; the act of discriminating contrary modes of writing in Dahlberg would have dragged Olson into a public act of disagreement, a "mixed" review that would have obliged him to explore the negative side of Dahlberg's prose and imagination that would carry the greater weight. And Olson knew any such act of weighing and disagreement would result in a new crisis in their relationship. Instead, Olson found ways to put off the ordeal of having to come to terms with his judgment of the work. Gradually, he hints more and more to Dahlberg of his reservations. Dahlberg vacillated between two categories of thought, the one where experience had primacy and he dwelled on the ancient cultures of the Mediterranean, the Thoreau-like side of Dahlberg's imagination; in the other, he raged and condemned whole categories of people. In the second mode, Olson saw how Dahlberg needed hardly any instances before he would generalize one small truth into a moral principle, and there was no appreciable difference between this kind of fevered assault and the Christian sermon full of fire and brimstone. The word Christian is tossed around a good deal by both writers as they accuse each other of resorting to abstraction and an irrelevant moral system.

The moralizings added up, for Olson, to a blanket condemnation of American civilization, even in their own time. Perhaps Olson came at the social commentary by way of the technical rudiments of Dahlberg's prose. But it came down to the same thing: that Olson could not accept Dahlberg's view that the New World was corrupt and irredeemable. Olson's "Projective Verse" essay proclaimed the present as filled with promise and new discovery, and his poem "The Kingfishers" notes the eruption of powerful new revolutions (as in Maoist China) that are not only sweeping away a decadent past, but preparing the present for other epical transformations. Not the least of these transformations is the speaker's own, who rejects the Greco-Roman heritage of earlier Western life and adopts an Aztec-Mayan one as his New World birthright.

In time, perhaps, and with Dahlberg's patience, Olson might have finished his critique of the *Flea* and published it in a journal like *Origin* or the *Black Mountain Review*, where his strong blend of analysis and theoretical pronouncement would have been welcomed. Olson tells the truth when he demurs from writing for newspapers or popular journals, where a quick summary and opinion are all that are required. He was incapable of separating himself from the act of judging; his method required that the process of judgment be central to the act, which meant reproducing all those channels down which his thinking moved toward a point of conclusion. And his thinking required the close sifting of language, the threading of particle to particle, if the process of conception or critical discrimination were to occur. The "puff" or quick endorsement that Dahlberg, in his desperation, needed was just the demand that left Olson paralyzed and incapable of satisfying.

In the end, *The Flea of Sodom* garnered only four short reviews, two of them in predictable journals: the *Freeman,* where Dahlberg was a frequent contributor; and in the *Montevallo Review,* edited by Olson's friend Robert Payne; the other two were in *The New Yorker* and in *Poetry.* The book sold poorly and, like other of his books, soon went out of print. Even so, it may live to be a more important text than many others of Dahlberg's canon. Its grotesque satire of New York literati and the social fringe anticipated the humor and exaggeration of Beat literature to come, in particular the comic hyperbole of Allen Ginsberg's long poem "Howl" (1955), and of Jack Kerouac's *On the Road* (1957). Dahlberg's pastoral idealism and brutal caricatures of modern American life anticipated other dark comedies of the era, including William Burroughs' *Naked Lunch* (1959), Ken Kesey's *One Flew Over the Cuckoo's Nest* (1962), and Joseph Heller's *Catch-22* (1961), which work the common theme of an alien civilization where an outcast protagonist ekes out his life clinging to values the rest of society had long since abandoned. The theme of alienation writ so large in *The Flea* anticipated numerous other Jewish comedies on the subject of wanderers in the contemporary wasteland, from Salinger's *Catcher in the Rye* to novels by Mailer, Bellow, Malamud, and Roth. Though the *Flea's* much purer heat and darkness kept it out of the mainstream, it covered ground many of the minor and major classics of the mid century would soon retrace.

Even Olson appears to have taken in the influences of *The Flea* in writing his *Maximus* sequence. Its dark history of colonial America, where community failed under the pressures of mercantile greed, and its bleak descriptions of modern Gloucester falling away under the blade of the bulldozer, express a profound despair over the blind forces in American life akin to what Dahlberg saw in his own dark vision. Olson struggled to maintain his optimism as a writer and only occasionally gave in to despondency. It's possible Dahlberg's pessimism struck Olson as the poison that would distort his own life, should he agree with it or promote its searing indictments. Instead, Olson reneged on his commitments, and chose to defend himself by calling Dahlberg's rage and rejection a kind of wisdom—abstract, generalized, deductive in its logic— which he could not bring himself to publicly embrace.

The friendship lingered on, occasionally rewarmed by the tireless Dahlberg, whose ventures in publishing were always cause for reengaging Olson in correspondence. Though things ended badly between them in two or three of their worst battles, Olson did not bear Dahlberg any deep-seated grudge—though he was chastened and noncommittal thereafter. Only in their final sporadic crossfire did Olson let loose with pent-up feelings and old resentments on the score of his failure to write a review of the *Flea.* For Dahlberg, these were years of mounting literary success. Reviews, poetry, essays began appearing in a wider range of magazines; and now a steady flow of books in the voice of his prophetic persona began appearing, leading up to his major success—the penultimate version of his lifelong preoccupation with his own story, *Because I Was Flesh* (1964), reviewed widely in the U.S. and England, soon after translated into Italian, German, and Dutch editions. Dahlberg had arrived. But even success could not remove the thorn of Olson from his side; in his autobiographical tale, *The Confessions of Edward Dahlberg* (1971), a more chatty and opinionated version of his many retellings of his life, he reserves the symbolic chapter 33 for his acidic portrait of the now-deceased Olson, whom he coolly vilifies as a confused, self-destructive, selfish betrayer of his friendship. But even then, he could not refrain from admitting, "I shall always love Charles Olson and condemn him."

Olson, for his part, was far more discreet in discussing his feelings about Dahlberg. He never publicly admitted his feelings, but only confided some of his misgivings to Creeley in their correspondence of 1950. Thereafter, Olson was only heard to have remarked that *Because I Was Flesh* was a "dirty book."

Though Olson's literary successes were confined to avant-garde circles while he lived, his following was strong and ardent; and his reputation as an initiator of new principles of writing was, by 1970, well established. He came to represent the mind and feelings of a generation of writers coming of age in post–World War II America, reconstituting poetry according to a shifting, still forming metaphysic derived from numerous new disciplines and political changes. Olson had emerged at the end of European imperialism, and at the start of America's own fretful course at governing the Western and part of the Third World. Much of what he had to say represented a renunciation of the culture that had cultivated the imperial mind, and was a determined effort to ground the imagination in other mythological and cultural systems. Perhaps because he was so eminently the voice of a new generation, he was fated to clash with the disillusioned, darkly suspicious mind of another spokesman, who represented in one of its extreme guises the generation of World War I and the Great Depression.

Dahlberg spoke for those who had depended too much upon a political utopia that had ended in disaster, and who could not understand either the pursuit of more ideological alternatives or the relentless reconstitution of the arts in search of a new visionary testament. Not only had two men come to assume the roles of father and son, they had clashed and parted on the very terms of political history that separated two generations of Americans. Emerging out of the chaos of emotion and dispute of these letters were some of the first glimmers of the postmodern imagination. Though caught up entirely in their disputes with one another, they were sometimes baffled by their closeness, the interests they shared in common. Their feud prevented them from knowing how closely each had come to inventing their times.

The editing of these letters and the job of tracking down names and reconstructing situations and backgrounds would have been an arduous task without the help and counsel of many other persons. In particular I am grateful for the generous assistance of Harold Billings, Dahlberg's friend and bibliographer, and of Jonathan Williams, a friend to both figures. My thanks are also due to Clayton Eshleman, who originally commissioned this edition for the first three numbers of his journal, *Sulfur* (1981–1982), and to the close readings and corrections of that edition by Ralph Maud. Heather Walters, librarian of special collections at Brooklyn Polytechnic University, and Elizabeth Swaim, archivist at Wesleyan University, were able to supply the identities of several figures close to Dahlberg and Olson. Ephraim Doner, who appeared in thin disguise in *The Flea* as Ajax Proletcult, and who later married Rosa Shuser Dahlberg, resolved several riddles for me. My friend Carlos Salinas and my wife Catherine read manuscript with me for long hours, and Nancy Snyder typed and corrected portions of this edition. Others who came to my aid at different stages of this edition include Paul Metcalf, Geoffrey Dahlberg, Coburn Britton, Richard Schimmelpfeng, Johann Köbel, Joel Myerson, Jerome Loving, and Ann Charters. I am indebted as well to Catherine Anderson of the Humanities Research Center (University of Texas at Austin) for furnishing documents and for permitting my use of the Olson manuscripts in this publication, and to Richard Schimmelpfeng, director of Special Collections, Homer Babbidge Library (University of Connecticut) for supplying documents and permission to use the Dahlberg letters, and for his eleventh-hour magic in acquiring for me Olson's letter dated December 22, 1937, published here (among several other letters) for the first time.

And I am grateful to both Richard Schimmelpfeng and Coburn Britton, executors of the Olson and Dahlberg estates, for granting permission to publish these letters in the present edition. I am also grateful to Ralph Maud for supplying additional letters to make the edition complete.

My deepest gratitude is to my friend and colleague George F. Butterick, whose lifelong dedication to the study of Olson and postmodern poetry was not only good company through the years, but who set a standard of scholarly dedication which one could only hope to approximate. This edition is dedicated to his memory.

A Note on the Text

I have kept the rules of editing very simple. Where it is obvious that mistakes were merely mis-struck typewriter keys, I silently corrected; but where I found peculiarities of punctuation, or phonetic misspellings, little lapses in convention that seemed hints into the personalities of the writers, I left them as is. Brackets indicate either indecipherable or missing language, or editorial intrusions—to give relevant information on various figures or details that would otherwise seem puzzling. Three or four names here remain unidentified. Dates, when not given in full, are indicated in brackets, and with question marks if not fully ascertained by internal evidence.

IN
LOVE,
IN
SORROW

[2 Grove St., New York City]

Sep. 14, '36

Dear Charlie—

Had to leave Gloucester hurriedly. Doubt whether I will get back. A mess of things here to straighten out. Soon as I am more tranquil will send you books. Meanwhile, hope your sinus & your knee are healing. Remember, start work on the Melville book. I believe in you. I think I know. The sooner you start the better. Inaction spawns inferiority. This in haste.

Your friend,
EDWARD DAHLBERG

[Cambridge, Massachusetts

December 22, 1937]

Dear Edward—

I'm too ashamed to put a date on this letter. Nor can I really explain my failure to answer your letters and thank you with whole heart for the thorough & clairvoyant criticism of the essay ["Lear and *Moby-Dick*"]. I mean, something happened to me this month which has obliterated actions & time & *memory*. I've been seriously ill, just how seriously I'm just finding out. A hideous trauma of my whole system. It is as though I had slept away a month: actually I have slept many hours, forced to bed, neglecting everything. I seem to have awoke only yesterday[.] My mother, for example, phoned me long distance & in a frenzy asked me what was *wrong*—she had not heard from me & yet I suffered under the delusion that I had written her. The experience has unnerved me.

I need to get away. I cannot, however, afford a trip. I should like to come to New York for a few days next week, Ed. I shall disappoint you, for I have done very little. But it would be good to see you and talk with you. What I really need is strange country & stranger peoples, a shock of new life to antidote the poisons which have brought me my recent trauma. Tentatively I plan to go to N.Y. Monday or Tuesday. I'll let you know definitely when with the hope that I can see you.

Paul Christensen ▪ 3

Right now I am too shaken to write about your letter of the 2nd and your criticism of the essay itself. I must say it is about the only life I've had in this month.

I've had no reply from [   ] Massine. The [Charles S.] Pierce [Scientist, philosopher, taught at Harvard] Manuscripts are tied up, but through [Kenneth B.] Murdock and [Bliss] Perry (the men in charge) we may get something for the magazine [Twice-A-Year]. I am writing Dorothy Norman [co-editor with Dahlberg of Twice-A-Year].

Remember me to Rosa [orig. Shuser, Dahlberg's third wife]. You'll have a letter from me in a couple of days, Ed. This is to tell you what's wrong.

Sincerely your friend,
Charley

■══════════════════════════════════════■

[2 Grove St., New York City]

Jan. 21, 1937

Dear Charlie:—

Please pardon my delay in answering your letter. I was, of course, most pleased to get it and had intended to sit down & write you promptly. For I know your problem and it touches some of the most porous things in me. But I have been writing—and reading without a let-up, and after my day's work I have shunned paper and pen—could not go near either.

I have seen [Alfred] Stieglitz & he speaks most highly of you. I hope you have written to him. He is an old man now. I think you should not hazard losing the precious moments of knowing him. Did you ever read Sherwood Anderson's "Story Teller's Story[.]" There is a beautifully sincere and deeply felt dedication in the book to Stieglitz. Do look at it when you are in the library. Waldo Frank is now in Mexico. He is the honored guest there of the International Writers' Congress. We exchanged a couple of letters before he left, but I did not see him again. Tomorrow I am calling on Ford Maddox Ford (you remember E[lma]. T[hayer, pen name of Alix du Poy, Chicago journalist and activist, published stories in Ford's *Transatlantic Review*]'s references to him).

I wish you would settle some of the seething things within yourself by writing: otherwise, you will go along at a zero level & say to yourself

in your most dire moments: ["]My god, nothing is happening to me."
And of course, nothing can happen unless we make it.

However, I am not too worried about you. You have an
extraordinarily warm and fluid personality to which people are strongly
attracted so that even in time the cold blizzards and profound psychical
wastes and moraines of harvard will melt to you. That, of course, on
the human side, & important, but not the real problem.

To return to the thing you must face, why don't you write and why
are you waiting. Maturity, like a maid-in-waiting, will not come to
you. Besides, all books, no matter, when they are written, in what joy
or quasi joy of ripeness, are [n]ever anything but mistakes. So don't
needlessly harass yourself over the young years traipsing in your bones.
The bones are yours and so let's see their signature on the printed page.
As I have said, once you get the book on paper, I will see that it gets
published. But write!

I have been reading Poe's "Eureka." Poe interests me enormously but
I don't know what Waldo Frank sees in that long piece of tedious
godhead! Have you read it?

As for the magazine, I am deeply interested, but things like that
must evolve slowly. So I have not pressed it. Will wait till Frank
returns and then we will see.

Let me hear from you. Rosa wishes to be remembered to you & I
send you warm friendship.

EDWARD DAHLBERG

P.S. Does [John] Finch [Olson's roommate at Wesleyan Univ. in 1931–
32] still feel the effects of my anger at the surrealists. It is always better
to face a sound anger than to run away & hide in the crannies of Mt.
Vernon.

■ —————————————————————————————— ■

[POSTCARD]   [2 Grove St., New York City]

Feb. 11, '37

Dear Charlie:

I am seriously thinking of coming up to Cambridge next Wednesday.
Could you suggest some reasonable hotel that I could stay at? I don't
know just what your own situation is at present, therefore suggest this.

Paul Christensen ▪ 5

So don't misunderstand. I am only thinking of you. I wrote you a letter some time back, but as I received no answer, I imagined it was too difficult for you to write. And then maybe my letter was an inadequate reply. But believe me, I *felt* your letter, have thought of you much since. Do let me hear from you right away. I have been driving away, [am?] tired—

EDWARD DAHLBERG

■══■

October 27, 1937

Dear Charley:

I have already spoken at considerable length to Dorothy Norman about you and your piece on Melville. We are both, I assure you, very eager to see it; as soon as you come down to New York I want you and Dorothy Norman to meet each other, as I believe it will be a very mutual pleasure.

The following is something of a sketchy idea of what the magazine is all about. Dorothy Norman is the editor, and I will act as associate editor. The magazine will be called *American Quarterly*. In naming it *American Quarterly*, we are shunning, we belive, the gimcrack propaganca titles on one hand, and the cute foppish ones of some of the little magazines on the other.

We hope we will be governed by taste and by a sense of the humanities, and *not* by any set of doctrines or political propositions. It is my own belief that doctrinaires and political prophets monster their own truths.

It is our wish that the magazine have coherence and a thematic structure. We desire to include and relate the arts; to deal with the times, to be of them without becoming a literary looking-glass.

Issues are now being planned, one on the state—man as bondsman to any state: one on Randolph Bourne, author of "Untimely Papers" and "History of Literary Radicalism". American writers from Melville to Bourne will be given "alms for oblivion". It is our special kind of humor that when an American writer has been dead, Americans are generally literal-minded enough never to question the fact: so that Bourne lies in limbo, his books scattered like the buried fragments of Osiris.

I would like to give something of a rebirth to certain neglected writers; to print forgotten essays that we believe should be seen and read again, and to constantly revalue and reinterpret truths, superstitions, beliefs, literature and man. We are ambitious, but have no desire to make claims.

Do let me hear from you right away and please send your manuscript without further delay, as we have to know what material we have at hand.

As always, your friend,
[Edward Dahlberg]

Edward Dahlberg
237 West 16th Street
New York City

■ ══════════════════════════════════ ■

December 2, 1937

Dear Charlie:

Thank you very much for your kind and warm letter. I was exceedingly pleased to have it, as you know. I am glad that what I had to say about the manuscript did not disturb you. However, let me add that upon second reading, I find your Melville essay even more impressive: particularly the latter part which deals with Moby Dick. That is the best piece of imaginative criticism on Moby Dick that I have ever read anywhere, and I think it a real contribution to criticism.

I have edited the manuscript this morning, and have indicated in brackets the passages which I am suggesting that you use for the essay. There are many things which I have had to exclude because they make the essay less compact and centralized. I wish, Charlie, that you would make the Moby Dick the theme of the essay, and use the other material to illustrate that theme and to give it some of the atmosphere which you have achieved so beautifully in parts of it. Will you please set to work upon this immediately, so that we can have the manuscript as soon as possible? I don't know how many words the essay will be, because I did not go at it in that manner, but without thinking of that, make it as tight and as astringently cohesive as possible. But use all the material I have suggested that you employ for it. Both Dorothy Norman and I are very happy to have it, and are using it in our first issue, and may I re-emphasize, don't delay, as we need it.

As ever, your friend,
[Edward Dahlberg]

P.S. I got a very fine letter from Ellery Sedgwick, and am answering him today. I am most eager to see his piece on "Pierre."

Edward Dahlberg
237 West 16th Street
New York City

December 13, 1937

Dear Charlie:

We have changed the name of the magazine to *Twice A Year.* With a quarterly, we were unable to solve the waste that summer publication would involve. Each issue will be twice as large, about 150 pages, and will, we hope, be much more coherent and thematic.

Will you please send the Melville essay back without delay? I do hope that you have not let any time pass without work at it. We must have all our material at hand as soon as possible, and a manuscript in the hands of its author has only a metaphysical existence.

Besides, I would like very much to hear from you. What are you planning? Will you come down to New York, and if so, when? For the time I shall stay right here, as I have an enormous amount of reading to do to pull my own book out of the mess it is in at present. Have been seeing a good deal of Dreiser, and also had a long and warm letter from Waldo Frank. Do write me as soon as you can.

As ever, your friend,
[Edward Dahlberg]

Edward Dahlberg
237 West 16th Street
New York City

---

237 West 16th Street
[New York City]

January 10, 1938

Dear Charlie:

This is one of my form letters to you, so be prepared for the magazine lash. Thanks very much for your letter and for what you have to say. May I remind you that this is the 10th of January and that I am supposed to have your manuscript by the end of this month.
Have you had time to see about Melville's letters? When you see Mrs. Metcalf, please give her my warm regards. This in haste until I get your MS from you.

As always, your friend,
[Edward Dahlberg]

February 9, 1938

Dear Charles Olson:

I wrote you a letter a week ago, but have not heard from you. Needless to say I am very suspicious of your nefarious silence. Ease my wrath by sending in your manuscript which has become a veritable blockade against all publication, publishing, writing, conceiving, creating, and misconceiving!

Your friend,
[Edward Dahlberg]

P.S.
One of your breathless, panting, pulsating, special-delivery letters, would be very timely—provided the manuscript accompanies it.

237 West 16th St.)
New York City   )

Dear Olson:

It was good to get your warm card and to hear that you are working at the Melville essay. I hope that it is nearly done, as I am most eager to have it in my hands.

I want to thank you again for so kindly talking to Laughlin, and for writing to Houghton Mifflin for the right to re-publish Melville's letters. Have you heard from them?

One other thing—We wish to re-publish Melville's essay on Hawthorne which was reprinted, as you know, in the lovely book you gave me. To whom should we write about this?

Have you had a chance to talk to Sedgwick? Please let him know how interested I am, and how sorry I am that he took my own letter amiss. An essay on Pierre would be something that I would want to get very much, so, if you can pull him up and make him feel that that is all that I really wanted to do, I would be grateful to you.

Please have the Melville essay here not later than February the tenth; otherwise, we are "stuck."

I had lunch again with Raymond Weaver and had a very fine afternoon with him. I like him very much and he likes you enormously.

As ever,

> Your friend,
> [Edward Dahlberg]

■ ══ ■

[New York City]

April 28, 1938

Dear Charlie:

Many thanks for your kind card. It was good to be with you in Cambridge. Thanks very much.

The other day I picked up a copy of Postgate's OUT OF THE PAST. It is a rare out-of-print book and I don't think you'll ever be able to get it even here, so I am sending it to you and hope you will enjoy it as I did.

Please tell me whether you had a chance to look at the PIERRE.

Another thing, this is to remind you again, Charlie, that I am deeply interested in the "Melville and Democracy" essay.

And one more thing before concluding—We got a place in Gloucester, staying with Ray Adam's mother-in-law. So we'll get a chance to see a good deal of each other this summer and I am very glad of it.

Forgive this dry little note.

Your friend,
[Edward Dahlberg]

■ ══════════════════════════════════ ■

[New York City]

May 24, 1938

Dear Charlie:

I have not answered you because I have been writing for the past eight days. I have been at work on an analysis of the State in my Bourne essay. The original essay has turned out to be just the details for this one. I cannot tell you how abortively restless I was before I began writing.

I am so glad you got the Postgate book, and hope you have enjoyed reading it. Also, I am deeply glad to know that you are at work on the Melville and Democracy essay. Both Dorothy Norman and I are very eager to see it when it is done.

Charlie, I expect to be in Gloucester about the middle of June, and hope this summer to complete all my reading for the entire book, and then to disburden myself of it.

Incidentally, did you ever find out about the "Pierre"? Please let me know if you have the time to do so.

This is just another perfunctory magazine letter. I have many things to say to you when we see each other. Rosa sends her very best to you, and I am, as always

Warmly your friend,
[Edward Dahlberg]

237 West 16th Street
New York City, N. Y.

■ ═══════════════════════════════════════ ■

[WESTERN UNION]   [John Winthrop House]

1939 Mar 18 PM 7

CHARLES OLSON

DEEPLY HAPPY FOR YOU KNOW ONLY TWO IMAGINATIVE ARTISTS WHO HAVE RECEIVED THIS TRIBUTE [awarded first Guggenheim for a study of Melville] HART CRANE AND YOU THANKS MUCH FOR BEAUTIFUL LETTER AND BOOK DEEPLY TOUCHED BY BOTH FORGIVE ME IF I AM A LITTLE BLATANTLY PROUD OF ALL THIS MY FAITH AND LOVE

EDWARD DAHLBERG

■ ═══════════════════════════════════════ ■

July 16, 1940

My dearest Charles,—

To leave you, there, with those scummy shantied creatures was pain. It is homelessness for you; without natural touch; grace.

But to other things. I have been drinking at those sweet and sharp springs, Shakespeare's Plays. I have thought much of you while reading Lear, Macbeth, Troilus; thought of how you led me to these Founts; how wholly you had possessed the FOOL, in LEAR. You must return, apace, to your Visionary Cap and Bells; and make for you, and me, those Quickened Unheard Words.

Now, Charles, to look at your MYTH [regarding an early (now lost) version of *Call Me Ishmael,* part II "Shakespeare"]; and now for some seeming, sere pedantry from me. You know how unfraught

Shakespeare's Lines are; either he Speaks in Angered Adjectives, unfettered by phrasings, prepositions; even articles; or he Cries:

Tomorrow and Tomorrow and Tomorrow

or to return, his spleen is Pure Epithet: Reechy, drenched, murky, without a clinging Substantive. Or when he hazards a Slow Detour, it is shaped in words of a syllable, in four to five letters:

You do me Wrong to take me out of the grave

Your own sentence, here, is balked by flattened verbs, adjectival, with barnacled fastenings of prepositions; redundant articles, and too many nouns. Of course, for the moment, have you lost your own Path; for everything you have done is against your blood. But again, and further: You are, yourself, most magical, in the seeming slow line, of short syllables: "springs of myth can mean"; "Dreams stop the machines" (Here stop, for me, is not thrusting enough); "Edenic springs"; "Rappacine in his garden of false flowers"; "We are the last 'first peoples' " (Here, you weaken your phrase, so good, with "of the world"[).] You overburden your perception with obstructive words that add nothing to seeing, hearing, breathing. The Verb, as Huysmans said, is the central force of the sentence; and the power of the sentence lies in its Crisis. One begins a line to finish it with a Cry, a Moan; to get to the End. The thing, above all, is to Finish. But, see, Charles, how such uglified words impede, subtract;—in effect; like; maturity; in order; accident of the industrial revolution; maturity. Shun, above all, the word, maturity; it is a mare's nest, not to be pursued, mentioned; a gibbet-word. And, avoid, definition; it slackens anger; makes a polemist, a didactic out of the bursting wrathful tongue. And do not, to repeat, elucidate. Speech, must always be, unguessed, ecliptic. When one knows all, beforehand, or later, or too much, ennui, supervenes. But let me cite a few more words you should eschew; point of departure; spiritual life; temporariness; singularly; compulsion; adventurism; materially.

But enough of my quasi-pinnacle. As you know, I stand, aloft, on a foot-stool, and like the elder Maccabee, from this height fall off and break my neck.

Let us move to the meal, the mead, the grassy, flowered intuitions, in the Essay. I shall cite: "Homeless in his land, in his society, and in himself, he found his place in space." "There was in him an attraction to the origin of things, the first day, the first man, a centrifugal movement to the distances of the universe, to the Pleiades, to the unknown sea, the buried continent." I have, here, clipped your line a jot; it is very fine; question, however, centrifugal, and also, attraction. Or, to continue, and I am making emendations to compress your own horizon; "Melville warmed himself by the first fires of man's life after the flood". What follows, is, deeply good, too; "He sought origins so primary he was able, in *Moby-Dick,* to discover the lost past of America and establish a myth for a homeless people". Very lovely; but I don't like, establish. Or take this; here is something exceedingly probing, vitiated by the anticlimax "essentials"; "Melville lived wrong, but he lived so intensely his and his people's wrong that he forged something in Moby-Dick" and now the drooping "essential there is beauty in it". Perhaps, you might follow, Charles, wrong with "his people's Guilt."

To go on; "*Moby-Dick* is ultimately a private vision, in essence as antagonistic to man as Satan." The rest, refuse of phrasings I cast out. Here, again, and very lovely; "Lucifer has the beauty of the morning star because he is, wholly himself, in all his evil, as Moby-Dick." I have garbled your wording, in ungainly correction.

You have, Charles, already, the Seed, of a Book. You have uttered truths known and knowable only to an artist; and I uncover before your Monuments, Temples, before your Sphinx, as I have so often before. What I am doing is to return to you your own Memory; telling you, what was Foreknowledge to your Self and which in the night of doubt, misery, ennui, we forget, and will always forget. Could we remember, continuously, we would be, again, in Eden; with the tasting of the Tree, of the Fruit of Good and Evil, we Forgot. How Jehovah looked; how to be naked, unashamed, how never to Hide, as Eve did, after she had listened to the Serpent, and Puzzled Adam.

Write, work, and believe in your Ilium, my dearest Friend.

Stanley [Burnshaw, poet and critic] asked after your book, again. I am seeing him, for lunch, Thursday; and when the time comes, we will combat the world, and take our Honey out of the carcass of the Lion, as Sampson did.

Let me hear from you, soon.

Yesterday, I bought the [Edward Hallett] Carr book on Dostoevsky [*Dostoevsky* (London: Allen & Unwin, 1931)], for a dollar and forty cents. Went to eight bookstores before I could put my hands on it.

I pray this is of some little worth to you, Charles.
I send you my warmest love, my faith and uncrack'd loyalties.

Your devoted friend,
EDWARD DAHLBERG

The ride back was a Boon to Doris [orig. Huffam, Dahlberg's fourth wife, whose half-sister, Constance Wilcock, married Olson] and me; the afternoon was a raiment of breeze, sea, sun. Thanks for that. Doris, of course, sends her love to you.

■ ══ ■

August 1, 1940

My dearest Charles,—

Your deeply good letter came to me; what a pity my own thanks to you had to go to Dallas before reaching you. So are thanks given in this world. But, again, my pleasure and happiness I announce to you in the PIERRE you so generously gave me, and the shirt, too, which I have been wearing in contentment; delight.

When you mentioned the sad brevity of the Poet's Life, the few Plays, I wondered, had we spoke. For I had been thinking so, with pain, of Shakespeare kneeling in his Orisons, The Tempest, after he has freed Ariel and Caliban, and his 'power is o'erthrown', thinking, 'What a falling off was there.' This is the Anglo-Saxon burden, which Shakespeare carried, and which we have inherited. And no Englishman, or American, so far as I know, has eschewed it, nor Chaucer in the last part of Troilus, the last Christianly humbled lines, which, alas, are not the earthed irony and laugh, as it should have been; nor the Sonneteer, nor Melville.

This little isle, whose width from shore, bay, to tangled, wildish ocean, can be spanned in six to seven months, and whose length of pure beach line, is forty miles long, is likewise without an Ariel or Caliban. In its dunes, pines, spray, toads, frogs, it is an Encantada; in its imaginative life and habits,—the skull and bone church, the clapboard, shantied cottages, without design, or heart-deity, or manual love, the witch-like faces of the natives—it is the corporate town. Thus, it is New England, the Cape, where, you, I know, must be right, about the sluggish shore, the way the sea sluttishly inclines upon the

Paul Christensen ■ 15

muddish land, America. Much preoccupied with Shakespeare and Dostoevsky, I, too, have been so near the final abyss, of 'barren hate.' My affliction in man is so accursed at moments that I am ready to fall into that slime-pit, there, where the kings of Sodom and Gomorrah fled. But it must not be; to go the other way—forgiveness is everything—I cannot go. It is a giant lie of the flesh and the bones, and I cannot so govern my organs; nor can I do the opposite, for I cannot live with such a disgraced and chaffed palate.

Now to the days here; they have been rather agreeable, save for those graveled glances, encounters which drop like coarsened things upon my veins. Of women, there is a little pentecost here; license, the riot of appetite prevails. When women take off their clothes, as they do in a resort, they really disclose all, and rush out to man with a louder trumpeted lust than is man's. It is somewhat expensive, though; I pay ten dollars a week for a room, facing the sea, the sands, and eat out. There are no other expenses but that; for in the evening, one walks with a woman under the Milky Way, and that is the shortest path to the haven we seek, to the Breasts, the long upheaval of the tresses, the Euphrates Valley, the Womb.

[Harvey] Breit [editor of the Sunday New York *Times* Book Review] has been very ill; should he be well enough to come, he and Clara [Breit] will be here for two weeks. Dora [Shuser, sister of Rosa] may come, too[.] The fare from New York is only a dollar thirty five cents; an hour by train, and a forty minute journey over a sweet, billowy sea in a motor-launch.

Doris has not been here yet; last week we had too little money for her to join me; but tomorrow she will be here; it has been much anguish for me to think of her in the fumes and fires of New York heat. I wish, deeply, I could ask you to come as my guest; forgive me, I cannot, although nothing more would I desire. The evil is not in my bosom, but in my purse. When you want to stay at the apartment, let me know; whenever you are ready, we will make arrangements.

How is [   ] Korin? Did he receive the book I sent him?

I have finished note-taking; now I must read them, over; and begin. I fervently hope you are writing, seeing, hearing, murmuring, as in a beauteous shell, ocean-shell.

So with all my Faith in the Book, in your pure, jetting Gifts, I give you also, my heart-friendship, and deep love.

EDWARD DAHLBERG

■ ══ ■

Edward Dahlberg
General Delivery
Ocean Beach
Fire Island
New York.

[HANDWRITTEN ADDENDUM:]

From Notes

From Underground—

Petersburg—"the most
theoretical and intentional
town"

It's in on page 4 or 5,
Charles—

■ ══ ■

April 9, 1947

Dear Charles:—

I did not know of the existence of your book until Easter Sunday. I rejoice in this small, mythic volume. A little book, no longer than the Song of Solomon, Amos, The Georgics, or Call Me Ishmael, is the mead, the honeycomb and the Jerusalem for my insatiable Soul. I love a book with no other mortal deposits in it but the pith of gnome and parable.

Literature is the pious commemoration of extant relic, ritual, and you have deeply understood this. No one before you has really perceived Herman Melville, the fabulist. There have been some goodly guesses about the albic Bull Leviathan, but the mythology of Moby

Dick has been sealed and mummied. 'Who can draw out Leviathan with an hook' says Job, and there is no better remark than this upon those who would fathom the American Continent, the occidental Jupiter, the White Whale, or art and letters without going back to humanity's birthplace. Herman Melville's head-devouring quest for Beginnings, his cry for the First Winds that blew upon Oceanus and Nilus and Pisa's springs where Father Zeus was born, has been as hid in the awful Book of Ahab as your own Enceladus underneath Anta's Heap. Call Me Ishmael is the same priestly pang for First Causes which will always eat up every man who has a Deity in his brain; until we can fathom the Semitic and Phoenician mysteries before Sidon and Tyre and Gaza, our knowledge is gross.

But now to garner from your book: the son calling to the Father, the stricken skald weeping in a middle English, 'O fahter, fahter, gone amoong' brings the tear from my heart, for my mother, too, has been lying in the darkling and dreamless earth for fifteen months, alas, not close by Absalom's Hand or Obadiah's Cave, but in alien and untrembling clay in a Hebrew Orthodox cemetery in New Jersey.

The Prologue, the record of those infernal anthropophagous acts, is done in a doughty prose. But the book begins for me with the Shakespeare, or the discovery of Moby-Dick. Your speech wavers at the start; sometimes just by the dropping off of an article your line loses its natural force; then you fall away from your own poetic nature into the vernacular. But this is debris and the sea-lees you can sweep out at some later time with Poseidon's Trident. These are the exterior flaws which will make the literary Barabbases mock your lovely book. I cast out almost twenty pages from Do These Bones Live for the English publication, and it may be that I was still too gentle to my own skin. This is a little matter, something for you to consider when the book is reissued. I doubt, unfortunately, that this will be your present problem. Unless I speak foolishly, the citizens of Philistia will give you neither lucre nor honor, not for at least two lustra. Genius is a stumbling-block in a cold, boreal land; this you know. But to return: I am your vassal-reader in the entire Shakespeare portion; your understanding of Melville's need of warming, pagan gods, Scamander and hot Triton and sweaty, priapic Vulcan who cohabited with nymphs and begat heroes, which every American poet requires if his genius is to have a hearth, is deeply moving and pulsant. I could call back to you so many lines and passages that you have written, so heavily marked is my copy. The book of the law of the blood is remarkably recorded; your citations from Melville are in themselves discovery.

I want to thank you, of course, very much for your words about me, very much. I have changed the title of Do These Bones Live to Sing O Barren, broken from Isaiah. Routledge in London is publishing it sometime this year, with a Foreword by Herbert Read. I have also another very small book, almost verse, done in the gnomic prose, called The Rational Tree, which the Mint, a Routledge publication, is printing this year. I had intended sending the two of them to you when they appeared, as I wanted you to have my tribute to you, and my feeling for you, in the English book, in your hands.

I am, as you know, an Ishmael in solitude; for the most part, the waterpots of Cana are empty for me, and I have to fill them by reading the ancients, or walking or in my life with Winifred [orig. Sheehan O'Carroll Moore, Dahlberg's fifth wife, originally married to Harry T. Moore, a professor of literature, critic of D.H. Lawrence], or from the robust adamic laughter of my year and a half old son, Geoffrey, who is Jew, Irish and Norwegian.

Call Me Ishmael is a little piece of Melville prophecy, and you have my promise that it will be remembered, and with this my affection and friendship.

EDWARD DAHLBERG

■══■

Edward Dahlberg
58 Barrow Street
New York 14, N.Y.

Please do not give any one my address; this is not a booby pretence, but a caution which you probably understand.

■══■

[Washington, D.C.

April 16, 1947?]

[DRAFT OF A LETTER BY OLSON, WITH CANCELLATIONS AND HAND-WRITTEN REVISIONS THROUGHOUT; A SUBSEQUENT VERSION WAS POSTED TO DAHLBERG ON OR NEAR ABOVE DATE]

My dear Edward:

My deepest thanks for the bounty of your letter. It is most moving to me that the book earns your particular word. And I take it as a mark that is is you who points to the lines to my father, and the Moses, for they seem & are the forehead and the heart of it.

I rejoice, in my turn, that Herbert Read is a man to give you place, and I shall eagerly await the promised volumes.

It is a peculiar delight to have you tell me of your son Geoffrey, and of this [mixture?] of your blood. For in respect to both I am his like.

Yours, as ever,

[CANCELLED, IN HAND:] My affection & my friendship, and the futile hope that

Charles Olson

■ ══ ■

[58 Barrow Street / New York City]

April 17, 1947

Dear Charles:—

You have written a little book of genius. This I told you in a letter that you have not answered. However, your book, no less than your life and your churlish silence, has been a sore trouble to my heart. Your greatest faults are sloth and untrembling bowels. I rebuked you often for your sluggish spirit until you became dainty and effeminate about your time, until you became a sick, busy American. 'Must you dung as you run?' said Aesop to his Master. I have never had the coarse effrontery to tell another man that I was busy. However, I succeeded in word-flogging you into writing your book, and all the Grace and Goodness and Courtesy in it you conceived when you were close to my identity. The rest belongs to the world (O I have overcome the world! cries out the Nazarene in Luke), the beginning where man is just the fat gobbets for Cyclops' hideous gullet you must sooner or later reject. The Noah, the Christ, and the Moses, I believe you garnered up from the MS which I implored you to rewrite. I knew at the time that the book was to be dedicated to me. But now, because I took you unto my identity, gave you my table, and whatever knowledge had come to me from hunger and all the mortal and perfidious aches, you have bequeathed the volume to your poor, dead Father; your acknowledgement to me has the same bitter obituary taste in my mouth, because you in the same manner of a perverse Balaam and a dainty and vain Absalom that you were to your Father, alive, are now offering to me, deceased, unto your own character and spirit. What is to become of you? You cannot feed any longer upon that brute Minotaur Leviathan or upon Oceanus. This is no mirthful human meal for a man whose soul is already too watery. A man should have a dry soul, said Heraclitus.

You have not been a Judas to me; that is a warm-livered error; your sin toward your nature and me is of a cold, stygian decoction. Your silence has been brewed in that foss and marsh where the muddy and mangled shadows abide, and is a portend of a stilly and fetid cessation in your spirit. You cannot ripen so, neither in the rain, nor in the sun. Nor will those brackish and Mammon-caitiffs of Parnassus, Brooks, Van Doren, Pound be of much avail, unless you further submit. The other one, whose Gomorrah vice I find abominable, cannot sustain you.

You cannot have a culture in a land, especially in this mechanical, doomsday country, where everybody is so vilely separated, and each man spills his spirit like the defiled seed of Onan. Poe could not go to the Quacks of Helicon, nor could Melville, and neither had any real unfolding. Man must talk to man, if there is to be a vision and a human spirit; otherwise everything is in the hands of Barabbas, the poetry, the handicrafts, and the thievish loaves. Could not Christ and twelve ignorant fishermen produce a legend!

Sodomy, which is the neutrality of the sexes and the human heart, and the ache for a united Babel of the world, all go together. This reminds me: about three years ago, I saw Harvey Breit, now a first-class citizen of Philistia and a sodomite, and I said to him: Why don't you give up Blake and Dostoevsky so that the whore in you will flourish more easily?

EDWARD DAHLBERG

April 21, 1947

Dear Charles:

I have no need to withold or even to change by one jot the epistle I wrote you on the 17th. My first letter to you was dated the 9th, so sharply uneasy was I about your depraved silence. As a pure, unknown nobody, your words were sent to me in great haste. What sorely troubles me now is that you are very likely to become a well-known nobody. I have in my hands your exsanguious, American syntax letter of thanks. You are discerning enough to know that you have given me a base and wily affront. I could have so requited you by not acknowledging the homage you make me in your book; but I do not know how to be lofty or to premeditate a cold and sly jibe for another mortal. Cato preferred to tear out his entrails rather than to expose them to Caesar; and every day that I go out into the streets, I cower in my mind before the thorns and the mischiefs, all the pismire Golgothas, one is likely to get from a tradesman, an American or a Charles Olson.

Your little transhuman volume of genius also disturbs me very much. How will you get over into the warming humanities to the other side of the Pillar of Hercules. Your book, the central text of your vision, is beautifully-wrought literary metaphysics; your citations out of the Journal Up the Straits are in themselves apocalyptic discovery. You first divined the Melville pining for the Cresent of Mahomet, for the Balm of Judea, for some human wedlock with Mediterranean and Asian pulsation. Your intestines quiver, but there is a mocking Pilate in your intestines. That is why I was so *useful* to you. At the root of all intellectual antisemitism is the laodicean serpent that hungers for the Jew's liver.

I foresaw your perfidy years ago. Your own Father's death was not enough of an admonitory lesson to you. You must also do the same to the man who fed your spirit, fathered your book, and deeply cared for you as the Nazarene must have loved John of Zebedee. The Thief may go to Paradise, but if a man mire upon his own Seed, his Father and his Vision, he will rot impiously unto himself.

Yes, I know the appetite for pragmatical comfort and mediocrity in this land. I understand why you run after exterior people, why you grudily hanker after the artistic mountebank who puts Topeka and Telemachus together to make a canto. I comprehend the necessity in you to consort with the mediocre friars of syntax. But take heed lest monkish merchant Brooks bless you, lest Van Doren put the mouldy hands of Benjamin Franklin upon you. Take care lest the hypocrite College of Arts and Letters give you a National Award.

EDWARD DAHLBERG

■ ══════════════════════════════════════ ■

217 Randolph Place NE
Washington 2, D.C.
April 23, 1947

My dear Edward Dahlberg:

I am damned if I can see by what right you send me the two letters I received from you today. If it is under the cloak of friendship, then let me unclothe you, and tell you it is not friendship, and you a man without shame.

They are more like you, though, thus more authentic than the letter of praise I had from you earlier. By your own act you prove that letter false. I found it so, except for the moments when your perception rose above yourself, and it was they I marked in my reply. I made one error in that letter, a matter of tense: it should have read, where I compared myself to Geoffrey, I *was* his like. I wish I might hope you'd be a true father to him, for you'd then once understand some secret of love, and not make mock of death, which is digestive with you. You offend me deeply now, on my father, as you did once upon the holy grass offend me on my mother. Who are you, sir, that you think thus to cover with your own gross those who have permitted themselves to come close to you? Who, sir, do you take yourself to be? Short of Jehovah I do not think you know an answer, and that, my friend, is pathetic of you.

You outrage me. And why? because you are outrageous to your self. I shall be the last to take from you the brilliance of your sights but, Edward, this one thing is clear: what you spit out as sights of others are but the sputum of your own mouth. You eat, and if my Cyclops is too much for you, you are too much for yourself. You read me fables, here is

Paul Christensen ■ 23

one for you, more useful, if you now wish to talk to me of use, than your Empedocles: Euripedes, in exile because of Aristophanes, was set upon by dogs and torn to pieces.

So much of what you say of me is true. Of course. It is the easiest act to stick my finger in another man. We are all open, exposed. The shame is that a man like you thinks he has a right to beat us with our own sticks. We are each Euripedes, and it is only dogs and Aristophanes, he who longed to be the Thirty First Tyrant, who set upon us.

It is not love you offer anyone. If it were you could not take it back like money on a table. You buy, that's the verb, and its tense forever present. You traffick in affections, deal. I would say it to no one but yourself, for I would not expose you, but see yourself, once, gently, as an American production. Why is your critique so apt, so sure? For the reason of the hidden E at Delphi.

Or do I jump before myself? For that is also key to the single seed you hold so carefully hidden in you, the unblown seed. Of Sodomy you speak so easily, of neutrality, of dung, of death, and it is all supposed to be a 'guilt' we others, who impinge upon you, are the victims of. I do believe we are, but you, unholy holy, are you not one of us? Or do you prefer your image of the Nazarene?

Invert yourself, or speak a straight word, a word unfolded, neither of praise nor of your fraudulent damnation, for they repeat themselves and are not very interesting. You can. I've hear[d] you. I've caught sight of the seed. It is nothing to be frightened of, in fact, you would be the terrible creature you may fancy yourself to be if all the mighty armament were based, so based, so rooted where life, which others do participate in, is. They do participate, and that is the confounding fact you, with all your arms, shall have to meet. Even with your own death.

Do not ever again, please, praise me, use those nouns of genius and its like, for I am sure I shall not be able to give you back the price [that praise is marked with, to repay you with the coins] you think are love and friendship. I thought once I could, for I did not know how cheap you make them, how they have a market value which you, a Kansas City merchant become a monogod, presume to give them.

And do not, above all things, ever again think that I or anyone ever gave and gives you the right to dirty with yourself what birth has meant to me, or death. My father died. This attempt of yours to

intrude upon it is an act the grossness of which you cannot
comprehend

Cover yourself.

(signed) Charles Olson

■ ══ ■

[58 Barrow Street / New York City]

April 25, 1947

Dear Charles:

I know the fable about Euripides and the dogs that tore him to
pieces for his impiety. But what sacrilege have I committed against
you? Did I say it, or did it not come out of your mouth, "I have
betrayed two persons, my Father and Edward Dahlberg." You revile me
as a base merchant. Have I shown gluttony for praise or reputation. Do
I whore after people who can help me? Am I the consort of the
merchants of Toledo, Carl Van Doren and Van Wyck Brooks? Am I a
companion of the lucre Pilates in Washington? Are these the seers and
the political male Cassandras who perceive the world better than I. If
so, you will please let me leave the world. In the Chester Plays one of
the three curses is the world.

You say that I am outrageous to myself. Of course, I share deeply and
covertly in the Guilt of man, and I do not say so to shed my own sins.
My errors were not against you. Your book, written under the dominion
of my identity, is the proof of that. Why should you be so angered
because I do not relish dungy Cyclops. Were you not queasy when I
committed the same sort of fault in endeavoring to understand the
nekrophiles and the scatologists. Did you not cast away many of those
pages, with my total acquiescence? Why do you revile my sputum.
What preterhuman dust and spittle do I find in your letter. Timon once
upbraiding Plato called it bile. You speak of simple and uncrooked
words. You have said I speak and write so. What really angers you is
that you are too perverse to own a fault. In our friendship I labored for
you and not for myself. Even now, after sending you in my first letter
good savory words of the heart about your book, how do you reply? You
cunningly smote me with an affected and fatuous note. I do not know
why it took you three weeks to compose so few platitudes; in that

length of time you should have done more. What is baleful is that you have sly enough bowels to know that you were smiting me, and it gave you atlean and lofty feelings. But never mind that: I did not raise my hand or heel against you; you did that. You are very irrational and untruthful when you say I buy. What, pray, do I buy and sell, my limbo, which you have no intention whatever of sharing! In our friendship, did I labor for your benefit or for mine. What was my earnest for being a co-editor of Twice A Year: I received one advantage, I saw to it that Lear and Moby-Dick was published. How did I fatten my blood-stream or my so-called reputation when I ran around getting your essay into the hands of authors who could help you. Was it not my mirth and advantage to give you the fellowship of authors which an unknown would have not had in at least a decade. I did not have it without pang and hunger and denial. You had it without any, because of me. Did I work for you or for me in getting writers to speak for you for a guggenheim award? Now, for the matter of paying some irreverence to your mother. You are again unjust: the one time I was your guest, I got the water and you the wine out of the Cana Pots. I am not a gross feeder, and what food is put before me does not matter, provided my host has the same frugal fare. You happen to be a rank eater, and if Plato and Socrates and the fable of Euripides and the dogs could not teach you that it is base to give your guest dingy food while you sit opposite him and eat large chines of beef, then your belly and your unflagging appetite should have given you such breeding and wisdom.

If it will give you more felicity to have the newspaper Barabbases, the Van Dorens and Brooks call you genius rather than I, I will try to bridle my tongue.

I imagine you have gotten some astute saws and apothegms which are more available for comfort rather than a life of ritual. You cannot go the way of the world and be a human artist. Nor can you pity the aching denials in Herman Melville while you denigrate mine. You can't be both spirit and mammon save to the low Yahoos. You see, I am much too pathetic and abject and obscure for anybody to bother trying to tempt me.

I do not know what you will think of this letter; it may bedevil you, or you may see, later, that though you now regard me as the watchdog Cerberus baying at your entrails, you will come to understand that I was the one Guide of your spirit and nature and gifts.

You will pardon this penultimate piece [o]f human malice: May God make Charles Olson a failure, may Call Me Ishmael go as unsold and as unread as Thoreau and Herman Melville. Should this happen, maybe then some day in some chasm where Dante casts those caitiffs, like Edward Dahlberg who was for himself and not for Charles Olson, we can talk about grossness and shame and the dogs that tore Euripides to pieces.

EDWARD DAHLBERG

■ ══ ■

217 Randolph Place NE
Washington 2, D.C.

April 29 [1947]

[CARBON COPY OF LETTER, UNSIGNED]

My dear Edward:

I want to be clear with you, and without the humping of the blood when I last wrote. Yet you anger me, when, in pieties, you wrap and hide your greed. Now you would eat my book as you would diet of my father's death and curse my mother for the food she gave me!

Why don't you ask of me my name? I'll give it to you, and you'll have it all. I am Nobody, he said.

Cut away these holy wrappings, cease to play Christ and to quote me Chester plays, so we can speak together, now, for I am unread by you and do not wish to wait for posthumous Christian places imagined by literary men. If you were able to distinguish between us you would know from ISHMAEL, especially the CHRIST, what a lie I take a path to be which leads a man to make himself a Cross and cry, "I hate the world."

It is thin of you to think I go the way of the world because I stay in the world. Or that comfort is the alternate to a Cross. It is mechanical conclusion. Your Essene rite of self blinds you, it would seem, and makes your fine ear dull. I miss active thought, and intent, when you speak as you now speak. You repeat, and in incantations which do not speak but hypnotize—yourself. Brooks   Van Doren   Pound, repeat, Brooks   Van Doren   Pound. But what do you know? You miss now as you so flatly missed seven years ago, the meaning of events, of who and why I see. For behaviour is a long bow. It can only be confused with identity by those who confuse the ritual in life with ritual in individual behaviour.

If you would play Christ, to succor yourself, do. I said as much, and wished it, with the heart, for you. But when you come down and seek to flagellate others with these outworn rods, these pitiful weapons of a literary religion, it won't work. "Sacrilege", "betrayal", nonsense. You kill a friendship when you make yourself so pious. I do wish you'd left things as they were, contained, despite our disagreement, for I took pride in you, valued the many things you'd given me, had learned, as a young writer might, from your critique. Now you must regurgitate.

Have you no sense of another's man's memory? Do you know memory as anything other than a rosary of your own acts which you tell over as you walk with yourself, you and yourself in long monkish robes? It's a crazy business, friendship with you, a game, I'm damned if I do and damned if I don't. You offered me many things. I accepted them. Obviously I could not give them back in kind. How I give them back is, is it not, to be my way, not yours? If you gave them, now only to blackmail me with them, then, surely, anyone would wish they had not been given. That is why I say I regret you have chosen to misread my note in answer to your gracious letter on the book and to judge me, judge me, judge me, three times down the wind, with dead leaves.

Yrs,
[Charles Olson]

[58 Barrow Street / New York City]

May 2, 1947

My dear Charles:—

I do not know whether you are purblind to my letters or just forward. I have never spoken one profane word about your Father. I too deeply revere the remains of the dead. My poor, smitten Mother lies in an open sepulchre in my breast.

I do not envisage myself as Christ, or even as some wayward or fallen essence of him. I am a sick, nervous Jew, a base and whoring issue of Noah, Seth and Japheth. You know my attitude toward the Nazarene.

All that I said is that I had the same feeling for you as Jesus had for John of Zebedee. How does that make me utter crooked words? Or how do I eat your book and your identity? I have never had any disciples; you were my friend; I taught you how vile our [occ]idental earth is, how loathsome the American naturalists are, and I made you write. All that is astonishing and choric in your lovely and memorable Call Me Ishmael was written under the influence of my identity. Had I eaten you there would have been no book. What you added to the volume disturbs me. I told you why, and I do not see that it is outrageous of me to get queasy when Cyclopes devours human corpses. That kind of anthropophagous prose belongs to your inferiors. I say so now, and will say so later, because the book for me is a Fable and a Pilgrimage.

Why am I foolish when I abhor the world? and why is it literature when Timon moans, "Why, this is the world's soul." When Melville underscores this remark you are deeply moved, but when I say that in the Chester Plays one of the three curses is the world I am just repetitious and indulging in incantation. How many truths do you own? How often are you garrulous and repetitious and just squalid to your own soul? Wit and wise sayings do not come from a man's mouth continually. Solomon could write no more than two books, and Amos no more than a modern chapter. Would you then discard them as bores from whom you could not learn, and so turn to profligate Egypt or Sidon or Tyre for wisdom? The error would be yours. Do we not go constantly to the Masters simply to be reminded of those heart-truths we think we know? The greatest human spirits have had no more than seven or nine apothegms in their mouths, and only the coarse will say I have heard that man, be he Mark or Cervantes or Plutarch, say that before. Let us take your life and book as an example: How much profit do you think I have gained from your epistles to me? What have you said in the second letter that you did not repeat in the last one. Does that matter to me; no it does not. I have a deep feeling about you, and if at times you bore me, well I bore myself perhaps more often. I have not seen you in at least six years, how many opulent and profoundly gifted lines have you been able to add to your book. According to my own sights what you have added, I am talking about the beginning, and am not in any way trying to diminish your Call Me Ishmael, has been exterior and an error. That does not matter either, because the book is so entire without the five or six or seven years that were added to it.

How to speak as simply as I can about the time when I was your guest; does one have to be clever to make you understand that it is base to sit at table and eat better food than you offer your guest. Aldington told me that Gerhardt Hauptman once invited him to dinner; he set a bottle of vin ordinaire before Aldington while he drank rich Sauterne. You will be lenient if I find a dismal cleavage between Hauptman's socialism and his hospitality.

How can you endure what even a Henry Adams found abominable. How can you be a companion of pusillanimous and low politicians whom Thoreau abhorred. How do you propose to guard your own vestal fires in the Augean stables at Washington? Shun the fleshly denials that Melville had, but don't think you can associate with boobs and Barabbases without punishing your nature.

Had you disavowed me for some Timon or Lear or Amos, I would have been stung, but I would have had to own that this was ripeness for you. But you forsook my friendship for the world, and I believe you know what I mean, and how I mean it. "Will ye go away?" asks Jesus. "Whither shall we go?" replies Peter.

You fumble in the human spheres in the book; your pose, so plangent & kelpy in the many pages on Melville's mythology, is American in the beginning. It is a perfect little book once you take those pages out. Well, you will have to wait awhile, maybe months or years, before you feel less greed about your own lines, and know that you will have to peel away the dross until you get to the quiddity of your own nature which I honor.

At this instant, I have a deep and persistent feeling that the Herman Melville you so pity and kneel before in the Text you would have deserted in the Life.

Charles, we cannot always be as interesting as we think we are. Doubtless, while you were reviling me for writing you letters that were not as remarkable as I thought they were, you were unmindful of the boring observations you were making.

Be patient and ruminative, like Buddha and the Cow. If you are fortunate, you may, after a decade of ennui and stupidity and vice and reading, be able to gather up enough parables and feeling for another small book of genius, like, Call Me Ishmael.

EDWARD DAHLBERG

[CARBON COPY OF LETTER, UNSIGNED]

My dear Edward:

Anthropophagy AND anthropology: your letter is of such depth and of so much beauty it asks, to be answered, such determinants, as well as the personal. It is how we see these man-eaters. I am so made I see all that has been already gone, and the egg of chaos already broken by the horns of the bull of the Lord.

No one has disclosed the omophagia of the west as you have, in the substance of DOGS / and FLUSHING, in BONES as critique. I shall have occasion to remind our stupid contemporaries of you as revolutionary. (The inscription in ISHMAEL was meant to be otherwise, personal, for I was the double gainer: I knew you, as well as your work.)

You are wrong to say I forsook your friendship. It could be you forsook me. But again (I anticipate your rejection, because of the word) there is an anthropology among men as among societies. Differences arise from, CON NATURAM, different identities.

I think you are quite wrong, "purblind", to see ISHMAEL as governed by your identity. I should myself have to admit another man, Melville. And you will excuse me if I note that it was written by a third man and, unsatisfactory as the book is to me, have the impression that it does declare a—to use part of a man's phrase whom you introduced me to—"sense of life" different from Edward Dahlberg's or Herman Melville's. The anthropology is the common, ishmaels,—as well as the difference. From the man-eating tragedy, as you have with what truth exposed it, Melville turned away, you back. I can do neither. For I remember Orpheus.

My reason for FACT #1 is song as well as parable. You spoke of its doughty prose and it gladdened me. You also reject it, and confuse it with your own clean indictment of those victims of matter, the American naturalists. You see, Edward, if I keep throwing at you the image of Christ, it is because you do have a morality by which you choose to judge, and its sanctions are, as I take those of most of the great reformers of these past hundred years, Christian.

I do take space ...... But no capitals with you. I would be quiet with you. (It is the tone which you yourself achieve in this last letter.) ((As in the dream of the death of Wilkes.)) Do see the quiet—the identity—as merely the absence of a morality I do not believe in. And the presence of ANTHROPOLOGY.

It is another way to record ANTHROPOPHAGY. I want to correct my public words: the central fact of man born in America is anthropophagy. Not space, or rather, space not yet taken up and used as an element of anthropology and thus a container of anthropophagy. (To hell with this: erase it, typewriter. I am more interested in the fact that the Thracian women, scorned by Orpheus, tore him to pieces,— and his head washed up on Lesbos.

Also, as of this letter, to hell with Orpheus.

I am no man to write a biblion. It would be a repetition of work. And besides, you are doing that, apothegms, Aesop, Amos. I should much prefer to make a thing come out a sphere. It is a Moebus strip which invokes my imagination more. Perhaps you would find my attention to object "worldly," but it might just as leave be what a painter has. I would tell a story and, if I might, mount it in intensity so that in itself it is fable, not in a moral tag written in at the end. "He looked back."

Nor should I be surprised if I were not a friend in your mode to HM were he alive. For I should have been impatient with him too. Men's egos are competitive, no? I also have a deep and persistent feeling: that you are too pious, that you too would have left him dry.

It would be to our gain if we knew even remnants of life out of which we might put together, with blind imagination, a Phaeacia. We don't. And to dream it up is, for me, a sentimentality. Or mystic business. I do not dream of a city of the sun. I dream of my father.

I eat, and am eaten, and would put a stop to it.

An obsidian knife is a terrible instrument, but used right, has an edge. Otherwise, men are knives to cut each other.

I so value your perception your praise is a delight to me. And I would register your critique more if you did not hang it on behaviour. Again you take a high tone about something you know nothing of, Washington, quote me Adams, Thoreau, Christ, and the labors of Hercules, all to prove I punish my own nature, endanger the fragile quiddity—the vestal fires. It is automatic of you. "Washington", "politicians", "the world", and you're off. Actually the facts are quiet. They mock you, your boobs and Barabasses. They are yours: you dream them up.

But you come up head first. Agreed: a man gets little, has little. I don't know that I want to be like Buddha and the Cow when I am a blood-letter and a Bull, but you are right about the end. And I would condition it, as you have, "if you are fortunate"; though I do not threaten myself when I add it. But there, we invoke different gods.

Yrs,
[Charles Olson]

[58 Barrow Street / New York City]

May 17, 1947

My dear Charles:—

Thank you very much for your letter. It is my deep delight to tell you that your prose has the sea and the kelp in it, the murmurous and plangent sound of low, evening surf. No wonder Homer worshipped Oceanus!

I have been brooding about you and your letter and for that reason did not reply at once. Besides, I have been in a defiled, syntax classroom at Brooklyn Polytechnic College. But I would rather do that than get money out of books, not because I am pious, but because I know that lucre and reputation are the same thing today. Have I not observed Waldo Frank run after reputation with sainted bowels, and is he not furtively hankering after Mammon. I do not see him any more, because he writes so badly, and that is a good enough reason. In his upside-down aesthetic prose are all his monkish affectations. However, in a European country, even in England, where people are less sick with hurry and some homage is still given to a writer, he would probably have written one good book. But here, like a man who is uncertain of his potencies, he has to keep on writing to prove his powers. I'll get my Ilium in other ways!

You feel that I am some kind of United States St. John of Literature, content with the aching genials and penury of the wilderness. Or maybe you think that I am wooing oblivion slyly, really hoping for a headstone Immortality. What makes you think you know American or Washington any better than the author of Bottom Dogs or Flushing? What makes you so sure that you perceive the world more sharply than Edward Dahlberg, street-urchin, orphan, laborer, vagabond in these States? Is it not intellectually perverse of you to inveigh against the world in CALL ME ISHMAEL while you defend it in your letters? Am I a fool for upbraiding such dove-vendors of Moloch as Van Doren and Brooks, and am I garrulous for repeating over and over again until I am ashes and dust that a thief is a thief and a liar is a liar. When I stop doing this, then you had better be on guard against me. Why should it irk you if I cannot have bland and lukewarm relationships with people who are to be despised and revealed for what they are. How long do you think you can get succor from these people, just so long as they can patronize you. You'll have to be a toady, and a sensitive man is more likely to make a more charming and gifted sycophant than a dullard. It is quite simple, a peasant or an illiterate charwoman can smell such a truth and understand it. You cannot be a member of the National Democratic Committee and expect to go up to the Mountain of Frankincense with Saul's timbrel, wine and loaves. Saul relinquished his heritage for the cattle of the Amaleks, and that is precisely what every young American iconoclast has done. I believe that a breaker of images in a beautiful human culture is a wicked person, but that he is a seer and a poet in a low and lethargic civilization. But what is the little American cycle: first the writer is a young, acerb Timon, but as soon as he gets into comfortable, pragmatical relations with his environment, he is a pickthank friend of the national culture he once abhorred. Sherwood Anderson, who was much less gifted than you, he was half a Philistine and half a poet, would not go to Hollywood. Look at William Carlos Williams, the baby doctor with the obituary satchel of pills. He had talent and defiance, but during the war he was a police-sergeant of American shibboleths. Ibsen said that it is not necessary to make a definition of art, but what was important was the struggle with those who are against it. The people who hate arts and letters and painting at present are the artists and writers.

I was clairvoyant enough to recognize you in two to three minutes. Do you imagine that if there were a covey of obscure souls and geniuses in this poor, smitten and coarse country I would not somehow know about it. Tell me where all these pulsant and hidden human beings are and I'll run after them so that I won't be so lonely and neglected.

Another thing: It does not matter who influences whom. What is important is that Book. I never patronized you, I argued with you vehemently to make you shed Mark Twain and Hemingway and a number of other literary boors, and you in the end uttered your identity and not mine, and so you proved your own pulses and our friendship. If I am foolish enough to believe that I had a deep influence upon you and your work, and you think I have not, that, too, is insignificant. What we did prove is that two people, with tender feeling, could labor each for his own spirit together. It is the separateness of those individuals who pine as solitary figures for Thebes, Ithaca, Sidon, for the spice-producing countries, that makes it impossible for us to have a literature. Each of us alone is a polluted Onan who spills his seed and his vision.

I have been reading the ancients, making ready to do a book of poetry, and be sure I am not looking for the Cana Pots with which to quench my visionary thirsts. I ache for Arabia Felix and tender human climates washed by the Father of Streams. If, in the meantime, I go back to the Cape, and find nothing there but a little of Matthew's Salt, I at least can take Strabo with me.

EDWARD DAHLBERG

■ ══ ■

April 20, 1948

My dear Charles:

You say I am obscure to myself and perhaps ought to be. I do not gainsay that; he that gazes too deeply into his nature is likely to see either Minerva's owl, dragon, and the people, or Jeremiah's three beasts. Man we know is more automatic than intellectual. Write a book, and all you can do is to pray for your powers, and then nobody

Paul Christensen   ■   35

knows what may happen. Whatever my vices of Baal may be I am haughty rather than overweening; I am too much of the Iscariot waif to be otherwise. Of course, I know more than the American; but such wisdom is penury. Besides, man's knowledge, like the poison of Demosthenes, is drunk from his own quill.

I am deeply mindful of your good nurturing words, and for an instant I go up as Saul did to the Mount of God with the loaves, the flagon of wine and the timbrel, only to drop down again into Lethe's region, America, where the earth is accursed and the fable dead. Jupiter fastens the isle, Delos, when Latona is pregnant with Apollo and Diana; and we, too, when we are teeming with our visionary progeny must have something graspable, or be without vision and poems. You understand this so profoundly in *Call Me Ishmael*, and this I pray you will never lose. The foolish infidel American believes he can write without going to the founts of Helicon, to the hills of Judea, to the Nile lily. "Canst thou draw out Leviathan with an hook?"

Perhaps you should know a little of my life; my fate you can augur; I will never be what I never was; though I walk in the meadows of the asphodels for whatever little books I may conceive. I have almost completed a small volume [*The Flea of Sodom*] about the size of *CALL ME ISHMAEL*; but I live so apart from the world that I do not know what I will do with it. Herbert Read tells me I have a small, loyal following in England, but I see no one pursuing me. I have another son, Joel, named after that lovely minor Old Testament verse, and I pray that his tender head has been blessed and shaped by some ancient Prophet by the Eurphrates. For the rest, I have been teaching this past year at Boston University, and am looking for a better place, where education is not a basilisk or the Medusa that turns the bowels to stone. The summers here are hallowed, the ocean a deity, but the winter has been a Cimmerian and misty Bosphorus in my soul.

I do not believe in Jesus as you know; I hardly think he was more than a hurt and wandering Word, as the Gnostics conceived him to be. However, I have no rude phrases for him, be he the Word or the several messiahs that must have come out of Isaiah as Russian literature issued from "The Cloak" of Gogol. There are many parables in Matthew and Luke that have dropped like spikenard into my heart. I tarry to reread a line, a gnome, and to use it as I can.

As I told you, I have read no modern book since *CALL ME ISHMAEL*. I never looked at a book by Ford Maddox Ford until he died, and I peruse nothing of Herbert Read's. This is not my food; my rapture and my eden are in the ancients, and I go to them to comprehend my perplexities or to give more form to my opaque identity. Of late, I studied The Hyperion with great amazement. His use of mythology, such as "Where Cybele and the bruised Titans mourned" is my conception of homage to the Muses. Your book has been read by my students and by admiring academics. I have little relish for the herd academic mind, but he has not such stygian cunning as the writer.

You must know that I have always been a truthful friend to your genius, though you once said I forsook you. Had I coarse vanity I would agree. When I said to you, "Go," you had already left. I had labored for your spirit, and when I saw Actium almost won you took your sixty vessels and fled.

At the moment, I am weary; my Cana waterpots are empty.

Thank you again for your words, Charles, I savor them as I do your inscription to me in CALL ME ISHMAEL.

My affections,
EDWARD DAHLBERG

■══════════════════════════════════════■

Edward Dahlberg
Wellfleet, Box 42
Cape Cod, Mass.

[NOTE IN SCRIPT AT TOP OF PAGE:] Charles.—I am mentally wounded by silence; it is more destructive than the tongue.—EDWARD DAHLBERG

THE FLEA OF SODOM

> "O my friends there is no friend."

ARISTOTLE

Let us admit, going over the Atlantic
was a tragic mistake, and that he who drinks
the vile, oceanic froth of Cerberus
loses his memory, and goes mad. Hercules
took his cows no farther than Cadiz, beyond
which men haunt the pitchy fens of the
cormorant and the unclean ibis.

Homer's geography is purest Metaphysics; Cimmerians
occupy fetid, purblind Bosphorus, which is near Hades;
Tartarus almost touches the Pillars, more perfidious than
the Sirens. Hera went no farther than Europe's Oceanus
and Odysseus trod upon the marge of the sea at the
Gates, and retired. The lotus his companions ate yield
spicy, Afric sleep, not Atlantic's horrid Lethe.

Do not pass the Pillars, hankering after new places.
Shun hyperborean lands: impious Prometheus was banished
to the blizzards of Caucasus. Recall how soon Cadmus
forgot the Phoenician shores girt with shells whence
Helen's robes got their Tyrian purple, and sowed
dragon's teeth from which the gory Theban buckler,
spear and iron javelin were wrought. Unknown
countries are Sorcerer's regions of baleful ore. It
is better to be slain by a bow of cornel wood or
face a warrior in a helmet made of the rind torn from
the cork-tree than perish by metal. The weapons by
which man dies reveal whether he lived with the roe
and the hind close by the founts of Helicon, or in
Boreal, gloomy towns. The fleecy Ram of Colchis,
Jason's cargo of copper, iron and coal, is Caesar's Furnace.

Forsake the metal cities, brewing Chimera's noisome
breath, lest you disappear. Zeus' docks are in soft,
Lybian climes. The Bethlehem manger is not far from
Apollo's Ethiopic stables. Jerusalem, Sidon, Crete,
Egypt, Demeter's Basket, is the Kosmos. The dog-
parent, Atlantic, is the sea of oblivion: unhallowed
people, return to the tender fig where the MUSES
sing.

■══■

June 6, 1948

Dear Charles:—

I spent the whole sunny afternoon with Herbert Read on the banks
of the Charles River. He gave me a clymene plucked from
Agamemnon's tomb, and I put into his hands CALL ME ISHMAEL
which you never bothered to send me. But then you have your Graces
and Dis-Graces. I showed Read lovely lines I had marked, and since I

had *bought* two copies of the book I persuaded him to take the one, hoping he might find an English publisher for it. But the Adamic Shame is everywhere, and the small tribe of artists is rapidly disappearing from the earth. I cite Read's remarks: "I enjoyed his book (Charles Olson's) immensely, but wanted to acknowledge all the time the debt he owes you, and which he admits in his oddly interpolated tribute. I think the book has faults—it is willfully disjointed, unconstructed. But the observation is keen, and keenly expressed, and it moves on the heights of imagination. It is worthy of its great theme—touches the 'inmost centre' of a tragic genius."

Of my own little book he says: "I wish I had some consoling news for you, but my own enthusiasm for FLEA OF SODOM has not met with the response in the office. Raggi is still a sick man, or I might have relied on him for some support. But to the sales people you are just the author of an unsuccessful book, and there is no inclination even to look at another manuscript, especially one which, on account of its size (very small) presents a special problem in salesmanship. To argue that it should be treated as poetry is no argument at present . . . My own deep pleasure in your writing is not unmixed with a certain appreciation of the saleman's point of view—he can sell cakes and ale and even savory spices, but you are asking him to persuade a constricted multitude to buy a dish of aloes." You see then how it is; either you turn to Pontius Pilate and mock your own entrails or you kneel to Vision, praying that along with the gall and the vinegar you ascend the Mount of God with the loaves, the flagons of wine and the timbrel. You, my dear Charles, are taking neither. You write me a very long letter, giving me frankincense and all the spices of Arabia, and when I reply to you, you simply don't bother to write me again. You are discontinuous, or you've got the occidental disease, being busy. Had you continued to be my friend, the book would not have had those faults in construction, which is simply saying that in the beginning the perceptions are not so swiftly formed as the blessed lines, verdure and sea and ambergris cropped from your Atlantic Ida. Ah, but do not get vexed with me! All that I can say for myself, dwelling as I do on my lonely, and rugged Parnassus is that "Oblivion cannot be hired."

Do you recall how froward Waldo Frank used to be with you, and how irascible you became, and how you even sat in your drawers in his presence to humble him. But you, too, have a perverse heart, and somewhere in this little book which none will have I have written, The froward heart breaks the bones. What are we to do? to lie while we rot; I hate a thief, cannot endure Barabbas, but the roundabout man makes me rave.

I hope you won't mind any critical remarks Read made about you, since he really cared for the book, and that is what I wanted him to do. All books are errors, or else how could we conceive them?

My affections to you, Charles, and I pray that you try to be simple about simple things; do not mind my counsel too much, you won't heed it anyway. I am a zealot and a quixote fool, that you know, and I have to persuade people, alas, I have nobody to convince save you, I furtively hope, and Herbert Read. The others are gross, of the world and Caesarism. Meanwhile, I read with quiet mirth and benefit Livy and Strabo, and make ready to do a narrative poem about my poor, hapless Mother (about whom you never so much as mentioned, though I sent you sweet, consolatory words of the heart about your Father), going back to ancient common weals, Judges' and Numa's and Cadmus', pouring into the vial of Remembrance the Missouri, the Euphrates and the Nile.

I write, praying to God to bring to my parched stones the Angelis Fountain. O I revere Mnemosyne and Helicon, but what would I not give to put upon my lips some granule of dust where Elijah tread.

EDWARD DAHLBERG

Edward Dahlberg
Wellfleet, Box 42,
Cape Cod, Mass.

■ ════════════════════════════════════ ■

[Wellfleet, Box 42
Cape Cod, Massachusetts]

July 1, 1948

My dear Charles:

I thank you deeply for your fervent letter. Some one at Harvard, one of the business men of the nine Muses, told me you had received another Guggenheim award, and I am very happy that you did. I can not get any of the five barley loaves and two fishes from them. [Henry Allen] Moe [Trustee, Guggenheim Foundation (1945–1966), President

(1961–1963)], one of the ward heelers of the arts, will do nothing for me. They have made very few mistakes, and you are one of them. As you know, some gray-haired syntax boy gets their spices which we require to put those holy words of the heart on papyrus. I think the dismembered body of Osiris was put into a papyrus boat before it was cast into the Nile.

I am very glad you sent Waldo Frank, a dove-brained effeminate of Ephraim, a waspish epistle. He abhors the two of us. The other evening I was at the home of some one who had dinner with Dame Frank and Edmund Wilson. The pair of anti-artists were giving applause to the Paris cafe charlatan, Henry Miller and assailing your book. I said to the man: "Waldo Frank is a sodomite liar. Could he write one of the lovely, sea-pulsing lines in CALL ME ISHAMEL I would be his friend."

You are right, of course, in your anger against Herbert Read. But an English man of letters is so far above the American writer with his cormorant gullet, that lascivious Adam's apple for prurient newspaper notice. You remember how gracious Ford Maddox Ford was, and there is not a doubt that he would have given you lovely tributes for your book. I have never had a civil relationship with the American mountebank of letters. Yes, there was Sherwood Anderson; I enjoyed being with him rather than talking to him. And Aldington, with his blemishes, had not the pretences of a Barabbas and a buffoon.

I must tell you, that Waldo Frank did not even bother to reply to my petition. I only hope that the Erinyes will pursue him. He never committed any great sin or adamic vice; but let him be cast to the fish for his spite and his coarseness. I suppose we must not forget his gluttony.

Read, I am sure, does respect your imagination; but he has that frugality of the hyperborean. I sent him my MS and he said it was poetry and wanted to find a way of publishing it as verse, but he had fewer words to say about it than he had for CALL ME ISHMAEL. Yet when we spent the day in Boston together he took out two clymenes from Agamemnon's tomb and gave me one of them. Do not be severe with him; he would be deeply impressed with you if you and he talked.

I am deeply sorry that you and Connie cannot come up for the week. There is a genial covey of people here, summer scenery, of course, Paul Magriel [friend of Dahlberg, lived in California whom you know, and [Xavier] Gonzales the artist. All pay me homage, and I know none is a friend. It takes great genius to be a friend; doubting Didymus, nor timorous Peter was, and though John of Zebedee leaned upon the Master's breast at the Passover meal, what did he do for the hapless man who took the hyssop and the gall for a Kiss!

You have my heart-gratitude for what you say about my Mother whose pilgrimage upon this doleful earth was such a pang and wound. I have been reading for over two years for this book of verse. Fools call me arrogant, and yet I dare not write one line without the succor of a Master. I have been reading Dionysius and Diodorus, ay, even the rhetorician and poet Ausonius shows me how to form a winged line. A poet is always a journeyman, a humble and fumbling apprentice. I am only arrogant with my adversaries whom I recognize on the quick of my soul.

I would like to see you do the Moby Dick ballet ["The Fiery Hunt," written in April-May 1948]; it would please me so if you could get some money for it,—that dragon, money, that spews forth its noisome fire at God, and who is, perhaps, peer to him who creates, or greater, for is not destruction in the flesh of man so much deeper than the will to prune a tree, or build a littoral city, or to make a piazza where good men can talk. How I pine for Abydos, or Sidon where Paris got his purple robes for Helen, or mourn for Rachel's Well, or go out of my wits for Sais. We are born in a most unseasonable century, and if we do not gather together, four or five of us, we will all be lost, and the cicadas will be mute for a thousand years.

I want to get a copy of my MS. I wonder, then, Charles if you would read it. It is a very brief book. Oh, I must tell you, that is why the men of Gaza and Ashkelon so abhor us. Our books are too short. What know they of Joel or Amos or the Georgics or Bucolics? Do they recollect that the whole of Heraclitus' fame rests upon five hundred lines. The same is true of Empedocles. A line of his I love so much is this, "The blood around the heart is the thought of men."

If you and Connie can find a way of being our guests, it will be our savory delight to have you.

I am very sorry about the postponement of the French translation of CALL ME ISHMAEL [a French translation did not appear until 1962, *Appelez Moi Ismael* by Maurice Beerblock (Paris: Gallimard)]. That may bring you English publication. That is why I gave your book to Herbert Read. If I find an English publisher for my little volume, be sure that I will labor to see that your own book is printed in London. I am not hankering after many readers; it is a dismal folly.

Forgive me, if I said anything about the PREFACE that irked you; do pardon me. I do not covet your Gift, not because I feel too sure of myself,—believe me, underneath my little rock of Peter sings the Worm. Give me for my life and spirit two or three Charles Olsons, Men at Mamre, and I can sit like Abraham meditating underneath the Terebinths waiting for Vision. But I ask much, too much!

Your friend,
EDWARD DAHLBERG

[Washington, D.C.]

tuesday, july 20 [1948]

My dear Edward:

I am going to make this a note deliberately: I must get out of this humid house and go to the gallery where it is cool and a man's head can be Duccio Buonisegna's sea, which is grass, and the fish are fish in grass, and Jesus and Peter and James are fisher men and Siena was a christian place when spirit was alive as fish are alive, and grass.

(Which has not been true since? I picked up a book of Dostoevsky's short stories the other day and read it on a train and was not interested as I once was interested and was struck again with the accuracy of your discussion of Dostoevsky's ennuie [cf. "Woman," part VII of *Can These Bones Live*, pp. 156–159], and the root of it in sex.)

Saying these things I am suddenly aware of why I am interesting myself at the moment in Giovanni de Paolo. It is a double search, against suavity in art and spirit. I prefer his "St Clare" and "St Nicholas of Torentino" to Sasetta (I do not know his "St John the Baptist" in Chicago). I take it, his awkwardness is a clue. He, and Domenico Veneziano. And the insistence on the small subject. All quantity has sickened, and suavity is the Picasso of that big and competent world. I begin to see why I want small plays, 2, 3 people, woodwinds, no sets: chamber theatre, music, painting. It is a point of beginning.

I said a note. It is two weeks late. Something told me I should have shot off to you a card, even, to say, do send the FLEA when you have it. I await it. (I thought to write a letter and, instead, went off to Philadelphia to rub against the beast and make my own fur rise.)

Yrs,
CHARLES

[ADDED IN SCRIPT:]

A propos Keats:
have you noticed the hidden poem called
an epistle
a letter   to Reynolds?
It is in the 1925 ed. of Poems & Letters, Houghton Mifflin, p. 241)
   (March 25, 1818) (Also see letter, p. 295, & note, p. 461)
I honor him as much for that as anything.

■ ══ ■

[Wellfleet, Cape Cod, Mass.]
July 29, 1948

My dear Charles:

I have not replied to your kind note at once for a simple and plain reason: I am retyping the MS. and making corrections, generally curtailments, whenever I can. Should the heat become too rancid for you and Connie, or should it be possible for you to get away to the shore for Poseidon's brine, please come up.

I respect Keats deeply; that you know; I cannot mention him without *speaking feelingly* of him. I intend to look up the letter to Reynolds.

I wrote to Read suggesting that we form a small Anglo-American-French group of writers. We know that the real poets are hid in some grassy crevice of the earth, in Provence, more likely in the gutters of Paris and London. Otherwise, who is going to print a man of feeling, and who will read him? There is even more coarseness in the world than depravity. There are no simple, stupid people in America. That kind of peasant brain has vanished. Ignorance begets malice as Isaac begat Jacob.

I wonder why you who have so many graces of the heart sign yourself yours. It was that kind of little secretarial epistle that you originally wrote me that so irked me. I cannot endure, American lack of feeling;

and I cannot stomach, I beg to be your remains, or I am insincerely yours, or untruly yours. That sort of thing in the pachydermatous American makes my navel sick.

I have always had profound affection for you, and I send it to you again; you know John Keats' remark about the friendship of two men, "passing the love of women." When we speak of Keats, we are not thinking of Ham, or the dove-brained effeminates of Ephraim. Once you asked me about the rites of Moloch, which was a homosexual idol, I am sure; they passed their seed, through the fires of Moloch, or put their progeny into the oven of that loathsome image of Philistia.

Your friend,
EDWARD DAHLBERG

[Wellfleet, Cape Cod, Mass.]

August 3, 1948

My dear Charles:—

I have just finished, and I am infernally depleted. This is my autobiography since our infernal cleavage eight or nine years ago. I always wanted you to understand that I was never in competition with you, not because I am so sure of myself. Nothing could be less true of my own pulses. All I care about is to utter some Edenic Truths, and perhaps either in dream or in trance to lower my eyes as Helen descends the steps or to bow my face to the ground as Abraham did when God spoke to him. Alas, no one has spoken to me, "neither Jehovah" nor man, and here is my little monologue, part fable and part essay.

People have said I have deeply influenced you. This is a foolish remark. Of course, I probably have, and that is why you wrote as you did, very beautiful, murmuring sea lines, and not as I could. There can be no literature without a small tender group of men of feeling who are constantly sharpening each other. What people who do not understand such a simple truth as this is that I could not have written CALL ME ISHMAEL, or even one lovely line in it.

If we are to continue in our friendship, and I wish it for my sake and also deeply for yours, not because I deem myself a purer imagination than yours, but because you require my guidance. Take this, please, from a man who says this without pretence, who is not flamboyant, and who is sufficiently obscure to have plain truthful words in his soul. I want to use Sir Thomas Browne's "Oblivion cannot be hired" as the superscription for this very small book if I can find some one who will print it. I do not say publish it. I do not hanker after many readers; what I want are a few friends, ay five or seven or ten, if that is not too much. If God were willing to spare Sodom and Gomorrah if he had ten devout kneelers for his frankincensed altars, should I be so overweening as to expect more or as much.

I pray to God and to my poor, tender Mother who are the Cherubims of what Truths I may know that I have written without deceit or any surreptitious vanity.

> Your faithful and affectionate friend.
> EDWARD DAHLBERG

[WESTERN UNION TELEGRAM, AUGUST 4, 1948?]   Washington DC

EDWARD DAHLBERG
WELLFLEET, MASS.

FLEA DELIGHT. I GREET IT AS FIRST LEVITICAN FABLE.
BEAUTIFUL.

> Charles

August 17, 1948

My dear Charles:

I sent you a telegram from Boston. I have bursitis, an abhorrent word. Little wonder that the fabric of language is so wounded, for what is more indecent and base than the medical, the economic, the sociological or psychological vocabulary, which is the source of modern literature. I must return to the hospital for a general anaesthesia for a bone-manipulation.

I sent you another wire in reply to your own that came to me when I was as mortally slain as the vile kings in the slime-pits. I give you then my deep, deep thanks for this revivification. Your letter, which I had not answered, because my faculties were drugged with codeine, I keep as the plaister of figs for my afflictions.

Your rearrangements I have accepted almost without change. Your omissions I imagine are correct; I say it this way intentionally. Recall Charles how deeply vexed you were with me when I suggested certain deletions in CALL ME ISHMAEL. Only in the full, amatory excitement of writing, when one loves every word, am I sure. Later I am very uncertain, for my brain is too drained for such knowledge. You remember that amazing line from Empedocles I use in The Rational Tree, "The blood around the heart is the thought of men." But after that blood has ebbed, after one has come down again from the Mount of God, having worshipped, eaten the loaves, drunk the flagon of wine, and played the cithera, the deity in man's breast has expired. Again I must say, I can pray that The Rational Tree is what I had asked heaven for. Suppose what I thought was the Burning Bush is sumach, as I believe some ancient has surmised, am I to be brazen-necked about it. If you put your heart in Esau's hairy palm, and he rejects it, you must then fight the wild Ancestors of Edom with all the weapons of your soul.

The Mint in London was supposed to have brought out The Rational Tree; two issues of the Mint, an annual publication, and a subsidiary of Routledge, have appeared, but I do not know whether there will be a third. Twenty thousand copies of the second were printed, and only eight thousand were sold. I am always in the issue that does not appear!

I cite a droll paragraph from Herbert Read's letter to me: "Last week an American publisher came into my office and asked me if there was anything new in the world of letters. I said that the only new thing of importance was by an American writer. I gave him your name. He knew you—it was James Laughlin, and he went away in a meditative mood. You may hear from him." I have not.

I have suggested to Read that we organize an Anglo-American-French group to publish those psalmists hid away in the grassy crevices of the earth, and whose songs only the pastures and the cicadas can hear. Naturally, should this happen, I know of only one American writer who has the lute and a timbrel in his spirit whom I would ask to join this little band of chanting augurs, and his name is Charles Olson.

I know I have not thanked you enough, but then no man can ever be grateful enough for truth from God or balm from man.

Know that I love and esteem your Imagination.

Your friend,
EDWARD DAHLBERG

Black Mountain College
Black Mountain, North Carolina

[*September 16, 1948*]

My dear Charles:

I want to send you my bounty of thanks for your gentle sympathy and companionship. I am very sundered at the root of my identity, which has become a widowed waste-land where I weep with the cormorants and the bats for my angelic infant son, Geoffrey. I cannot fathom these furied Medusas who bedung your soul while uttering words of mercy for your hindrances.

I earnestly hope that Connie is quickly coming through. These would be sweet Oceanic afternoons on the sands for you and her, and a plaister of kelp and brine would heal her as Isaiah cured Hezekiah.

I am too torn to write more.

I do not know whether I can endure the life here smitten as I am. Could I get part-time teaching in New York or Washington I would leave at once. I have not the sinewy courage to go out into combat against pachydermatous students. I have already given two lectures and it was vanity and a striving after wind. I am sick unto nausea of trying to prove myself to others who lurk in the thistles and the cockles waiting to snare me.

I wanted to give Sam Rosenberg [friend of Olson, active in Democratic Party in Philadelphia] a copy of Sing O Barren, but he ran away.

My love,
EDWARD DAHLBERG

Edward:

No, the Tree and the Flea are not one. It is the Book of Edverbs, the Mount of Dahl, pressing. It is wise as men are not. It is thick, as though around the heart. It is apothegm, apothegm uttered, uddered, and thrusts, from your appetence. It is a Book, of itself—or the Mother of other Fleas. It is not the Flea.

I have just read it, marked it, would wish to make immediately selections from it as you have from Laertius, Chaucer, Hesiod, Amos, to put into my blood its sayings. If I sit on my chair, the ass's stool, and make recommendations, you will know I know the ears are big, and a man's mouth wide.

If I had my hand press (others bake bread) I would print FLEA first, then TREE, both such things as we recover from the ancients, codex, incunabula they call them, seeds, I prefer, papyri, biblum, out of pyramids.

((Such sentences as:

. . . . . a Roman Egypt whose figs give suck to the asps in Cleopatra's Basket

Ishmael, in his wild ass's solitude, will bite off his flesh for a soft look. (Do I not?)

Culture is conversation

a man of feeling kneels in his heart at the mention of Solomon and Chaucer

the energies of the soul parched

Evil and spoiling are in the imagination of families and races

the children of Israel preferred to eat the leeks, the cucumbers and the melons as slaves in Egypt than go to battle

The whole trembling Part 5: The seer was he who sat (Beautiful sentence! And the paragraph:

Be quiet, my ribs; stay home, lambs and goats of Ai. Rest; the ships of Tarshish are in your room: Eden is in a chair. Sit, my heart, and Schechem and Uz are thine

Argos was the udder of the land, according to nourishing Homer

copying down everything he said on the shoulder-blades of oxen

Or, Dr Swift, and the horse

Shame is man's portion, and where there is no modesty the Cicadas are silent

Famine and scab do not plague the heart like insolence. (Or a sentence not in Tree: Ignorance begets insolence as Jacob begets Isaac)

Courtesy is the handmaid of learning
Vice is not so miry close to the Cherubims . . . (and the images of the Proof)

Hebrew literature is admonitory lore

If a truth is uttered by a froward person it should not be heeded until it rests again upon pure lips (and the mighty lines which follow)

What matters most

On haste: dung as you run

And the Words of what can the mind do . . .

TO USE WORDS WRONGLY CREATES EVIL IN THE SOUL

The lovely phrasing "When the past was beginng to fall somewhat feebly on Homer's ear"

THE OBSCURE REGIONS, OR THE IRRATIONAL, ARE THE MOTHER AND FATHER IN THE SON

Testicles—by Ceres!

The ass that made the grapes more plentiful by browsing on the vine-shoot taught men how to prune

Pascal on fear

The will empowers the soul

The passage which begins: "Eden is a shepherd's culture in which there is no time."

The head which jibes more than venery

ennui and fire will roar in his veins like the Fires of Gomorrah

and not to interrupt the Festival of Ceres

It is not difficult to say why I separate the Tree, Gomorrah, from the Flea, Sodom. It is the presence of the narrative, which is the Judas who is not present, even tho his creator is, his creature, in the Tree. Nor is it the narrative or the I as decoy: it is that the Horror, that which is, is juxtaposed. The eagle AND the cow.

> The Tree is the "Sayings of Dahlberg" as those of Socrates which you could not tell me where to find.

The Flea is one of the lost tragedies of Diogenes.
End: you will guess, if you know me, that that I read the Tree proves today was the first chance TO SIT. And these notes will tell you plain what you know that it takes more rumination than I have yet had to speak.

Constanza improves most slowly. All I was able to do was to divert and prepare myself by buying Bohns and Loebs: Athenaeus, Hesiod, Catullus, the Anthology, the Morals, Theocritus, Herodotus, Percy's Reliques, John Lyly's Plays, Elizabethan Lyrics. I traded all week: Lowdermilk was best, tho Reifsneider is now in my hand. But I have lost Ornstein: he could not stand that Reif gave me 13 dollars for what he offered 7!

Do not, please, be upset by what I have said. Am I so wise? I am not. I am in love with FLEA—and as I told you, I am of such a nature . . . . TREE is very beautiful.

Your friend
CHARLES OLSON

Hotel George Washington
23 Lexington Ave. at 23rd Street
New York 10, N.Y.

September 29, 1948

My dear Charles:

Would you please send this letter on at once air mail. I have picked up some teaching but must find an inexpensive room. I got a much softer letter from Winifred. What chattering, mournful doves we are when we have no need to be a serpent. She needs money, and so I must earn money to send it to her to help keep her and my two infants.

This in haste, Charles. Please let me hear your decision. I have interviewed about five Columbia graduate students, none of whom I could send down with any assurance. Am I to appoint a teacher for Black Mountain College who will praise Hemingway and syntactical Tate and so help remainder our books.

That reminds me, in conclusion, American neuter style, I beg to remainder your books; you need not bother about mine. I have always had the most chivalrous publishers who have taken care of this for me.

I do earnestly hope that your Constanza is thriving again.

> My love,
> EDWARD DAHLBERG

■ ══ ■

Edward Dahlberg
General Delivery
Church Street,
New York, N.Y.

[ADDED IN PRINTED SCRIPT:]

I got your book for nothing, a pure metaphysical price, signed by you!

[ENCLOSED WITH LETTER TO OLSON:]

My dear Winifred:

On October 28th our darling Geoffrey will be three years old. I should like to buy clothes for him and to kiss him. I must tell you, Winifred, I prefer to be the raging Furioso rather than the soft and nimble Iago. You do your self great wrong in heeding the counsel of easy spoken deceit. I wish for yourself you would depart from the vile [B]osshards and Moore. Why do you go to people whom you abhor; you ever looked for Moore's death and the Bosshards you found dullards; a dull man is always a baleful basilisk.

I am perplexed to have your letter proffering friendship whilst you prepare in your heart a legal document designed to purloin whatever I have. As I said in my previous words to you I do not smart at the loss of possessions. Can I eat the pewter, the pottery, the chairs bought with so much tender feeling; eat them, Winifred, but in the end it will fill the gullet of Charybdis. Abstract the gold from my poor mother's blood, but it will do you no good. I am certain of that, knowing how we are tormented for our baneful acts. I shall oppose you in nothing; I am simply amazed at your fond and erring nature: you value my friendship yet you rush to lawyers to filch from me land, house, goods,—ay it is sad that you should do so. You tell me you are not avaricious! maybe not; but tell me how you spell your deeds. Have I not repeatedly told you that I had no wish to slough away any burden I owed you and our tender fleshed infants. When you wrote me the letter saying how little money you had, I had less than you, and could not then get any. Olson's wife was in the hospital and his Guggenheim dollars were not released. I had already borrowed heavily against my salary. Yet do not think it was painful to me not to be able to send you money at once. Of course, I realized you might take money from me and then jibe at me in your soul. Winifred, if you have not Clytemnestra's liver you will tread more gently upon my life. It cannot be wholly opaque to you that you kindled the greatest rages in me. It is a fine and wily subterfuge to tell lawyers, police, jackanapes, foul-livered and rank lipped dolts how cruel and darksome and blackamoor is my soul. But what do you say to your hidden self? Did I grudge you dollars; did I spare my skin when you required protection; did I benefit in any way from your trust, a sore evil to me always? Pile on my head the plague of your own perversity, and you drop ruin upon your face. Neither you nor I can shun the fate we woo. The property you are taking perforce from me will be dust; neither you nor our hallowed children will have any benefit from it. Without my counsel the trust will moulder too. And what will happen to you, Winifred; you will cry out in your affliction for the man you now gull and despise. I beg you to do one thing; yes, get the divorce you pine for; take the belongings perforce; disport if you must with low, cankered skin. Just let me see and touch our two infants. I will clothe them and do all that I can to help you; you know I am no skinflint. Let me spend the day with Geoffrey, that is, the 28th of October; if you wish, come on the 29th, bring Joel, please, and any doughty protector you wish. If you will show some heart's civility I can relieve you of hardships and will do so freely. You can shed the bland tear upon legal shoulders, also, and make your own court-room exactions. That won't do you much good, Winifred; the houses have their dangling, taloned roots in loathly sand; I have not. However, I beg you to know that it is in my free desire to be an advantage to your life regardless of what fetters you forge on what stinking stithy of fate. That, alas, is your doing. I will not deny, that if the varlets you trust at the instant harm you, it will be grievous to me.

Naturally, I will take care of all expenses. I suggest meeting you in New York because Washington is too far; besides, I detest Massachusetts more than Poe did.

Have pity on Geoffrey and Joel; do not orphan them so long as nature does not. You know how I dote on Geoffrey; without him I walk a sundered Lucifer on asphalt and bitumen. The very little I ask you for is that benediction you must not deny our infants, some touch with the nature of their father.

I am reading constantly, Shakespeare, Josephus, Philo, Horace, a Christopher Smart translation Olson has given me, and gathering my forces together to assault Pisgah. This time I shall see Canaan!

Will you, please, Winifred, send my overcoat and my corduroy shirts, and the books and the photographs of my mother. I asked you for these in my previous letter.

Read this epistle carefully, and see whether anything in it is not plain and straightaway. See whether I urge you to drop any action you deem a protection to yourself although you procure this by wounding my name and pressing your heel hard upon the very essence of my spirit. I want one thing: I believe the issue of Edward Dahlberg should have some palpable connection with this impalpable image. Had you been the Beatrice of my soul, you would know that every apostle of vision from the beginning of time has been roughly spat upon by the mediocre. You wanted a poet to have the easy and pliant acquiescences of the rude, the liar and the fool. Like the admiring rout we had around us; you admired my book but fled from the wisdom therein. But time will hear me out, and all the revolting dust that now wickedly lies upon my name, will go to their burial place of oblivion and Acheron filth, but my words will breathe like the Ephesian sod. I know that and I need no one else save my own pulses to give me the oracular knowledge.

Take care of our beloved little stalks of innocence who make a quiet covenant with me that will be goodly for our infants. Ask yourself, whether I ask much; remember what I have often cited from St. Shakespeare; use these lines as your aegis when you are prompted to run to evil mouths and pustular lips for a judgment of me, "Goodness and wisdom to the vile seem vile; filths but savour themselves."

EDWARD DAHLBERG

[POSTCARD, IN PRINTED SCRIPT:] [New York City]

Dear Charles:—

Thank you very much for the Book & for the Words: I love Both.

Soon as I have some tranquil moments, & can in some way dissolve the melancholia in my bones—ay, I am as sad as Saul, knowing not how to avert fate & Mt. Gilhoa, I will write, & earnestly thank you—

My love—
EDWARD DAHLBERG

[HANDWRITTEN, BOTH SIDES OF A POSTCARD]

[Washington, D.C.]

Thursday afternoon [September 30, 1948]

Edward:

A note, as I take the mss to the p.o., to send registered: it should be in Straus' hands in the morning. Very much regret I was not home to talk to you: you have a register and tone now to tell of the Dostoevsky furnace you are being burned in.

I wired and wrote [Joseph] Albers [rector of Black Mountain College]. All you said of it was true. I need it, and have left myself in a money state I don't know the way out of. But interior things fix me here. I shall have to find work, some appointment in this swamp where I find ground.

I also sent off the letter. And the book to you will go to Church Street, unbeliever.

Your friend,
CHARLES

[Robert] Payne is out: has had all his books refused, his time in the U.S. is up, and, with his tail in his hand, he must go off to Persia, Tibet, and Delhi, poor man.

■══■

[New York City]

Oct 4, 48

My dear Charles:—

Thank you deeply for your letter. Did you mail the book, or am I to continue to be the first infidel, the alone & the dark that Adam begot before Seth. The harpy harrys, Harry Moore, Harry Bosshard (with the help of Anne [Bosshard], who has the glazed eyes of the rodent) are working with her. So would you, please, Charles, say that I'm living in a room in Washington should any one ask. I must keep this N.Y. residence hidden.

I could get you part-time teaching in N.Y. if you wanted it; but you would have to move with celerity. Did you send [   ] Cloutrem a letter?

I earnestly hope Constanza is much improved—

Forgive these bleak, tombed words [   ] Sam Rosenberg I think of him & his wallet, as skinny as the Jade Rozinante because of me——

Your friend,
EDWARD.

It was very good of you to send the Ms. so quickly——Thanks, thanks—

■══■

[POSTCARD WITH PRINTED SCRIPT:]   [New York City]
still at Broadway Central Hotel

Dear Charles:—

I earnestly hope you are out of bed now; would urgently advise you not to make the journey south until you are stronger!
Professor Oscar Cargill, an admirer of "Call Me Ishmael," wants to meet you & have lunch with you when you come to N.Y. I saw a copy of the volume in a bookshop, "Call Me Ishmael" & could not resist buying it.

2. There are a few others who would like to know you. I put your book in everybody's hands.

I toil for my life, my spirit, & pray heaven, my wrath will be no less than Achilles', & my words as sharp as the Delian Ash when I get to my book! Ay I pray,—so many of my petitions to heaven have been bootless cries. Would you, please, ask Albers to have my books, all in cartons, sent Railway Express, to me——I have also there [Black Mountain College] some clothes, a student lamp, a couple of pieces of pewter, Navajo Rugs, a hat, an aluminum spun study lamp——I would be grateful if you could get a student to pack them very securely. Perhaps you would be good enough to see that he does. Almost everything is tied up in cartons except Friedlander's 4 volumes on Roman Manners & Habits, very scarce——

Please send the verse as early as you can——, take care of yourself &
all love to you & Constanza——
EDWARD DAHLBERG

You are [right?] about Sam R[osenberg].

■ ══ ■

Washington

Thursday [October 7, 1948]

My dear Edward:

Albers has written, accepting my decision not to leave Washington this year, but inviting me to come down for a week now to lecture and give seminars. It fits, for Constance needs such a change before returning to her job, which she is now determined to do. So it looks now as though we will spend next week down there. And what I'm hoping might emerge from it is some arrangement by which I might go down there a little of each month, in such fashion to make it possible for us to get through this winter financially. I'd hazard the guess some such plan is in Albers mind. So, if you will now add your blessing to what was born in your brain in the 1st place, Black Mt may be the magic to solve what has, up to now, been a knot in which I was so bound I was unable to use my sword.

((Your mail, or messages, from you and to you, will be forwarded with ours, and I shall despatch them to you, Edward.

And do write again. Your postcard was a golden leaf in this drear fall week, and I am most anxious to have your news of the diseaseion of Farrar & Straus.

Sam grunted. (I gather he is Rosinante. The Institute [at BMC] don't pay, have 17,000 deficit)

I have spent two days in Crete and Mycenae, following an Ariadne thread of my mind, and feel somewhat refreshed. But the words do not go down on paper and you know, cher maitre, what that means to such a neolith as I.

Constanza is now almost a woman again and joins me

in love,
CHARLES

■ ══ ■

[New York City]

October 9, 1948

My dear Charles:

I wish I had the grassy quiet of the early Genesis Giants. There has been word from her. A legal document which I refused came from Wareham, Mass, and that is doubtless her word and gift. It will, perhaps, now go back to Wareham, and then be mailed to Black Mountain or to you. I must keep my New York whereabouts sphynxed. It is registered and requires a return signature. Will you please handle it as skillfully as you can and send it to me so that it will not be known to her that I am in New York. There is the base problem of finding a lawyer here. I do not know to whom to go. Worst of all, my tender Geoffrey is still hidden from me, and that is "The cankerous wound that bites my flesh." If you have, Charles, any suggestions please let me know. Meanwhile, I walk a solitary Lucifer upon bitumen and asphalt.

It is a felicity to hear that you're making arrangements with Albers that will be helpful to you. I earnestly hope that Constanza will benefit by the change. Should you want me to write to Albers suggesting that you go down once a month for lectures and seminars I will do so at once.

I regret to hear that neither Sam nor his Rozinante wallet is to be fed barley, hens, or wine for his teaching. You were as wily as Odysseus about that school; little wonder that Roosevelt wanted to appoint you the assistant secretary of the treasury. Such exchequer olfactories!

Your judgments on the Tree are doubtless very good; the obscurity which compression brings is still unresolved. It is a fault. I have always believed that the path to perception is perception, and that all else is waste, Dead Sea prose.

The MS has not been read. Whether so small a book will entice a publisher is perhaps doubtful. I am thinking of following a suggestion you made and organically enlarging The Flea of Sodom by pilfering gnomes from the Tree. It is wholly your thought. What I will do is to fatten incident with more adages and add new ones too.

You see I write fumblingly. My letter is not sharply limned as yours. My soul and my knees are feeble, yea, as weak as the cony in the Psalms. You have now the books you need for your spirit and when you have fed upon Bashan and Carmel you will be more filled than when you wrote CALL ME ISHMAEL. So be patient; take your loaves, your timbrel and flagon of wine and go up to the Mount of God.

My head was my obsession, says Verhaeren. Mine is Geoffrey, and when I do not think of him my mind is upon my friend, Charles Olson.

Love to you and to your Constanza,
EDWARD DAHLBERG

■ ══ ■

Monday morning [October 18, 1948]

Edward:

We are just in fr Black Mt, and I wanted you to know your letter to Winifred (sent fr NY Saturday) was posted off from the P.O. I hope, for your sake, that that was the only letter you sent for mailing last week. I discovered this morning that the forwarding order I left a week ago got so fouled in the stupidities of the P.O. that all our mail but this one letter from you has been sent to Santa Cruz, California!

You must forgive me I did not write for a week, the more so I had a beautiful letter from you just before we left. But I threw my energies forward into that place, and neglected all else, in order to pierce it to the root.

That done, what shall I say? It is a lovely girl with whom I am in love. You were right. In some karmic fashion, the place is very right on this prick of my time. Albers has asked me to return in the middle of November and again in the middle of December, and I shall—for three days each time. But I am seriously considering reopening with him the offer of settling there for the winter and spring—if, now that he has had the fountain, he should want to repeat it. I gave him an abundance: a class each day, Monday thru Friday. And three public goes in the dining room in the evening.

We are both deeply in your life for the giving of it: it was an illumination when we, unknowing, craved it, and fed like hungry animals. And you are remembered with the proper ambiguity: the best have you hot in them like a discharge from a mortar. It is a measure of Albers size he carries you as fire.

I am most anxious to exchange stories with you. And shall, soon. When, now, I don't know. But I must go off to New England shortly to bed my mother for the winter and shall get in touch with you when I am in N.Y.

Do pardon this rapid note as I am in the door. It is inadequate to our gratification. But hear the love

Your friend's & Constanza's
CHARLES

[POSTCARD]   [New York City]

Oct. 19, 48

Dear Charles:

I would be very grateful, if you could send me ten dollars by return mail. In a few weeks I hope to be out of dollar difficulties: Would that I could get that devil out of my life—would that I had the asses & oxen of Jacob!
It is a pulsing felicity to hear how good Black Mt is for both of you, & that it is the physic you need. I know few delights more tender to me than to serve your Muse & your imperial necessities. I am at 193 Waverly Place; should you get here, on the sudden, as I surmise you

will, & I am out, leave a note & tell me where I can reach you—I see people & so dissolve the pinching ache & the gall.

Both you & Constanza have my love—

Your devoted friend,
EDWARD DAHLBERG

■ ══════════════════════════════════════ ■

[Washington, D.C.]

Wednesday [October 20, 1948]

Edward:

Constanza goes now to the post office to see this off to you—yr card just came in the afternoon mail.

You are right, I probably will jump on new york like an animal. Yr address leaves me in a quandary where to send this ten dollars. I shall send it to Church St.

So do excuse these bare words—it is an act of despatch.

Love fr us both
CHARLES

■ ══════════════════════════════════════ ■

[POSTCARD IN PRINTED SCRIPT:]   [New York City]

October, 1948

Dear Charles: 1.

My grateful appreciation for the ten dollars—I am too sundered to write you as my heart dictates. This woman has put her hece upon my spirit, & it is so flattened that no blood flows. Your troubles, too, are another stinging defeat upon my head. Should you & Constanza wish to go to the Wellfleet house (it has an automatic oil furnace, brand new, & neither you nor I could blow it up, God or Devil-willing).

2.

I wish I could write, & assault the heavens——All my Pulses urge me to——but one reading of the Psalms of St. Shakespeare, & I will wrestle, till my thigh is wrenched, with the Angel at Peniel——These are the blades in my throat & my pain pierces so——————

My love to you & Constanza—
EDWARD DAHLBERG

Does Constanza know some woman who could put thru a call to Chicago from New York——some one in New York, with vocal secretarial efficacy, who could be representing a teacher's agency—I hope, maybe, to get Winifred's address, & see my Geoffrey! darling stalk of pulsing innocence. Please let me know by return mail, Charles——

Your friend & Constanza's

■ ══ ■

[New York City]

October 29, 1948

My dear Charles:

I have had no word from you and pray that you and Constanza are not having hardships. I want to thank you again for sending the ten dollars so promptly. I am concerned over my debt to Sam Rosenberg, but so far have not been able to dissolve my debts here. I had to borrow money from the chairman to get through the month.

I write no one but you, my sometime spouse, and her Cape Cod lawyer, a fine and stygian triune. Of the three you alone have my healing word as doleful and wanting as it is.

I continue to read; it is my sole balsam. I am trying to find another room. Where I live at present is the house of Sodom, the man who lets out the rooms being a half-dame from the plains of Gomorrah.

Nothing came of the publishing incident. The head of the firm said he did not have enough learning to read the manuscript and that he could not afford to print a book for a private audience, you, Constanza, Sam Rosenberg and three other maimed and sorrowing spirits who read and petition heaven for three privy readers.

Tell me, please, whether you have shelter and what you and Constanza are going to do.

I do earnestly hope to see you soon.

Love to you and Constanza.

Your friend,
EDWARD DAHLBERG

[POSTCARD]

[New York City]

Oct. 30, 48

Dear Charles:—I am very hindered. Whenever it seems I might see my Geoffrey, my letter does not get to my erstwhile spouse, or you disappear. I phoned you yesterday & was told the phone was disconnected. I sent a letter to you to her lawyer trying to make arrangements to see Geoffrey. You, Charles, are the breathing witness of my love unto cracked distraction for Geoffrey. Please put an air mail stamp on the letter to her Cape Cod lawyer. Get it there, with Mercury's golden sandal, I beg you! & let me know where you are. I cannot even receive my mail so desperately needful at the instant. My tears fall on dry potsherds. I must keep my N.Y. residence a secret: otherwise I would not bother you. I still hope to form a group with Herbert Read & in which I deeply include you. A letter came from him today, giving me the name of 2 anarchists who have a press. He is working for publication of the book. Be sure you will be printed when you are ready! Read writes in despair of the "fat, pursy times": "We vent our indignation (if we have your prophetic force) on a seething mass far too preoccupied with its own dissolution to turn an ear to our lamentations." If you are my friend, as I have ever been yours, [   ], I entreat you to get my letters to the baleful Scylla, the state of Mass. And let me know where you are!

Your loving and deeply torn friend
EDWARD DAHLBERG

[HANDWRITTEN NOTE:]

Ed—

a slight hold-up   i don't see how i can get out of here, to worcester,
& to ny by tomorrow
we better plan it   for *wednesday* afternoon   if by any chance i can
get there tuesday you will have heard from me by 3   but all signs say
wednesday, around 2
christopher smart is beautiful and it was a beautiful evening, turning
on the Wheel of Sheol

love
CHARLES

■ ══ ■

[HANDWRITTEN NOTE AT BOTTOM OF A FORM LETTER FROM
POLYTECHNIC INSTITUTE OF BROOKLYN, DATED OCTOBER 25, 1948, FROM
DEAN ERICH HAUSMANN ASKING CORRESPONDENT TO COMPLETE A
"PERSONNEL BLANK."]

[New York City]

Dear Charles:—It was deeply good of you to phone me—I go now, I
think, to 143 Lexington Ave—phone—Mu 3-0019. You say nothing
of Sam Rosenberg; please assure him as soon as I can make some stable
life for myself. If I hadn't taken those accursed planes I could have sent
my wife money—I am quite sick about the whole thing, so heart-
wounding— Please mail this to her lawyer as soon as you can. Tell me
how you came out of your own eviction turmoil. Do you have a roof, &
do I have a mailbox in Washington!
As [?] we sing, "when shepherds pipe on oaten straw", if we
could—
When will the Poems [Y & X (Washington, D.C.: Black Sun Press,
1948)] be printed—
I read & lament & walk—

All my love to you & Constanza,
EDWARD DAHLBERG

■ ══ ■

Nov. 2, 48

Send all mail, Charles, to Broadway-Central Hotel, Broadway & 3rd St. Am staying there now.

Dear Charles:—

Evidently none of my letters are getting through—I sent you [two?], & one to the lawyer in Hyannis. I phoned yesterday, using a subterfuge, & learned he has not received a letter sent out a week ago to you. If Constanza has the letter, please don't mail it. I want to rewrite it.

I *must* have, Charles, a Washington address or some city other than N.Y., so as to conceal my whereabouts & at the same time be able to negotiate. If I am ever to see my son Geoffrey, I must get my mail through to the lawyer *now*. Otherwise, it means denial, the rack, & unpurging lamentation. Please see my friend if there is not some way.—

There was no talk of lowering salaries; on the contrary, Albers was going to increase them.

How deeply it pleases me to hear the Poems are at last to be born, or at least to have the ripening light. Nothing came, Charles, of the Straus encounter. I want very much to return my MS, but have no copy. I wrote you yesterday Read wrote a very sweet letter. You, Read & I will yet, alongside others, form a group to publish our work. Any thing that heaven sends me must include you—All my love to you & Constanza—ever.

& please answer right away, so I can begin negotiations with the lawyer. And give me an address, please. Not knowing where you were, & not being able to consummate anything, was a bleak destroying angel for me for a week. I was reft of reason. If I could yield up that fetid spectre, & keep my senses, if I could—I would not rave on bitumen & asphalt—

EDWARD DAHLBERG

[Washington, D.C.]

Monday afternoon Nov 22 [1948]

Edward—

The enclosed in the afternoon mail.

I returned fr BM yesterday morn: our friends here brought over paintings & [Caresse] Crosby contributed [? ies] & the 1st 2 copies of Y & X. So today we have a little money to stave off the summons & hold our house, for the moment. With the BM money I can begin to go ahead.

Yr goods will be sent to you paid. They are boxed & ready: done by Mme Bodky [wife of Erwin Bodky, pianist and professor of music at BMC]—and yr "bete," Jackson [BMC student?]! All that is required is word from you direct to Ted Dreier [founder, with John Andrew Rice, of BMC; originally at Rollins College, Winter Park, Florida, left with Rice in 1933 to become a professor of physics at BMC, ousted by faculty vote, and departed for good in April 1949]. He asked me to ask you to say to him where you wanted them sent. I hope that pleases you.

And soon we must both get free of difficulties & have the chance to let breath & words in. For now

my love,
CHARLES

■ ━━━━━━━━━━━━━━━━━━━━━━━━━━━━━━━━━━━━━━ ■

[New York City]

November 25, 1948

My dear Charles,—

Thank you deeply for your note. I take joy in your book of verse and wait to have a copy inscribed by you, my dearest friend. My sole physic has been reading; I have seen many people, but I go out to be entertained to find that I am the entertainer. Tonight I see a group of painters and sculptors. I am taking Berenice Abbott, the photographer. She should do a camera-portrait of you! I don't particularly care for the one on the dust-jacket of the book. It appeals to me because I am so fond of you; this sentence I shall not consummate as I see you grinning and making ready to pierce me with some bodkin word or other.

Maybe, today, I will find a typist who can make a few copies of the FLEA, and then send you one. I am so pleased that the books are going to be sent and to be paid for by Black Mountain College. O that is a benediction, a beaker of brine. Thank you, my bow to you and to Albers.

In a month or two I will begin fumbling with the Word. What my surging soul so pines to do I fear to begin.

The other day I read that Paris was reared by a hind,—a lovely legend that succored me for days, and is in the season of my own spirit and hungers.

It is very good of my bete noir Jackson to take care of the books. Give my oaf, my imp, my trauma, my gratitude; tell him he begins to know learning and has an occult being that Ben Jonson would have reckoned to be mineral for his pen.

Do I laugh? ay, it is the smarting laughter that rends the bowels. I know no other simple save lamentation.

Many times I have been sorely tempted to go to Washington to spend a day with you, but I cannot afford to do it. I still owe you ten dollars. What has become of our giant of Anak, our six-fingered man of vision of Gaza, Samuel Rosenberg? You are much too silent; let us have prayers and divulgations. I owe him money, too, and were it not that I have been sending dollars to Winifred I would have paid you and him. Forgive me for being so laggard.

When do I get the POEMS? You know what a sack of cupidity I am for a book, particularly one by you. This will be the second contemporary volume I have read in a decade. The first one was by an author named Charles Olson.

Does Constanza flourish? When will you get here. You know how it is in America, you are either, au courant, or in the gutter; and so I have to make a valiant combat for my life, and I have by necromancy and the help of heaven to whom I have given such bootless orisons, gotten to know people. The women I have met have tried to snare me. Imagine a woman so infatuate as not to have sufficient lore of her own organs to know that she does not have to be any more guileful than she was ordained to be by nature. It is very droll, and very drying, to watch a woman employ stratagems. Oh what impotencies come from such an arid well!

All my love to you and Constance. I remain at the Broadway
Central Hotel, so please write me here. Should i by mischance find
another room I will send you a telegram or have that fleeting pleasure
of speaking to you over the telephone.

Your devoted friend,
EDWARD DAHLBERG

■ ══ ■

[Washington, D.C.]

Wed [December 8, 1948?]

My dear Ed:

I have just written a note to Albers to tell him I arrive Monday
morning at his whistle stop. And Jeremiah save us—I look forward to
it! What do you say to that, maestro? But I'm nix on settlin' there. Too
thin for steady wear. [Max] Dehn [professor of mathematics at BMC]
and I descend on the place like archangels and go away like banana
skins, and it is better that way. But it won't last, alas. And I need—o
do I need—their gold. (We have held the house. Friends raised 50
dollars, and that bone stopped the yap of Madame Bartlett and agent
and court but yesterday down they came again with a 175 slap. And as
for clothes I am at that point from which there is no turning, I look as
bohemian as I did in the village, aetat 1940. Not to speak of the
butcher.) How do you fare, brother?

You should not be mortally grieved. You know me, Brer Fox. Name's
Possum. And been mighty behind (and white) these many months. I
got back to this desk and several uninterrupted days last week and feel
properly chagrinned, for a change. (I have not your management, most
gifted friend! of language or of life, those *ars*. For me to be a knife
takes too much whetting. Enough:)

But I do some things. Yr mss., for example, went off five minutes
after it came, to one of the three, the 1st & most commercial. All we
can do is light candles by aloes. "This incongruous world of ours", sd
Herman Melville, as of his tale of one, Budd.—I shall let you know
the result the moment I hear. I imagine it'll be some weeks. You did
not include RATIONAL T. Unless you are rewriting it, I think it would
be better to present that too. I do not want to see you put off by the
slides they used on me—too slight to make a book. Fat slices, that's
what the porcine want, eh?

We are heating the house with wood, to avoid starting the cost of coal, and the smell is lovely, and if I were about my own work I might feel like a New England Orpheus. But I'm busy trying to make 40 dollars, writing a review of three new books on Melville, one of which will interest you, F. Barron Freeman's edition of BILLY BUDD, in which he prints for the first time the original version, a short story from which Melville tried to develop the longer one. It is a third as long and has all the celerity the "novel" lacks, rotted as it is by that sad, sad notion of poor Melville's that Hawthorne was the better man. What a blight that spinster needle was on his hebraic imagination! — You know how long I have stooped and gone aside on BILLY BUDD. It is satisfying now to have a version I can read, to be able to speak of a short story with enough respect to mention it in the same breath with Benito Cereno or Bartleby. The curious thing is, how Hawthorne is the tree that brought forth sodom fruit in Melville's ground, and crowded out his own Saul-David root; Hawthorne to Christ to the pain of the sentences of billy budd, Novel, is the dying off of a giant, a giant out of Samuel bred down to christian by a Nathaniel out of Salem. It is a dread, dread story, a fable, Edward, should be told to children of a golden age as warning. "Go not, with your flesh, to men of little blood." What is your wondrous quote, is it from Heraclitus, that to take thought is to thicken the blood around the heart?

I must go back to it. It is a delight to write to your ear.

And keep me informed of yourself. It was a very deep pleasure to talk to you last week and to have your delightful letter. You are resilient and you keep speech in your mouth like myrrh. I am glad for your sake as for mine. It is yr fatherhood.

Constanza returns your greetings. She is fine except for some peculiar pain and sense of calcification in the vertebra at the neck which her weeks in bed seem to have left her with. I too have trouble in the same region (without her cause) and live in dread, now that is again ugly winter, of a recurrence of that infection that laid me low two winters ago. But these are gloomy matters

> and I would send, end with
> love,
> CHARLES

My dear Charles, —

Your lovely book came last evening, and I am very grateful for it. I have done no more than glance at it. I had looked with some care at the TRINACRIA. Did not the infidel companions of Odysseus eat the oxen of Hyperion there? I was perplexed somewhat. I hear you say, Return, clodpate misreader, camel, beadle, egg without yolk. So I shall and very soon.

You have been deeply in my mind. The other day I saw Professor Cargill on the street and again he asked me to be sure that you called him when you arrive. Joseph Freeman [socialist critic and historian], whom I knew years ago, and who has a warm, Mediterranean brain, is eager to meet you. I gave him the [INSERTED IN MARGIN:] your book I bought. He is reading CALL ME ISHMAEL the second time. Every one asks after you, Monsieur Caviar, the women ask after the health of your navel and the unambiguous males enquire after your genius, beg for your address, and wish to know just what savings account you have. As a matter of truth, Joseph Freeman thought that a month hence or so we might make a little trip to Washington to see you.

I now have a week's vacation from teaching. Soft, archangelical words come from Winifred, but her acts are mortal foes to her low, sighing words. Nothing has been achieved. I am always poor because of her, and that is why I have not sent you money. I do not mean the small ten dollar debt to you, naturally it is little to me, since I owe it, and nothing to you as you have not got it. I am still sorely prone; she has powdered the very quiddity of my soul with her heel. She has the legal sickness; I would rather have the botch or the Neapolitan bone-ache.

Yes, I have met a number of women, one an icelandic dame, daughter of the prime-minister of Iceland who asked me to go there. O what a boreal place in which to sport. There is a Scotch woman, but she is married to a bad artist; he is a mongrel, Irish, Spanish, French, with a little poodle Balkan to it. A very hysterical man who promises to hang himself every time she threatens to leave him. Up till now I have always coveted the portion of the painter. He can hang his canvases; a writer can simply hang himself. I do not care for any more laceration than I have, and then I think my pulses are waning; soon as a woman is wary, my blood congeals. There is a Hungarian dame, very earnest and meek when she is alone with you; she strokes your thigh with the greatest integrity, but at a party she is spiceless, and I feel as knit to her as I would to a Eunuch at the court of Jezebel.

You will always require money, my dear friend, and so there will be time, a season for the peaches, and the deep pocket-reaches, ay, what a reechy couplet, were I ambitious enough I could get a Nobel award for such knavery.

Please pardon me if I fail you now; I am your friend in ACT, and when I prove it, as man must always prove his friendship, lest it spoil because it is not savored or eaten, and therefore was never ripe, then I can loosen my tongue.

I hear little of Constance, you send me her greeting, but it is such dry chaff it could burn without sun or fire.

Your devoted friend,
EDWARD DAHLBERG

[NOTE IN SCRIPT:]

Mrs. Sherwood Anderson may telephone you & Constance on her way back from the south. She is a fine woman, & both of you will enjoy her.

[Washington, D.C.]

January 15, xlix

My dear Edward:

Forgive me that I have delayed to write these abundant thanks for the grace and force of your letter to me about y & x.

But alas, it put me into my own despair. I have not been able to rise even tho the wings of your words let rise my spirit. For I am barren, and do not sing.

Instead, I shall include some days' work. You will understand.

There is a quarrel in me, and I am unhinged. You must excuse me if I have nothing to say. I do not know which part of speech to speak from, what organ. Some certain things have left me. Others are not yet born. I gnaw, and gnaw.

I have news for you, familiar news. Number 1 of 3 has said no on the FLEA. It was the most commercial. Suffering present, but not enough substance to make a book! Bah. I am sending both off now to 2: burn aloes and violets, if any grow by you, but keep the rue.

My thanks, dear Friend, my thanks. I am merely slain by my own perplexities.

my love,
CHARLES

[included with letter:]

TANTO E AMARA

I have heard the dread song

I had not heard, in the middle of life, I had not heard
I was all eyes, all things were, now they are blind
and I am, I crawl, do not know where I go
You who have heard the song will understand.
Death is a remote beginning.
I am rudimentary.
I grow a heart.

I stumbled when I saw, knew high passage, persons
one imperial nature whose conclusion was
nothing, it is nothing.
I know now it was nothing.

The wise man said, nothing dieth but changing as they do
one for another show sundry formes.
He lieth. I cannot have back my mother.

In the grave, before the dirt goes, will go my love

What shall I be, what forms will plague me then
where shall I go, in what ditch pour what blood to hear
her voice, the love I hear, that voice now mingled in
the song,
the song of the Worms?

CHARLES OLSON

< > [New York City]

January 18, 1949

My dear Charles:

Sent you a special, and then enclosed a note in another letter to be forwarded to Wellfleet. Would you please let me know by return mail the name of the school in which harry moore teaches and in what town it is located. Please!

My love to you
EDWARD

■ ══ ■

[New York City]

January 18, 1949

Dear Charles:

It is a deep pain to wound you. I send you my words out of the fat darkness of obscurity. Should there be truth in them, what good, alas, is it for you whom it prongs. Or what satisfaction can I have as a darkling, stumbling Tieresias whose penurious foreknowledge maims his friend. It requires years in Erebus to labor for a few poems, and one epistle to deny them! Did I not pay homage to your identity, knowing there are ideal images shadowed there more astounding than those in Plato's Cave, I would reckon myself an Iago to your Muse. Do not believe that I do not honor the imaginative strength of your line, or that I slyly hanker after the lucre clodpates of letters.

My own distraction has been so bizarre that I never asked you whether you received The Rational Tree. Horace Gregory read the two and his deepest yea is for the Rational Tree. He showed me some of his unpublished verse, one, My Lady Circe. He has our feeling for Homer and for the tripod. But how simple it was for me to locate his flaws, while yours so baffled me. They were as hard for me to fathom as sin, and as difficult to relinquish. I had to be two persons, a loving friend as well as the Conscience, the servant, and if necessary, the Erynes, of a Genius. Ay, speaking so, fate has been baying at my heels.

Nobody knows how to make a book; even after it has been written, and one or two or three human beings say yea to it, can the owner of the vision be sure he is not a lazar, a pickpocket, a lewd churl. How often can one read the most amazing line one has made without draining gall and hyssop? How long was Shakepeare able to stomach HAMLET? It was a spewing forth to begin with. Once Callimachus said, a great book is a great evil.

Yes, we know nothing, but such infamous divination is not the result of a Socratic syllogism. We go to the oracles slyly, but Apollo often gives hindmost replies or none at all, and in the meanwhile we are more plagued than the cattle who have murrain. No beast suffers so much as man. Man is miserable because he wants to be an animal or because he does not want to be one. The poet wishes to be a gifted beast!

Winifred disappeared from Massachusetts with my two sons. Would it be craven to say that were our calamities weighed in Job's Balances, mine would be the greater? I have had eleven more years than you in which to make a cairn of woes upon which no man pours oil or worships. What have I compassed that you have not? I have no verse printed or tombed in a drawer that remotely equals yours. Do I churlishly believe that SING O BARREN is as good or better than CALL ME ISHMAEL? I do not believe anything. The irrational god of my own powers and ruin does not let me so think. The only proposition I would earnestly ask you to ponder, or to dismiss, is this: the difference between CALL ME ISHMAEL and Y & X is the ultimate distinction between Edward Dahlberg and Ezra Pound. Now when I have said this, I am simply telling you what you are acting upon yourself. Your mountain springs and the Naiads of Helicon are in Statius, Chrysostom, Horace, Homer, Plutarch, and O merciless gods from whom we beg a basket of summer fruits and a BOOK, which when they give us we deny,—O such mocking deities, we have to fail or die! And death is the root and branch and flower of [ ]root of all literature, for Prosperpine, the consort of Pluto, is the Seed of those April, zephyry words that gull and cheat us, and for which we so pine.

Maybe, you could send a copy to Professor Oscar Cargill at New York University, Washington Square College; he is doing his second volume on American Literature and will be writing about you, and one to Horace Gregory, at Palisades, New York, Rockland County. I am thinking of some attention for the pomes. Would you send a review copy to Alexander Cappon, perhaps with your compliments and my regards. The University Review gets a good deal of attention. The address is Alexander Cappon, Chairman of the English Department, University of Kansas City, Rockhill Road and 50th Street, Kansas City, Missouri.

Let me, please, hear from you soon. I have a hundred examination books to grade, but I had to stop to write to you.

My devout belief and loving friendship.
EDWARD DAHLBERG

[New York City]

[January 19?, 1949]

My dear Charles:

Your POEMS kindle the greatest perplexities. I do not want to fathom speciously what you so plainly know. There are lines wondrously wrought, but I do not have enough of the darkling speaking heart in these five poems. Five small verses divulge the occult skill but not the minerals in the man. O I know we have less than five hundred lines of Heraclitus and Empedocles! It is not, perhaps, that you write too little, but that you do not walk forth upon the page as Empedocles or Charles Olson. I am a kindred of your vision, but the greater moiety of it you withhold for some riper seeding. Prosperpine descends into the dark earth to reappear in budding Spring. I wait for the leafage and parsley, and even for the choughs and the horned owls and the seagulls in the Cave of the Nymphs.

I do not comprehend all of your lines, and here I may be whipping myself. The riddle of a line should lie in its truth. Vision is the suffering pang of the bowels, but you have dismembered your sorrow and cast its Osirean body into the Nile. The pith of my meaning is in your beautiful, Learean chant, "Of bitter work, and of folly cockatrice and cockololly furiously sing." Here I am the vassal of your Imagination. The opening, though much less piercing, I pay homage to, because, I am such a fool as you, and dare you to be more the FOOL, "Go, fool, and hatch of the air a blue egg."

Your allusion to Trinacria I cannot understand; the definition is lucid, the text without ambiguity, but why should such a thought be in your imperial nature: "Who fights behind a shield Is separate, weak of the world Is whirled by sons of self, sown As teeth, a full armed crop Sprung from no dream No givers of a fleece Who bring their dragon blood inside Reality, half slain" Is not the world the baneful chalice? Who would drink more of such Medean ingredients? We sow dragon's teeth in the Cadmean fallows, and the armed men that crop up against us is the World from which we separate ourselves. The lines, penned in gore, not the ewe's, the goat's, the ram's, but the heart's, are too sententiously dried out.

If I have misread you, do not believe that some arrant knave who praises you will do better. The men who bring us laurels and chaplets are our Erynes.

There is only one jot of dross in all the verses. You will find no healing seaweed or salts in a Buchenwald. You are too abstruse to require *more* experience. Vent your Angers, and the Muses will give you fillets and sweet calamus.

Please do not be vexed with me. No man is a more steadfast Horatio to your Genius than I am, but I look for the crowing of the dawn in your nature, for the Morning Star, Lucifer, and for Isaiah's cockatrice that creepeth in the every man's skin to make its hiss, and I want to see the piteous Ghost that wails so secretly, and on the nightside of our selves, drop its filmy garment upon the head, and then disappear as one man vanishes from another after he has emitted the nether deposits of his identity.

At the moment, I am a nullity, and hear nothing but the song of the Worms.

Do not think that I do not consider these poems of dear Worth, or that I go hankering after some churl of letters for better ones. They are the best, but they are not good enough for me from Charles Olson.

Your loving friend who deeply thanks you for sending the POEMS and for the tender words you wrote.

EDWARD DAHLBERG

January 19, 1949

My dear Charles:

I wrote you a special delivery letter this morning, and pray you will have it by this evening. Would be grateful to you if you would send this right out to Miss Freeman at Wellfleet. And will you, please, send back any letter I may get from her, special delivery.

My love,
EDWARD

■ ══ ■

[Washington, D.C.]

Wednesday [January 19, 1949?]

My dear Edward:

All three of your letters came, and the letter to la dame sans merci was off and away from here at noon.

the worm moore crawls on ground I used to know well as a child— Wellesley Hills, Mass., where my father's sister lived (I learned to my horror a short while ago that she was struck down by an automobile in her age and her life was so taken from her)

moore is a small part of another knave's place, the Babson Institute (which also was a part of my life[)], for Roger Babson comes from Gloucester, and I was raised and attended by his sons who are physicians—Babson you will know as that gimcrack of business

I have just talked to La [Caresse] Crosby to try to get out of her the three copies you recommend be sent. I feared it would, at this moment, be difficult, for she just mailed 50 press copies, and as she has sold only 30, and is in debt for some 1200 dollars for the edition, she is copy-shy. But she allowed as how she would send one off to Horace Gregory at least. (Do keep me posted if he doesn't receive it fairly soon.) I am somewhat disadvantaged pressing her because some two years ago she paid me $100 for the verse and then, last summer, when Constanza was ill, advanced me another $50 against sales. (Which is, as you well know, high behavior for publishers for such low attractions as ourselves!) But in a short time I shall be able to acquire two more copies and shall see that Cargill and Capon receive them. It may be only that they will not have them until Feb 1st. How much further I can go with Mme will depend on what sort of notices, if any, the slim-thing receives.

You have all my heart's responses for your troubles, from 100 blue books out! If only Black Mt were in NY you'd have unshouldered that weight at least!

This note is a thin thing for such an ample letter as you gave me, but I am writing it to catch the afternoon collection and deliver the corpse of moore into your hands.

Do write me as many times again. It is a deep pleasure.

Your friend
CHARLES

■══■

[Washington, D.C.]

Wednesday Feb 2 [1949]

My dear Edward:

Are you allright? I have the feeling you are so involved in transactions in the Wellfleet-Plymouth-Provincetown triangle that you have no time except for that pool and billiard game of women you must play.

I have mapped out your present life in spite of your silence: it is clear you must be teaching at NYUWashSq, live in that fallen ymca the B[roadway]-C[entral], when you are not bedding yourself down in some of that Scotch-Rumanian-Irish hay you made my mouth water with, Silenus. But when do you read and write?

I reread THE FLEA before I shipped it off again, and I am the more convinced about it. Did you do any more with your own idea, to expand it as a narrative? Or to do another in a like form? ((In answer to your query, THE TREE did come, and I have it, still stubbornly seeking to have the FLEA published for itself. I hope you won't mind my critical stool, from which, as you once said, one always falls into the dungheap.

I read, go out, and do not do enough work—But why should I sting myself with lead? I am in a period of reading and question, and am desperate. Nothing as shape pulls me on. But today there are shadows of a shape, and I feel better.

Tonight I go to see for the first time Mr and Miss Graham dance. For Mr (then Erick Hawkins) I did that play with the obscene title [punning on "The Fiery Hunt"]. But Mrs (then Miss Hush) I have not seen dance. I doubt I shall be able to dispel Fannie Brice as Martha Graham in a Follies years ago.

Two things come to my mind to ask you: you never did give me an inscribed copy of BONES (I know I have a SING, but [no] BONES, sir). Nor have I any longer my copy which I gave away to Robert Payne when he left for Tibet. I have no way of knowing whether you have any copies, and I do not want you at this straitened time to buy one. But keep it in your mind that I have asked for one.—And one time when you have another copy present it to BLACK MT: I keep sending the men and women there (Yala [Heinrich Jalowetz, Viennese musicologist at BMC, known as "Jalo"], Bodky on around) to your text. And there is none.

This was a note to include bills, receipts, and like dregs, which I'd have no man receive like cold meat.

And your word?
Love,
CHARLES

[New York City]
February 3, 1949

Dear Charles:

I found Winifred and Geoffrey and Joel [Dahlberg's other son by Winifred, also known as Kevil O'Carroll] and Sharon [Moore, daughter of Winifred and Harry T. Moore] in a town [Croton-on-Hudson in Westchester County] just outside of New York City. It took the wiliness of Odysseus to locate them. Sharon cannot endure [Harry] Moore. I go up each week-end to see them. Geoffrey is extremely tender and very crestfallen when I leave.

I have been in Erebus. Have been reading some Statius and Plato. Did you see to it that the POEMS were sent to Horace Gregory.

Paul Christensen ▪ 79

I have been sorely troubled about the money owing to Sam Rosenberg, but what with taxes and mortgage payments and money required to take care of the children I have so far been unable to repay him. He will be paid, and with my heart thanks.

I am really prone; please forgive this epistle as sluggish in spirit as the waters of Styx.

> My love to you, and do write me.
> EDWARD DAHLBERG

It is a mistake not to send Oscar Cargill a book; he will be writing about you. Unless you crave fatter oblivion than is mine, you must guide your publisher. Moore said that Caresse Crosby hated me. She came to see me years ago, wishing to print proletarian literature. I at once advised her that that was an oxymoron, and saved her money and shame. I am as despised as Jeremiah, a derision on the tongues of churls. If a man is without arms or legs he breaks me with his tongue. Charles, please get this letter to the tax collector into the mail right away. I would consider it a great kindness if you would forward any mail to me with despatch. I must prevent the usurers from getting the property.

■══════════════════════════════════════■

[New York City]

February 7, 1949

My dear Charles:

I spend my week-ends with Winifred and the children. She is still deeply drawn to me, but I do not know what we will do. When a woman becomes rational I go mad, and like Christopher Smart, am ready for Bedlam.

Winifred had a long conversation with Edmund Wilson in Wellfleet not long ago. The quiddity of the conversation is something like this:

Wilson: I have the greatest respect for Edward's gifts; but if I read his book and don't care for it, he will become very angry with me.

Winifred: I don't think you should read it. I would not put it into the hands of anybody who did not beforehand have a quick sympathy for it. Besides, you don't have the culture to read it.

Wilson: I am very fond of Edward. Why don't you let me send it to England. A contest is being held and Edward might win $5000.

Winifred: I am not a literary critic, and my name never appeared in the New Yorker. But Edward has read the Masters to me so that I can tell the difference between merde and poetry. You have read so much contemporary filth that you no longer know how to read.

Wilson: I have real affection for Edward. Why don't you let me send it to Herbert Read so that he could enter his MS in the contest and win $5,000.

Winifred: I admit I have a copy of Edward's MS, but I know he would prefer posthumous publication to a contest.

Wilson: If a woman believed in me as you do in Edward, maybe even I could write something momentous. I know Edward is remarkable, but I don't want him to turn on me as he had done to others. I think he ought to send his book to the contest and win $5,000.

Winifred: Edward would never win a prize because the judges can't read or write. You never cared for his other book.

Wilson: Edward is a wonderful person, but I don't think I ought to read his book. But why don't you let me mail his MS. to the jurors in England. Sometimes people are so gifted that they totally misunderstand a book and award it $5,000.

I am still reading and teaching at Brooklyn Polytechnic College. As soon as there is quiet in my belly and frankincense in my mouth I will begin to fumble for words. I have a copy of Do These Bones Live in Wellfleet, and as soon as I can get one from there it will be my pleasure to send you one. I must order copies of the English edition. But I owe them money. Still, I should like to own a few copies and send you one. I will do so.

I think of your POEMS, and anyone who gainsays your GIFT is a churl. Did you mail a copy to Horace Gregory? I looked over CALL ME ISHMAEL, and it always pulses and surges against my trembling veins like the evening surf being easily raked in by Poseidon's Trident. I love the little book, and it awakens in me all our deep, lost origins, cairns of racial composts.

Do as you like with the Flea or the Rational Tree. I don't mind at all your critical feeling about the TREE. Not at all. I am in too much turmoil at the instant to be reflective.

Harry Moore has edited letters of Lawrence to Bertrand Russell and Harvey Breit has blessed them. Give me a doomsday curse, a Tartarian malediction when benedictions are so rife.

I am weary, but wan as I am your words made me smile and I wanted to send you some in return, as pithless as they are at the moment.

My love to you,
EDWARD DAHLBERG

■ ═══════════════════════════════════════ ■

[New York City]

March 17, 1949

Dear Charles:

Your letter was manna and quail in my wilderness. I have had your sibyl, Jane Harrison's PROLEGOMENA, and also the SHAKESPEARE IDENTIFIED. A rereading proves nothing; that he was no malt Balaam I knew before; that he made no money my own patrimony devoured by property taxes and Winifred, now divorced, is the best text. I will reread the Xenophon, and you may find repeated joy in Plato's PHAEDO. The Hesiod Theogony is a source for your MYTH; I make no claims for it as poetry, although the simplest record of fable is an homage to the MUSES. I am still pondering the character of Socrates, and wondering about that double-tongued and negative Zeno and his purificatory cross-examinations of eminent fools. How to write is still a great perplexity. I am inclined more and more to find a piercingly simple prose; let the legend of my heart be the oracle. Then there is that vile Gorgonian knot which I cannot untie, how to get lucre. My teaching ends in the latter part of May with no assurance of summer work. It had been my deepest hope to begin on the book then.

I am told by other members of the faculty that the chairman holds me in high regard. But how shall I translate such coin, academic esteem? I am not at this instant averse to going into the provinces. Aside from continual reading, and living out my life in a hotel room, I am in the hinterland. I see fewer people; the psychic depletions are great, the guerdon is small. I simply go out on occasion to sharpen my wit very much like the ancient Jews went to Gaza to whet their shares. Incidentally, the communists in Croton offered Winifred free legal service to pursue me!

Perhaps you might write to the man who wants a writer and a chairman to establish a humanities' department. I could do it and would be interested in doing it. If I can find repose, the sweetest pastoral simple for my unquiet spirit, more assuaging than the honey and butter of Isaiah, then I can write. I would be very grateful, Charles if you would send him a letter about me.

Homer is still a deity; the other day I read a volume on Homer and the influences of Tyre and Sidon on the ILIAD that was very pleasurable. Unfortunately, I learned little that I had not known previously. It always delights me to hear again how Menelaus took hold of Proteus in the AEgyptus stream until he forced from that wily god the oracular secrets he desired to know. Can we ever lay hands on Proteus and force him to reveal what our clandestine life will not divulge? This again brings back the knotty and baffling perplexity of prose or verse. Should the line be an Afric leopard, a water-hog of the Nile, or just a mild Pythagorean bee. Should we write humbly or fiercely or plainly? I know I have been too obscure; what right has man to be as darksome as a god in his lore? Ay, who will tell me anything? Meanwhile, my ruminative cud are bitumen and asphalt, and I walk alone thinking as best I can, but these miserable peripatetic exercises are in only a small way purgative, because there are neither gods in Hades nor mortals here for company.

I hear regularly from Herbert Read; for the most part, our relationship has been aloes and frankincense. But since the publication of his last book other odors have come up. He cited a line from CALL ME ISHMAEL which I had given him to honor and to publish to confute me! I was deeply heartened to know that the book had made an impression upon him. I cannot blame a man for wanting to feed his wife and five children; I sometimes doubt that he should feed the former. If we must live in Grub Street, we have to save our strength for vision somehow. I imagine poor Kit Smart was a literary porter most of his life in order to live and compose THE SONG OF DAVID and the Pascal Lamb poems. Unless we save our forces for the spirit we might as well eat the acorns, the mast and drink the drugged Pramnian wine, and go at once without boast or lies to Circe's Sty. There is no good feigning to be on the Parnassian slopes with swill on your shoes.

Now that I have sent for my books there is a strike. I am sure this is just malice! some demon told these workmen to hinder me more. Regarding the tender papyrus, I have been trying for some time to get Porphyry's CAVE OF THE NYMPHS. I want to know better how to roost with the horned owls and the choughs and the seagulls either in that hollow underneath the earth or in that cavern at Salamis where Euripides looked out at the beating white surge. What I would not give at this instant to hear the sea-cry of a gull or look at a heron or at that Arion's Dolphin that carries man out of the shoals.

Let me hear from you soon, Charles; I wish we could talk. I am more starved for conversation than crusty, wormy Lazarus was for a morsel from the rich man's table.

What does Constance do? I have had no sense of her since the hospital days when she was guzzling ice cream and being such a gay and foolish canary in the midst of trouble. I am not a canary. I am just gay and foolish.

My devotion and love,
EDWARD DAHLBERG

■══■

Washington

Friday March 25 xlix

My dear Edward:

Your bounteous letter guerdoned us both, caused us to dance, my friend, naked in this room! So one steals archaic pleasures, in a filthy time.

And tho you have not heard from me I have been at some things which concern you. FIRST, your book is in press—at least Cernovich is experimenting with type and space. I send off to you what came today. I have already written back to him, to lengthen the line and to try a Baskerville instead of this Bodoni. But I like the mass he has accomplished. Do you?

You must ignore his errors. It is a trial piece.

He overwhelms me when he says the cost will run 100 to 250 dollars. I have told him that is as much as you or I earn for a book, after ten years of Tantalus rocking the sun. I sd 100 is already too much. Question: do you have anyone who will contribute to same?

When I was there they asked to see THE RATIONAL TREE as well. They now have it, and will print both together if they have the time and number of people sufficient. (Albers, by the way, is delighted they do it. Whatever his faults as rector, he is artist enough to be a trout to a lure. I like him excellently. He leaves, as I told you, in a huff, this June. Bodky, [Natasha] Goldowski [physicist at BMC], Trayer unseated him when they meant only to unseat Dreier. A[lbers]'s wife [Anni, weaver, instructor in crafts at BMC] is an erinyes.)

And I have written to John Caldwell at Alabama [president of Alabama College at Montevallo, Alabama], and you should hear from him, for I said you were he— if he could get you to leave New York. I still question that you should. But there. Each man to his errors. And they are least important in you, because you rectify them so quickly!

But I doubt you think so these days.

All week I have been walking as many paths as days back into Greece. Today I sent off to a young composer Part I of a dance play called TROILUS for him to experiment with. Yesterday it was Euripides, his ORESTES, which I was trying to get to by way of WAY, angry that I do not have that language. The day before Odysseus (& Homer: would you please tell me what was the book you spoke of reading, of the influence of Tyre & Sidon on the Iliad? Do you know any writing by anyone on HOMER, which has illuminations? Even [Jane] Harrison deserts me here, though this week I found reference to very early book of hers [Myths of the Odyssey in Art and Life, (London: Rivingtons, 1882)] on the myth of the Odyssey in art. If you come by that, get two also, Ed. Edward, this is a note to haste to you the look of yr words in type. You must excuse this wretched thing in return for your lovely letter. So I, poor, ask another of you!

Love,
CHARLES

Dear Charles:

Your queries kindle me deeply. How the myth-producing mind, the mythopoeic faculty, must labor for FORM is our task. There are a number of books that I have not yet seen. For a year I have endeavored to procure Porphyry's THE CAVE OF THE NYMPHS. The entire problem of the gods without whose solution no ancestral or eponymous literature can be conceived is best summed up in Socrates' remark to Miletus: "You strange men, do you earnestly believe that I do not regard Helios and Silenus as divinities?" A piercing bit of knowledge is that Aristotle in his old age found in mythology his sole consolation. You know how Heraclitus reprehended those that did not accept the Homeric theogony. Now as other readings for you: may I suggest the long, doughty and remarkable essay on SOKRATES in Grote's History of Greece. I believe you will read with profit his chapters on The AEolids and the Pelopids, on Attic Legends, the Arcadian Genealogy, Legends of Thebes and Legend of Troy. His disquisition on the Homeric Poems is perhaps less satisfying. The volume, Did Homer Live, by Victor Berard is agreeable, but you will find that Sidon and Tyre in the ODYSSEY yourself. The best sources are the ancients; there was the adversary of Strabo, Eratosthenes. Soon as I get more of these books I will let you know at once. If I see additional copies I will buy them and send them to you. Our imaginations are kindred; let us be sure that before we do our work they are not rubble Titans.

The page pleased me; as you say, the print is not right. It is glutted with errors, but that you have already told me. I believe one line is missing, but I am not sure. I should like very much to see the two included in the book, that is, The Flea of Sodom and The Rational Tree. And let them go for what they are, while I retire to the bowels of Mount Aetna to work with the Cyclopes in Vulcan's Stithy.

The Four Seasons Book Shop on Greenwich keeps CALL ME ISHMAEL in stock just for me. I gave a copy last week to Professor Howard Dunbar of the English department at New York University. I asked the book people whether they were selling the POEMS, but they said the salesman or the jobber told them the book had not yet been published. Is that true? I see no periodicals and so do not know.

I am distressed to hear that Josef Albers is leaving. I do not think he should. How many people have been put into the maw of Kronos at Black Mountain would be hard to compute. The leafage and the fetid earth is a devil and a place for mania, suicide, and avant-garde pederasty. Still, I am very grateful to the students who are printing the book, and would be deeply pleased if you would give my full thanks to [Nick] Cernovich. I remember the thewy willow with the glasses and the daedal eyes.

If I can get summer teaching I will be able to send money for the book. Please let Sam Rosenberg know that if I have summer work he will receive the forty-five dollars due him with my deep heart-thanks, and ask him to forgive me. I still owe you ten dollars which I have not forgotten. The property is my bane and Acheron, it yields nothing but the bills of the she-Brirareus.

Read this to Constance when you are so mooded; it is from Thomas Campion:

> "If I love Amarillis,
> She gives me fruit and flowers,
> But if we love these Ladies,
> We must give golden showers,
> Give them gold that sell love,
> Give me the Nutbrowne lasse,
>   Who when we court and kiss,
>   She cries, forsooth, let go.
>   But when we come where comfort is,
>   She never will say no."

Winifred may give me a check for fifty dollars toward the Black Mountain publication of the book. If she does, I will have it made out to you, and you take care of the matter when you go down to Black Mountain.

I give you my gratitude, which is like the honeycomb in Pindar's mouth. And I give you my love and with it the fillets and the pears and the pomegranates to the Pierian Sisters who smile fondly upon your GIFT.

Your devoted friend,
EDWARD DAHLBERG

Friday April 8 1949

My dear Ed:

I have had another letter fr Cernovich, one half hour ago, which I have answered. He has gone ahead well. It will be necessary to use bodoni (in *any* font they have so little type they have to set 1 page at a time, and throw the type back before setting another) but he followed my suggestion [of] a longer line, and it looks good. C ran into trouble on binding, but he has solved it by adopting the Chinese design, the book is sewn when it is all done ((*rhapsodia* means to *sew* or stitch *song* together)), with two covers front & back. The problem he is beset with now is paper—which, and how to buy it. If you can get me the check Winifred promises, instead of waiting until I go down (not until the 25th) I would send it off immediately so that C can go ahead. (I have suggested an issue of 100 copies, with a colophon describing the book as a first special edition handset, numbered, & signed by you, done at the Black Mountain Press, design Cernovich, supervision Warren Jennerjahn [printing instructor, formerly a student at BMC].

NOW to what causes me to write in haste: (1) which of the two titles do you wish for the whole? Myself, you know, I favor FLEA.

(2) May I have your permission to put my hand into the text in some such fashion as I did into the 1st 3 pages of FLEA? I should keep my intrusions to a minimum.—If you consent, can you send me a second copy of both pieces? They have the blue text, and ought to have it by. If you could let me have another, I could keep filing pages to them as I finish.

Do let me hear from you on these matters just as soon as you can. C is beginning to get a little frightened at the thot of 75 pages, each set & scrapped before the other can be done, and with only two months left of his year there (he cannot afford another, the shame of it; he worked a year and a half to get himself there a year; he is worth the whole she-bang; I have got him, however, into a long story about his mother and brother: his blood is thick as were the Atreides, those Phrygians; have you any ideas (o we comrade ragpickers) where he might manage a life?) I sent him your message to cheer him up, the daedal.

Otherwise only Ovid is new (came on his Medea in the Heroides). And Berard, whom I have fed on. The English bk you, too, came to, is miserable, but the base text Les Phynicein et L'Oddyssee is fine & thick, and I am now trying to get his translation of the Odyssey in 3 volumes. The gain is the precision of nouns he can manage due to his documentation. (I am a gainer, because I was a loser two years ago, when I did the story of O and Nausicaa, and could not get through the bad English heretofore. Had to give it up, the story HE SLEPT. My interest now is a dance play) ["Troilus," to have been a four-part mask or dance-play; only part one was completed, "The search for Love," in July 1948; published in *The Fiery Hunt and Other Plays*, ed. George Butterick (Bolinas, CA: Four Seasons Foundation, 1977)].

We had Sunday evening with 'Orace Gregory & marya, here. I like OG very very much. I suppose she is the stronger but his weakness has more fruits. I could have fought with her but chose to be amused: she horns the pitch-pipe of p-o-e-t-r-y every quarter hour like the grammar school creatures. (There was only one, a Miss Lee, 2nd grade, who was a woman, we called her Melon she had such breasts.) Horace has a fine feeling for you, and it was a pleasure you sent us.

(As you sow the olson seeds, my johnny-a, I should tell you that the distributor of *y & x* is now THE ATLANTIS BOOKSHOP, 100 Fourth Avenue. It has had but one review, the Nation, and that a matter of SIX words!)

And my deepest thanks for the Socrates, Aristotle, Heraclitus triad. AND FOR THE CAMPION: it is strange how you and I have got to the same wafty bridge, the Elizabethan singers & the Ancients. At Black MT I took away a book called MELODY & LYRIC by JM Gibbon which you might care to look at (do not buy) for the lyrics there printed I do not find elsewhere. Another Campion, to music by Morley, is:

Now is the month of Maying
When merry luds are playing,
Each with his bonny lass
Upon the greeny grass.

The spring clad all in gladness
Doth laugh at winter's sadness,
And to the bagpipes sound
The nymphs tread out their ground.

Fie then! Why sit we musing,
Youth's sweet delight refusing?
Say, dainty nymphs and speak,
Shall we play barley-b[r]eak?

(I let Constanza come on the other lines by herself. Shall we say she
was perplexed? "Shall we play barley-break")

I was delighted when Gregory said he thought you were as spirited
now. Yr delightful letters confirm it. They are my joy. Continue,
friend.

My love,
CHARLES OLSON

[New York City]

April 12, 1949

Dear Charles:

I am sending you Winifred's check for fifty dollars toward the
publication of THE FLEA OF SODOM. I take the title you prefer. The
manuscript shall be in your hands in a day or so, and please do with it
as you deem fit.

I am ashamed I have no Greek. I cannot find the words I seek in
Homer and which I know are in the original text. On occasion a line
is winged speech: THE Scamander flows out of the mouth of Zeus.
This is legend and poetry. Euripides troubles me very much. I question
his poetic faculty, and though I consider this profane, I could say that he
is a thinker rather than a poet. This, too, is spurious; for thought that
is not poetry is not pristine perception either. Of some little value for
your purposes you might look into Paul Decharme's Euripides. But how
can a man be so iconoclastic and such a misogynist and yet dote on
the bestial multitude? THE ORIGIN OF BIBLICAL TRADITION by
A.T. Clay is better. It is kindling knowledge to be told that Erech and
Babel were great Amorite cities at about 4000 B.C. I have always
looked upon GENESIS as earthenware inscriptions or pieces of antique
pottery with figures of Enoch and Enos upon them. Perhaps the sherd
Job scraped his boils with had drawings of those Angels that entered
the sons and daughters of men. Legend is more history than scholiasts

have been willing to acknowledge. That is why Livy is so wise in being preeminently a fabulist.

Your account of Marya is mirthful and true enough. She has grown a little bulby since the days that she used to complain that she was a better poet than Horace while she swept moles of dust into the corners. One day she showed me her verse. After I read it I asked Marya to get her broom and sweep the dust out of the corners. You know how clairvoyant I am! A year or so later she got a Pulitzer Award for the verse. Her wish to make Horace great is the volition of Ligeia or Morella. While she stuffs Horace she so diminishes everyone present that somebody is inclined to ask Marya for permission to be just a little bit great himself. I will be content with some few pages if the Muses are kind and fortune not too severe. If a man writes one lovely line he may go to Elysium. All the great men of our day will feed forever on Lethe's weed.

Did you hear, Charles, about the college position? I am very worried about summer. My checks stop the end of next month.

Cargill will return from California sometime next month and I will show him your card to me. I imagine he will be pleased to make the exchange. What do you want the book for? I know nothing about it.

I want to get this into the mail; do let me hear from you soon; thanks for the charming song you typed out in your letter, also very charming. How is Constance, or I ask with more grace, Does she form her mouth to her liking, and is her hair softly trussed at back of her neck?

My love and my friendship,
EDWARD DAHLBERG

■ ━━━━━━━━━━━━━━━━━━━━━━━━━━━━━━━━━━━━ ■

[Washington, D.C.]

Wednesday [April 20, 1949?]

Edward:

How fine the FLEA looks on yr gray letter paper! I am rushing off a sheet of it to Cernovich, for example. —He wrote me this morning, acknowledging the check (I to you likewise now) but admitting he is scared, only 60 days left, and it takes him 2 days to set a page. I shall put his courage back ("Du courage a l'ouvrage", sd Verlaine) by letter now, and be there myself next week to see what can be done.—He is asking whether he better not limit himself to one of the two parts.

I am sending on to you a sample of the cover he proposes to use (it is scratched, he apologizes: it will be clear and clean!) You will recall it is to be hand-sewn in the Chinese manner. And the weakness of their design is the tendency of the cover to come off at the front-face hinge. I assume that is why he and Si [Sewell Sillman, art student at BMC] chose plastic. The question is: can you tolerate it?

FOUR SEASONS, thanks to yr sowing, lists ISH in its spring catalogue. I have returned them an order for books for Black Mt. (I like their tone, of 'em all)

But the fruitful books, one cannot find. I go round asking helplessly for the LOEB and the BOHN, but am already beyond them and have such needs that either I cannot afford or find. (Ran into a book in the former category I wanted to draw to yr attention: called THE WHEEL, a study of the use of praying wheels.)—I continue to feed deeply on Berard. Have now his translation of the Odyssey, which makes it possible for me, for the first time, to have it in such exactitude of language I can read without irritation. He opens, for example, with this characterization: l'homme aux mille tours. And, due to the documentation of the port of Alkinoos, is able to make the Nausicaa passage have the body I suppose it has in the Greek. (Shall we not learn that tongue?)

And I find Berard's argument the Odyssey is three "dramas" most imaginatively useful.

What is yr Socrates piece, you speak of rewriting? Did the Xeonophon reveal more of him? And what is the best Chrysostom?

Love,
CHARLES

No word fr that Alabama Caldwell about you & the position. Have you? Does the Cargill rise lead you back to NYU?

April 22, 1949

Dear Charles:

Read Chrysostom's Trojan Discourse in volume 1. According to this version only the *eidolon* of Helen was taken to Ilium, while Helen herself remained in Egypt in the reign of King Proteus. Look, too, at the conversations of Diogenes and Alexander of Macedon. Thucydides, Polybius and Pausanias are glutted with references to Troy town and Homer. Thucydides cites with some feeling the Hymn to Apollo in which the blind bard of Chios entreats the Delian maidens to look with favor upon his harp. I am looking for translations of Hellanikus, Damasters, Pherkydes, and will tell you what I discover.

I have not received the sample cover you mention. Horace Gregory believes the book should be printed and bound with real taste if it is to receive any attention. Otherwise, he believes it will be totally neglected. I think he wants to write about The Rational Tree. By the oath we make to the infernal damsel Styx, No PLASTIC! Let a plastic cover be used for a codpiece to hide what is lame or gelded. NO PLASTIC!

I have word from Herbert Read that an English publisher [Peter Nevill Limited] is interested. What will happen I am not sure. Anyway, I wish to make full thanks in the Black Mountain edition and in the English one, if there is one, to you, Cernovich, Herbert Read, and [Horace] Gregory.

The Memorabilia [of Xeonophon] I did not read with too much pleasure; it may be a plainer and blunter portrait of that gifted grammarian of ethics and churl of dialectics, Sokrates, than the Platonic figure. I have not changed my mind about Sokrates, but I do want to make a few alterations regarding the mythopoeic faculty. As pious as Sokrates is said to have been, he did disestablish Eros. Without Eros as a divinity poesy and myths and the whole assortment of incredibilias so urgent as aliment to man cannot remain. There is another crucial dilemma: how far can man go in his inquiries without blowing away the fine particles of dust which make up the ancestral and genealogical cairn from which the Hesiodic Catalogue of Women and the Odyssey are taken. There must be a limit which all the ancient sages accepted. Plato emphatically denounced any one who denied the divinity of Helios or Selene, and Herakleitus regarded those who questioned the mythology of Homer as impious.

I have been taking notes all day, and my back is very sore.

Please pardon this brief letter. Would you ask Josef Albers in my name, for whatever it is worth, not to leave Black Mountain College. We both have regard and affection for him, and I cannot see how the college can continue if he leaves.

I have heard nothing from the man you wrote to about appointing me as a chairman of a humanities department. Cargill will return next month, and if he is not a wily academician he should do something for me. I look for little from that invertebrood.

My love and devoted friendship,
EDWARD DAHLBERG

Very important: Please! Charles, send me by return mail the railway express receipts or checks, or whatever there is, so that I am sure to know how many cartons were shipped. Because of the strike the books are just coming in. Two cartons so far have arrived. And let me know, please, how many cartons were sent, and for how much insured.

■══════════════════════════════════════■

[Washington, D.C.]

Monday [April 25, 1949?]

Ed:

I am stupid. I might, three minutes ago, have given you some erhebung, if, that you are to be read by thirty young characters this month, is such. Even if it is at the cost of $1.50 to yourself. For I cannot find here, nor have the BM people been proficient enough to acquire DO THESE BONES LIVE. For I have just bracketed and assigned together DAHLBERG and HOMER: the ODYSSEY & THE FLEA OF SODOM (in mss), BOTTOM DOGS (which they have), and BONES, which I am asking you to send them, please, if you can, this day, attention Mrs. Nell Rice [wife of John Andrew Rice, founder and first rector of BMC].

Yr call upsets me. You sounded more raked than you have since fall. And it is a misery I had to add Cernovich's charge. For what it is worth, I advise THE FLEA, admitting that it will be still-born, that there is no distribution system, that it would give you no more than the satisfaction to have 30 copies to distribute and by which to provoke. It is little. But Cernovich has taste (you know his page already), can use a better paper, now understands plastic is an abomination, and will (with Hockstein's [student at BMC] help) wrap it in a simple rich paper. But there. You are shrewder than I, and you will gauge whether Read's bite leads anywhere or not. Cernovich will go ahead unless he hears from you to the contrary in the next two days.

Yr message to Albers was handsomely taken as he is handsome. But there seems no way to mend the break. He leaves, as does Bimbus [Charlotte "Bimbus" Schlesinger, instructor in harmony and composition], & Trude [Guermonprez, older daughter of the Jalowetzes, weaving instructor], with him (not to speak of madame aa [Anni Albers], whom I have no interest to speak of). The Dreiers have gone, now sit in Florida. Except for the plan of a Texan now there, who wishes to reconstruct a BMC outside Dallas (did you ever think of Texas? would you care for such a possibility?), Albers & Friends are going their separate ways. (Albers plans now to bind the year through three short stays in three small places). He is in good spirits, and painting gayly, though angry and bitter towards the revolutionists, Goldowski, Bodky, Trayer, and Mdm Rice. It is all very stupid, and has so riven the atmosphere none of the students do much any more. (Sd several of same last week: the more the time since Dahlberg taught us opens, the more we remember and value same).

These trips tire me very deeply. It is a great effort for me to go, and, back, to return to my work. But they have enabled me to keep this house, even if again, now, I am threatened with its loss, and I am most grateful to you. But, as you see, and sense, and said, I pay! I am very full of despair at my lack of accomplishment this winter.

Do write, and I shall at least to send you my affection. I have that for you, in your troubles, if little else to offer. Here again,

> then, my love,
> CHARLES

Dear Charles:

Thank you for your compassionate letter; I needed it. I sent a telegram to Cernovich asking him to go ahead with the FLEA. I still long to work on it. I would be grateful if you would let me see page-proofs in advance. So many errors that bring the deepest blush to the brain can be made. Maybe, please, you would look at it with some care. I bought a second-hand copy of the BONES and sent it to Black Mountain, care of Nellie Rice. My gratitude to you for whatever words you may have to say about me. I, too, feel shorn away; too much solitude engenders depravity and the worms of Lazarus. It was pious AEcus who begged Zeus for companions when he was alone on AEgina; heeding his prayer he translated the ants on the island into the Myrmidons. I would not be opposed to going anywhere if I might have some kinship to man. I am sepulchred away in this hotel cranny, reading and reading. Have you spent much time on Pindar? I have returned with very great pleasure to Aristophanes. He is a lovely, dithyrambic, decayed Levantine, witty as a Moor or an Arab. How he can write about millet and cheese-cakes and Minerva's olive and the Thesmophorium. Yes, I would earnestly consider going to a Black Mountain outside of Dallas. There is a student of mine down there now, and I have been thinking of going south on a bus and stopping over in Dallas for a time. I cannot go to Rome, or to Paris, or to blessed Attica. Were I to go to the latter place, I could only say what the Platonic Sokrates said: "What I would not give to converse with Homer, Hesiod, Musaeus." Perhaps, the person who is interested in a college settlement near Dallas could give me the names of some persons I could see there. Do let me know, please.

Geoffrey continues to be a piercing orison in my flesh. He is very tender and seems to require me. I cry out, whenever I muse upon him, or capture his face as I walk on asphalt, My Bowels, My Bowels!

I do not know what Cargill will do. You know the academic man. Could you ever link your hand with his, or call him Brother. The pulse of the heart glimmers away as one attempts to utter the name.

I walk on occasion through the square and pass the fountain of the sluts where the diseased muses sit. One little fantasical waved a dollar bill in the face of an Irishman whom he hated because he knew he was broke.

A little commune of learning would be good. There is positively no place, no jot of earth or verdure for a man of feeling any more.

Do not be dismayed if you have not had as many intuitions in the past year as you have prayed for. My entreaties to heaven are rarely heeded. I write solely to remain sane. Look, what swine there are on Parnassus. If wily Odysseus was not able to avoid the tusk of the boar, how can we shun the "middens and the piggeries?"

I am as melancholy as Heracles and Aristotle, and I ask you to pardon such a darkling distemper.

Do let me hear from you soon. When do you go down to Black Mountain?

Take my hand, weak, "indifferent honest," flawed, cunning, but man-fevered, and with it my loving friendship,

EDWARD DAHLBERG

■ ═══════════════════════════════════════ ■

Monday May 9 xlix

Edward:

The enclosed has just come. & I think the best thing is to agree, judging by the dirtiness of the press.

I'll look into the press business myself next week, & see what can be done about it, by fall. If this is the best the press allows, I'd say kill the project [BMC production of *The Flea of Sodom*].

But for the present I'd ride it over the summer.

It is a shame, & I share yr disappointment.

Love, Charles

■ ═══════════════════════════════════════ ■

[Washington, D.C.]

Tuesday May 31 xlix

Edward!

No deal dallas—yet. He has three houses to sell, and neither his will nor the tarot will cause who'll buy his houses. Besides, there has to be a tie-in, one Bobbie Dreier [wife of Theodore Dreier], if not Albers, there has to be a communitas. Which there may be. I'll keep you informed. I go back next week.

I dare say yr silence is expectation I should write first. Which is herewith done, if not done as I might have it done. Been sick three days (black mt fever) and am ajumpin today. Am secretive. Am writitive. How are you, I hope not croton-sick, it being the day after a holiday. Or are you blue (-papered)?

DURA

To come to the look in the sacrificer's eyes

the archaic sought, the harshness
unsought
          And the eyes which should burst
do not.

I read very much. Acquired Aristophanes today. But of whom I am suspicious.

O yes. Yr readers. It was most curious. You were the one who went home, of all of the year. And what will please you, BONES more, much more than DOGS, and, for the illuminated, the FLEA more than BONES! These, the new ones, read yr prose in a romp, the late prose. If any one had written of you well I'd have sent it to you.

This is a note, to awake you. And to say I should be seeing you inside of three weeks.

My love,
CHARLES OLSON

■ ══════════════════════════════════════ ■

[New York City]

July 11, 1949

Dear Charles:

I hear the bleating of sheep and the lowing of the cattle of Amalek in this appetite for Babel-America? Do you really believe you are going to deceive a great number of people. My poor friend, be at peace, you will not dupe anybody save yourself and three other readers. I appreciate your zest for all the arts and crafts and races; it is an exhilaration to watch you go out so valiantly to combat your identity and to return each night triumphantly alone! I would give you the chair of American Literature, but you would eat it like the companions of AEneaus devoured their trenchers. You should have then the chair of the dance, the drama, a portable bernard de voto, mark twain, the dreiser letters; I would give them all to you would you not grind them to powder as Moses did with the golden calf, making the bitter waters for you. What are we to do? I am aging as you so gallantly advise, and you with the vigor of Rahab, the Dragon and the Leviathan, are hungering for fame. Shall we break the head of the dragon in the waters? What shall we do? In the past eleven years I have grown more obscure? How shall you grow otherwise? Social adhesiveness is so sweet and the palate is so unsatisfied. I who walk around the rim of the earth like Lucifer should have some counsel for you. But I have not. I know you think I have a despot's will and that I would influence you more than you wish. Our problem is kindred, but not wholly the same. I would be content to deceive one person, Charles Olson so that he could write a book more wondrous than that piece of sorcerer's prose, CALL ME ISHMAEL. Charles Olson wants to gull many people by writing a book for the multitude. O I don't mean you are seeking a hundred thousand readers; you would be content to slay ten thousand Philistines like David or if forced to, one thousand like Saul. I should be satisfied with a hundred to two hundred foreskins of the Gentiles, one Hebrew, a Greek who does folk dancing and reads Homer and does watercolors over the week-ends, and perhaps a Phoenician and an Ethiopian. But not a Negro American style. Unlike yourself, I believe the Negro with the residual sorrow of slavery in his eyes is a more merciful creature than the free Negro of the north. Go to Harlem and tremble; or go not into those regions of Sheol with the stone tables of Moses and hope to return with your suit, watch or car. I have another perplexity; how do you manage to prevail upon the bowels of so many Abrahams Isaacs and Jacobs who own asses, oxen and sporting cars? You are more wily than Laban the Syrian. O yes I know, you are a furtive celt; with me you are double and treble, secretly reprehending my monotheism while you run after many american idols. But I know as much as I want you to have the nard and the calamus that Seth brings back from Eden to mitigate the pains of his father Adam, you will not have it by going into the camp of my enemies, the Midianites of American Literature. Fate is so sly that, perhaps, if you are very earnest you might write a bad book and get fame. Otherwise, you are doomed to be as obscure as Spenser.

Charles, I thank you deeply for giving the money to [Sam] Rosenberg; he is only a Jew by name, for the children of Ham and the sons of Gideon and Joshua are lost and their heritage is base.

I wrote a special delivery to Wilbert Snow [poet, professor of literature at Wesleyan University]; please tell me by return mail whether you have written to President [Victor L.] Butterfield [president of Wesleyan University]. I must support Geoffrey and Joel, and write and tremble like grass. I will labor ardently for publication for you in England. Would to heaven you could heed me; write the long, flowing Melville line, as form it is worth the three kids, the loaves and the flagons of the wine the three prophets took up to Bethel. But the great Melville as wisdom is the inedible fish of Homer and the wights of the sea the Galilean menders of nets caught. I repeat this banality; what else can a man do in his poor, wizened life, but reiterate three or four truths he has learned from someone else. We are always writing another book because the preceding one is a failure.

So much for ageing, repetitious and platitudinarian Edward Dahlberg; but I know my hapless limits, and so I wait mourning on the ground and praying for the noise in the Mulberry trees and the Truths I shall soon receive from the young, vascular Giant of Anak, Mein Herr of the flute, the psaltery, the timbrel, the pipe, the ballet, the pauline epistles of Jennie Gerhardt, euripides, pound and moloch.

Always your friend who gives you love and friendship; as for the rest of humanity, I cry to the hills, the rivers and to my spleen for remedy.

EDWARD DAHLBERG

[IN SCRIPT:]

Please send me by return mail the Flea of Sodom & The Rational Tree: I want to work again on the Socratic passages.

[New York City]

July 15, 1949

Dear Charles:

I am, of course, happy to hear that you are coming to New York. I am teaching two evenings a week at Brooklyn Polytechnic college and am at present living at the Paris Hotel which is at West End Avenue and 97th Street. The phone number is Riverside 9-3500. If I am not in, please leave a message and tell me where I can reach you. Am writing every morning, doing for want of better phrasing a Cape Cod novel with many allusions to the Book of Enoch and other apocryphal legends the mention of which should make you smart and pine like the Jews ached for the melons, the leeks and the cantaloupes of the Nile.

Forgive my silence. It has been singularly difficult for me of late to write a letter, even to you who are my kin and above all my friend.

Let me hear from you, or much better, see you soon.

Your loving friend,
EDWARD DAHLBERG

[Black Mountain College]
Black Mountain, North Carolina]

monday july 18 [1949]

edward

you must excuse me   i am having trouble even sleeping & eating amongst these barbarous & vicious creatures who now run this college, who drove albers out, who were pleased you left, and who are now after me whether i shall stay is now my question, tho i am somewhat trapped, & may have to hold

i have found that nick [Cernovich] seems to have taken the mss of the r.t. with him (i have the flea)   so i am writing now to have the 2nd copies in washington sent to you immediately

i sent the wire winifred requested as soon as her wire reached me it was left in the post office box (the carelessnesses here are beyond toleration) i am delighted for you both, & hope it insures you both economically for next year as well   does it?

do write me, and do not be upset if, until i can get something worked out here, i am irregular   i feel like a egg shell & a fool

love
CHARLES

a stupidity is enclosed [missing]

■══■

220 Sullivan Street
Apt. 3C
New York, N.Y.
August 3, 1949

Dear Charles:

I am deeply sorry to hear that your summer at Black Mountain is not giving you quiet. All that you can do to eschew human filths is to cleanse your soul each morning by writing a savory line or reading one. I saw Herbert Read before he returned to London and spoke to him most urgently about having Routledge publish CALL ME ISHMAEL in London. He agrees with me that this is the most memorable book done on Melville, and he is going to see what he can do [to] get them to bring the book out in London. I shall in the meantime write him again to hasten him to commit this justice. If a good book is given light then a little evil will depart from the earth. Now as for the poems, I have not sent them out yet, but will do so shortly. I do not think Cappon is in Kansas City at this time, and I want him to get the poems. They are gifted, as I know you are, for my Muse long ago advised me so; but I am still praying that you will return to some of the traditional forms in writing. I do not feign that I know how to write or even how to counsel you. I write, and then my writing advises me. And even then quite obscurely. I labor each day for my form in this novel, and at the moment am at work on a fragment which I have called the Vision of Uriel. I look for my own guidance to the four archangels in the Apocrypha.

If the London publishers can sell American sheets they will do the

Flea of Sodom and the Rational Tree, which shall then appear as you suggest as The Flea of Sodom. I think it inadvisable, Charles, since you shan't be at Black Mountain to have the book done. I don't believe it would be clean and mirthful without you. Unless you need the money, would you remit (what a leopard-like word, remit) the balance of the fifty dollars. I can urgently employ this little lucre. But let me know, please.

As I previously said, I shall make acknowledgments to you and Read for your human goodness in helping me find publication; that will be my timbrel with which I shall go up to the holy mountains if the book is printed in London. Unless I err grossly, I believe it will be done. I have here as bait for them some 30,000 words of this novel; little do they know that this book, too, will be, I pray, good for their spirit, but of no worth whatsoever to their cormorant gullet. I set out in my abominable misery to write a book for the vile world, but neither Michael nor Gabriel nor Uriel who is set over Tartarus and the world would permit it.

Winifred is very dual, tender but guileful, and she walks in the world with perjured feet as all women do. I adore the children as you know, and Geoffrey in particular is the Son of my entrails, and the son of my Vows. I should like to see you have a son without, of course, the hindrances that I know.

Be sure, my dearest friend, that I labor in your behalf, and that I shall not be content until I find an English publisher for this book and for any other book that you will write. Give up, I beg you, these experimental satans who have put the nails in the Word. Return to Ishmael and to your own Eden.

My love to you, and do let me hear from you soon.

I have found an apartment, very pleasant too, a good size room with kitchenette and bath, a block from Washington Square, and now that food is as high [as] pigeon's dung in the famine of Samaria, I have a pot and a stove for a little cooking.

EDWARD DAHLBERG

Black Mountain College
Black Mountain, North Carolina

aug 16 xlix

Edward:

Yr check sld come back to you in a few days. I hid it in Washington,
the house was empty until the 15th, now the people are back, & they
shall forward it. I have written to them.

One clear day of Odysseus the Sun—otherwise jungle & humid. No
wonder the creatures are small here, bugs, snakes, turtles. That Albers
shld have stayed 17 yrs raises questions abt him.

But I have worked on The Kingfishers, Poetry London will publish
the first two parts of it, and some poems, translated into Italian, will
come out in Italy this winter with drawings by Mirko. (Such unions I
no longer like, at least in america: but there, like prefaces, they go.)

And I make a production in ten days: of three different projections
of THE CYCLOPS, and of a poem NOT THE FALL OF A
SPARROW. You must suspend yr suspicion of drahmah. You yourself
use the word "novel" when you know better; I go blind, too. Besides, to
your despair, dear friend, I am an actor. (Dare I remind you that
Homer & Shakespeare were, o my serious one?) ((Another proposition:
those who do not know what they are, interest themselves in other
people))

I am delighted FLEA will come out in England. This is a wonderful
thing, and others should have it. Keep telling me news of it, who and
when.

Tell me, mine orakle, which do you choose of these two readings:

> o that this too too sullied flesh would melt,
> thaw and resolve itself into a dew

> o that this too too solid flesh would melt,
> thaw and resolve itself into a dew

You see what a moist weather does to my mind. I [   ] how are
your sons, & winifred: give them our love. And what you are up to.
Send me yr round speech, which hides in my ear like a berry

I must
go now to one of these desperate meals. How come such a man as you
did not warn us of this food? They are tantalian.

Love,
OLSON

■ == ■

Dear Charles:

Thanks very much for your good, few lines, and I hasten to answer
them before laboring for my penury. I am fearfully worried about
getting work to support the two sons. I have heard nothing from
Middletown; [Kenneth B.] Murdock [HARVARD ENGLISH PROFESSOR,
RECOMMENDED DAHLBERG TO BLACK MOUNTAIN COLLEGE] wrote a long
letter, and now Cargill is sending one to President Butterfield whom he
knows. Cargill is the new chairman, and that should be a help. It
should, but you know how canny the academic mind is, how wily it is;
and how it despises the suffering bowels. It is a fearsome thing to have
to tell another man that you believe you have some human vision that
should be protected, or that Gabriel touched your eyelids by the waters
of Chebar at evening. I had to do it, and I felt miry afterwards.
Suppose I were as wrong as Waldo Frank! He has become a worse churl
and now believes, someone told me, that the only two people who will
be recollected in America are Waldo and Erskine Caldwell. This is the
indignation of the last times.

What do I know about myself? I know that you possess seven vices
that I do not know [I] have, and I know that this is self-deception. I
look into those obscure waters of Styx, thy self and myself, and I hurry
away, though, alas I return to cringe again.

The poems I am sending this coming week. I wish to reread them
very slowly. I wrote to Herbert Read the other day, and, among other
things that I said was that two or three books on Herman Melville
appear each year, perhaps more, each caitiff author filching some
gnome or feeling or pulse of vision from Olson without making a single
acknowledgment to him.

Paul Christensen ■ 105

[Edward] Kammerer, a sculptor to whom I gave Ishmael is an admirer of yours. It is better here than in Washington, Charles. Yesterday, I met a young Italian poet and he had a rare piety for literature; Slater Brown who has written badly for years spoke with feeling about the Wheels in Ezekiel, and after our talk, thief that I am, I wrote a hundred words on Time.

The other evening I read with rapture the Book of Daniel; I continue to read the APOCRYPHA.

I always rejoice, as you know, in your own work of the heart, and it pleases me fervently to hear that more poems of yours are to be published in Italy. Even if I am wrong about your poetry, I shall stand guard over your Muse like Cerberus; for our gift is our pitiless Acheron.

Yea, yea, I know the serpent foliage of Black Mountains and the food the wild asses in the desert would refuse. But I feared for your poverty, and I thought, too, perhaps you are not as troublesome as I am. I felicitate you; you are.

Now I go to the Book of Ezekiel and then to write a just word or two that may be put, I pray heaven and Cocytus, in Job's Balance.

> I send you my love.
> EDWARD DAHLBERG

You think you have the eagle's heart of Odysseus, but you are a fool; I, alas, know that I am a fool while others regard me as wily. What do I know about myself, Sir Charles, nothing, nothing, save that we are both hapless and wily fools.

---

220 Sullivan Street
Apartment 3C
New York, N.Y.

September 20, 1949

Dear Charles:

My deep thanks for the check and for paying Rosenberg; my tardy gratitude is my discomfort about money. At the moment things are worse. I have no appointment, and I do not know what teaching I shall get. The English publishers have not yet come to a decision, although I thought they had, and those apples I smart for [are] as far [from] me as they were from Tantalus. I wrote a small, apocalyptic essay as a conclusion to THE FLEA OF SODOM, which I have called THE WHEEL OF SHEOL, based in some part on a rapturous reading of Daniel. Otherwise, my solitude is a kind of debauchery; it has all the marks of evil without any of the low satisfactions from it. When I am not inert, I write a little, or read Christopher Smart, Seneca, the Miracle Plays, Porphyry, Livy, Herodian.

I called you this morning and learned that you and Constance were in Gloucester. This is the first time in years I have not had Poseidon's salt on my lips. What I would not give to lie on the sands with some kelpy Naiad, a soft wind from Arabia Felix cooling and spicing my veins.

If THE FLEA OF SODOM is published, Herbert Read is doing a Foreword to it.

You might care for Smart's translation of the Psalms. But considering your sodden silence, your watery inertia in which your Celtic bones are soaked, I beg you to read these lines from the hand of Christopher Smart:

> "In Ireland's wild, uncultivated plains,
> Where torpid sloth, and foggy dulnes reigns,
> Full many a fen infests the putrid shore"

You have fallen into the habit of not replying to my letters, and then when I remind you, you say with great guile, are you so Euclidean as not to write me because I have not answered your last epistle?

The Homeric Poems you have written interest me very much. I imagine, when your lines become the chant of the heart, they will not only have the strength of your intellect, which I never fail to understand and fully value, but the misery of your flesh. My own days are the saying of Kadesh for my Mother.

My love and faith,
EDWARD DAHLBERG

washington

october 6 xlix

mydearedward:

yr strictures were more cruel than you knew   i have been so eaten
with my lack of accomplishment (it amounts to four months i have
been away from my desk) i got blind to get back here, where, in
isolation, only do i work
i have just this morning returned to this desk, and without ease or
sense, i insist on writing you this letter, to ask after you, to tell you
how fine it is to have had your words, and to seek assurance you are at
a less worst than your last letter indicated
yr letter reached me in Maine where my senses, at least, were full of
delight   what new england was! we were visiting Washington friends
in Damariscotta, Newcastle, Wiscasset where it all opens out, East
Boothbay, Head of the Tide, those places where the carpenter was the
agent of grace
i expect now to be in new york around the 1st of november   i had
planned to stop off to see you on this return but another emergency on
this house has arisen and i came straight through from Boston
overnight (my landlady is back from france, and wants to evict us
again)
the U of Kansas mag returned the two Sumerian pieces without a
howdy-do (included with it was my letter to you, enclosing the verse!)
also greeting me was the rejection of the long "Kingfishers" by poetry-
london, after i had understood they wanted it
about The Flea: if Read should fail again, would you not want,
though I shall not be there, to have me try Black Mt again? I am sure
Cernovich would be anxious to do it (though you and I have an enemy
who now dominates the place, the bitch Goldowski)
do forgive me i have been so silent, am   it is my despair, but i
cannot work, or feel spun up, when i am societal   is it possible i have
now learned to stay where i am and refuse all such enticements   (one
of the finest pieces of wisdom i acquired from you is, people do not
change)

108   ■   IN LOVE, IN SORROW

remember me to winifred and to your boys, and let me know that
you have teaching and are in less discomfort

> my love and admiration
> CHARLES

a host of your perceptions have been
alive in me recently

My dear Charles:

I do not know how I happened to put your letter in low, alien hands.
I ask your pardon, and tell you plainly it was the result of sick
distraction, and not done with any purpose. I gave ISHMAEL to a
doughty Irishman at Brooklyn Polytechnic College, Professor [Thomas
L.] Donahue, and he liked the sweet little book very much. I do not
know how verse or prose should be written, but a Godly line has
within it the ram of Abraham, Samuel's anointing horn [to?] a large
Nestorian beaker of brine to assauge the melancholy heart. Give me a
warm-livered [Pr ?   heart] line; so warm a line that not even the
Caucasus can cool or diminish it.

Forgive me, if I have trespassed against your identity. I do not wish
to err against your Muse, but to pay homage to it.

You say you are coming to New York. I have an extra iron bedstead,
not long enough for King Og, but I offer it eagerly, with pastoral
kidney lamb chops, ale, a copy of Christopher Smart's REJOICE IN
THE LAMB, which I am saving for you, and a copy of Sing O Barren
to replace the one your peripatetic friend took away with him.

Winifred does not let me see the dear, sweet children because I have
not enough money to give to her. My teaching is meager, and I do not
know what I shall do. English publication of THE FLEA OF SODOM
is still in doubt. But I read poor, hapless Smart, that beautiful Genius
in Bedlam, and Herodian, and do you know what loving lines Edmund
Spenser wrote?

Some dullard, with fat mushroomed ears who had done a Melville tome has said that pecking pederast Matthiesen discovered the influence of Shakespeare on Herman Melville. I always thought that Charles Olson had. But I am a very foolish man and really believe in the truth, and if you believe what is true you do not have to sow dragon's teeth in the ground to produce armed men all around you.

Your silence makes me uneasy; it wounds me more deeply than my obscurity.

Your devoted and loving friend,
EDWARD DAHLBERG

■ ══ ■

[New York City]
November 15, 1949

Dear Charles:

I do not believe that solitude is good for the liver or the blood or the bowels. The gregarious American makes a fetich of his solitude; and I do not think it is necessary to be more alone than man already is either to write or walk or eat. Dying and writing are private acts, but one can neither die or write all the time. There must be seasons, moons and suns for privacy and for friendship. I still believe that the True Poet says, "Will ye go away?" and the Peter of the sodality of trouble and pain and vision will always reply, "Whither shall we go?"

You blame me for not forming Andromache as you would form her. Do you pardon Cressid because she was so moist in bed? or lewd Clytemnestra? Why do you rail at me for the same misogyny you celebrate in Euripides? Was wily Homer a fool about Helen, or even Penelope. When we want to write about good women, it requires no more than a line or two. Mary Magdalene is painted for us in a sentence or two, and that is right. Unless we are very artful we are far from the truth.

You accuse me of not giving enough of myself to a woman. Well, nobody knows anything about that. You least of all. Of the four women you have known in the past twelve years or so, three of them you met through me, and the other I had known. Some you thought radiant at first, but later relished them less. The one you so defend you rejected and may well have driven into limbo. This was your decision and no one else's, and only a busybody would feign that it were his. Does it matter whether we turn woman aside because her flesh has not the fertility of the Nile, or for another reason. Would you despise a man for rejecting a woman because he was troubled about her nature. Then, my dear friend, make yourself ready to scorn all the poets in the world.

I know how tempting the ascetic ideal is, and I also know that if a man petitions heaven for denials the gods will give them to him in abundance. Do you wish to be alone; you will be. Do you want to be without friends, as lorn as Prometheus who has no other companions but Earth and AEther. Zeus will not deny your prayer. Do you desire to be a writer, an oracle, a MAN? Then let us argue about friendship, and whether a man who is niggard with his time, will ever have the time to be a friend, a poet, a lover of the infinities and the Milky Way. Art is simply the ritual we make of our lives; make then a ceremonial of your raiment, food, companions, speech, prayers. Who can laugh alone? or eat with Ceres or Bacchus in gloomy solitude? and after a man has made an hexameter or an iambic or a strophe, and after a man has died, who will hear his meters? and who will clasp his ashy and aspen-like hand in desolate Orcus. I make no credo of miserable privation; I accept Necessity, always praying for the springs and the fruits of the deities.

I do not yet know the issue of this malevolent connection with Winifred. I must somehow or other father my own sons; this in some way is Godhead for me.

You must believe that I have the deepest feeling for your Muse. The other day I had coffee with Horace; I had brought a copy of ISHMAEL along with me, and said in a testy voice, "Do you not admire this lovely little Melville book, and do you know how many caitiff thieves are pilfering his lines? Horace has since read ISHMAEL, and spoke with real respect of it. I was very pleased and relieved.

Do not be precious about your time, Charles. There is no way of avoiding folly; I will take instructions from you regarding women, provided you promise me I will not only have a benefit or two from you if I prove to be a meek pupil, but will not receive more injuries from Laid, Thais, Medea, Regan and Goneril than I already have had. In Proverbs it is said that Woman hunts for the precious fluid of life in a man. There are many such opprobrious remarks about ladies, courtesans, wives; in fact, the PSALTER, the Chronicles, the Five Books of Moses, the Greeks and the Latins are glutted with Rahabs and Jezebels, and female Nabals. It is even said that Jael offers milk and honey to Sisera so that she can drive a tent-peg into his brain. I know now that the poets were liars, and that there must be another approach to the woman with the rosy teats and the snaky trunk, and I am [ ] in this darkling secret from you, if, of course, you can take yourself away from those visionary cozeners whom you are always reading, and who, perhaps, are just deceiving me! O how many books I have misread!

My love and full-time friendship grounded in the olden lore and apothegms in return for a part-time friendship, Occidental style.

EDWARD DAHLBERG

■ ═══ ■

washington

wednesday nov 16 xlix

edward, my high fancy Bastard, stick to cases, don't throw those absolute thunderbolts and think to blind me to the in-work where "Life" (your caps) gets itself worked out

      we struck fire over one woman, and the use you had made of her (you, not Euripides, or Homer)   i would not presume, as you have, to make judgment on your whole conduct with women (i am too full of particulars about what you have meant to other women than Miss [Ladine] Young [PART OF DAHLBERG'S CIRCLE IN GREENWICH VILLAGE IN 1932]) as you well know (and as i carefully said that night we spent the week before) when you write on WOMAN as a creature, when you do a Theophrastus, when you raise up your generalization and sting with it as a tail or tongue, then, what you have found out by your means makes sense, suddenly the sentences form, the "olden lore" you have learned (as you once set out in Kansas City to learn words) gets folded in, and we have a Wheel of Sheol or the "I" of Flea

      i was delighted when you recognized yourself as a metaphysician, and talked of resting your life on your principles   fine, my Moralist   but send your Sermons from your mount to that abstract thing, the World, don't lacerate me with pronouncements about myself when you are not able to include all my particulars

                at this precise point we diverge
    i might trust you the more if, when it comes to particulars, you

were as fulsome as your praises   (i speak now of my mortality, not
Ishmael, dear friend)
are you scrupulous, when, each time it comes up, you moan i did not
become Asst Sect of the Treasury?

you see, i do not believe that art is simply the ritual we make of our
lives   then Christ is an artist

you whore after wisdom   good   have
it   i mark how wisdom & commerce have a way of going
together   how else could you come to the Americanism "full-time
friendship"?

PART-TIME CHARLEY

■ ══════════════════════════════════ ■

[New York City]

November 16, 1949

Dear Charles:

You forget that it was you who assailed me. I introduced you to Miss
Young to ease you. I did that, having the same judgment of her then
that I have now. You know that knowledge and acts are rarely one; if
they were, there would be no Zeus or literature or art. I do not see why
you should be disgruntled because I say that neither Homer nor
Euripides regarded woman as a moral animal. However, they put her in
the Balance just as Aristophanes weighs leeks, cheese cakes, lupins, or
as Socrates talks about Justice. One does not pardon bile in a woman
because she is moist in bed. I do not regard scratching and pleasure to
be more important than good principles. My failures are due more to
the Rahab in my skin than in my mind.

You say that I whore after wisdom. What advantages have I gained,
either in lucre or in reputation or in friends? If I smart, because I have
no money for my two sons, and because there is not a soul on the earth
to whom I could turn for a potato, a cruet of honey or a loaf, am I then
the harlot of Tyre? Is every man base who covets the asses and oxen of
Jacob? Are not the denials that the World heaps like an AEtna upon
my back sufficient for you?

What deity is there in the heart of man who assails a man as
stricken as I am? what jot of God, tender grass, or Klymene or Arbute,

is there in a man who is so niggard with himself as to refuse a man, who has been his buckler since he learned there was the Immortal Word, an evening for talk? At least my sins are not apart from a desperado fervor for the artful human beast. I have never been a skinflint about my time with you, and it would not be arrogant or gross to remind you that generally whenever I have given you a day or a week, you have departed from me with a knowledge of ancient scribes and sages you had not previously known. I never thought it more essential to rush to Homer or Strabo or Porphyry than to converse with a friend. I read the Masters to talk better to a friend. I believe that literature is the health of man, and that he who does not regard it so, will bring to himself the Erynes.

You question my praise of your Muse. Yesterday, I wrote to Laughlin, asking him to remove my work from the New Directions ANNual, and print in its place your essays on Melville and Hawthorne and THE TEMPEST.

I have always reckoned a friend greater than any woman; women pass out of our lives, like the sea and the tides and autumn leaves. The more, in a way, we die unto life, the deeper is our need for friends. I say a poet does not trouble himself about being alone. He has all the solitude that the soul can endure; sometimes it is a rapture and often it is abominable ennui. But no man with some judgment has to ask God or men or even a woman for privacy. We will all be privy dust in a short space of time. Let then death take care of our private nature, or the soul which is perhaps the same thing; I depend upon the Angels for my will and my fate.

Christ is doubtless an artist, because his Allegory is not at all temporal.

I regard your large, Jovean, laughing face with the greatest esteem and affection, and believe in your Behemoth dimensions. You are an extraordinary, gluttonous human animal, and for all your intellect, you are sometimes like huge Ajax when he is furiously slaying sheep he mistakes for men.

EDWARD DAHLBERG

friday november 18 xlix

edward, my sheep

   you turneth away wrath you make such beautiful language!   it is
hard for a fool of beauty like me to keep from falling in the honey-pot,
my knowing knave
   and who else but such a wit and brain as you shall i be furious with?
the rest, as Alyosha sd, (and was it not you who quoted?), shall be
treated as children or as the mad?
   i allow i am ajax, and thank you for exposing me to myself: to learn
and to educate, these are the only functions   the only trouble is, do
you, may you, learn from me?   i am honestly too modest—la!   to
know
   i abhor it, but today, and too often, i am as happy as sophocles is
reported to have been for 80 years   that narrow difference between
man and animal is such a matter of hairs
   do, edward, forever, hesitate to make up sums of what you
give   such addition has, against the Pleiades, to be made by the
recipient   every time you count coups you rob us of the future, for a
man must keep his scalp, at all costs, even the loss of the learning, of
the gift to come   i do not forget one thing: that you must always bank
on ingratitude, as Lear found out, is too easy a charge   do you not
trust a cordelia who heaves her heart out not easily?
   and you are a sweet fool to cancel you for me in Mister loklins
annual 1920: master, let us go hand in hand, you who are sure, i who
am not, and thus finish so little! [ADDED IN SCRIPT:] & know less
   i send you thyme for your lintel from my door in the quickest

      possible answer to your courtesies

              which is a form of love,

                YOUR CELT

[ADDED IN SCRIPT:]
they are the lighthearted races, & therefore enjoy nothing,
obviously, so much as cracking of skulls—
the Iliad is full of 'em
their morbidity is altogether pervasive, children of the sun.

The earth (darkling, you'd say) they flee.
Persephone is never of their making. Nor their Mother. So women are
always their sisters, or little girls, whom they run with, play with as
their equals, & whom they slay, as deers   It is true, the sun breeds
slayers, makers of spring, & slayers. There it is,—Celts   light, light,
thin with it, & only in love with the dark, which they never
know.   How can they? Their blood does not go down, races out. And
they like to see it, out. They remember nothing but what has stood out
in space. You dark men root in woman as cave. They, the splinters,
want to dance, only to dance, & slay. They are without suspicion,
stupid, gay, think the world is a banquet leading to a scrap. O, what
shall men do with these empty-heads, before they destroy us, we who
favor the heat, not the color of, blood? What shall we do, to bring
them down, the laughing ones who do not have beautiful teeth? [early,
first? version of "The Laughing Ones," revised draft published in *Ferrini
& Others* (Gloucester, 1955), rpt. *Complete Poems of Charles Olson*
(1987), pp. 95–96.]

———————————————————————————————————

[SMALL NOTE PAPER IN SCRIPT:]

[March, 1950?]

Dearest Charles—Please send the Homage [to Olson, a brief tribute to
Olson's *Call Me Ishmael* and an attack on rival Melville scholars, the
"uncivil, unhearted, book-Barabbases," and those others, the
"incombustible syntax-boys who steal your worst lines," misplaced by
the English printer as an addendum to part III, "The Wheel of Sheol,"
in *The Flea of Sodom,* instead of on the recto page beginning part IV,
"Bellerophon"] back right away. Must mail it to London at once.
Where's a reply to my letter, Autolycus? My love to you &
Constanza—

EDWARD DAHLBERG

———————————————————————————————————

Dearest Charles,—

I am deeply charmed by the BILLY BUDD COMMENT ["David
Young, David Old," *Western Review*, 14, 1 (Fall, 1949): 63–66; rpt.
Human Universe, pp. 105–108]. Your prose becomes more warmly
flesh, and is as toothsome and vain as Absalom. I am altogether of your
feeling regarding BILLY BUDD, although I was not so years ago, but I
think you are right; the mirth and the myrrh of your lines prove, as you
say, what the dullards cannot fathom. Yes, to cite you again, we always
go farther with our flesh; perhaps our disgraces teach us more than the
virtues we believe we own. Do you own a virtue? No one has even lent
me one. I relish, too, your desolate interrogation, "Is this a winter's
tale, a master's "TEMPEST?" And finally, a very brilliant line you
make in, "as though the hand that wrote was Hawthorne's, with his
essayisms, his hints, the veil of his syntax."

It was gifted of you, Charles, to send me your only copy.

I am just getting out of my Heinesque mattress-grave. Today, I
walked in the sun for the first time, with acacia-reveries in my hebraic
heart, and I pined for hazel-nut, the dog-wood, and the pebbles Numa
Pompilius employed to augur. I am still weak; but I want to go soon to
the anointed tables of the Masters and feed.

I returned the galleys to London, and the book should be out in
England in April, perhaps not till May. I added a small essay-poem to
the book, called BELLEROPHON.

I am pleased that the homage to you charms your palate, and I hope
Constanza will be delighted with the cadenced reference to her. New
Directions has already announced the forthcoming publication of THE
FLEA OF SODOM, and it should be done here a month or so after
London publication.

I have just had word that Herbert Read has done "a very glowing
introduction." In the catalogue, English, Read writes that "Dahlberg is
one of the greatest writers of our time." My dear, good Charles, I
appeal to your rogueish, and Mercury-fingered wit, Who is greater than
Dahlberg except Goliath the stupid?

I am glad that you care for the RATIONAL TREE more than you
surmise, and only beg you, you nimble-fingered Autolycus, that when

you pilfer from me, that you do so with more exactness. Heraclitus did not say what you aver he said. It was Empedokles who said it, and he wrote it quite differently. Let me sharpen that Mind of yours: "The blood around the heart is the thought of men." Your own garbling of this remarkable line is not bad, not at all; it is quite good. Now, if you can mutilate another writer's text with as much skill, you are likely to turn out to be a very talented man, almost as great and blunt as Anak himself. But I confess, you steal as only a Genius can, and who should know better than I?

Did you ever get Maximus of Tyre? Soon as I have some health I shall look for it, and when I find it, I shall tell you. By the way, the allusion to Eliot is quite droll; the exchequer saint of anglo-american literature should have more such Aesopian sleight-of-hand.

I shall send this to you, special delivery; the mail-carrier will doubtless awaken you about three in the afternoon, and you will revile me, until you read all my Volpone flatteries, and no man who speaks of frankincense so lovingly as you do, will be able long to resist my epistolary gaities.

Do we all live in the Garden of Sodom, Charles? I can tell you I want the sweet, nectar-apples of Venus. Am I as feminine as the Earl of Oxford? I will love a man amorously with my mind, but not after the stygian manner of Galba or Nero or Caligula.

Let me hear from you soon, my good, gifted friend, ay, very opulently gifted, and take with this my love for you and Constance, the low hills, the sweet Pleiad Milk Maids, and may Heaven be kind, for I am pining to leaf and to flow swift again as an evening, pebbly river piercing through a moon-painted vale.

Your loving friend,
EDWARD DAHLBERG

■ ══════════════════════════════════════ ■

[Washington, D.C.]

monday [April 17, 1950?]

my dear edward:

i have sd so much about you, now to speak to you is an act of the strangest familiarity! And to enclose y & x, which was to be an act of intimacy, after i have used it to breit, [Wilbert] snow and kruse, as (and had i better, to [Homer] woodbridge [English professor at Wesleyan (1920–1938)], whom i abhor?) as lime to catch them on the twig of a job for you, is also strange

all of which proves how only discrimination matters!

as of wesleyan, the smartest idea i have come up with is kruse, cornelius kruse, professor philosophy, who, with snow, gave me the little the place gave me   he is a thin dry high literate, but he has power, was two years ago head here of the Am Council of Learned Societies (the circus top!), and is, with [Fred. B.] Millet, pretty much the boss, I gathered, of the honors college   you should have no trouble engaging him, for he is philosopher enough to feel the edge of a fine mind (if its sharpness is unclawed!), and gentle enough (though it is the faded flower of weakness) to show heart: his wife katherine is "literary!" i suggest you call them when you arrive just on a friendly basis, friends to friends of olson   let yr charmism do the rest, for i have cued him, by letter, of the possibility of a post and also of the short appearance of the FLEA

as of reviewing i have not yet come up with any addition to breit   i have accomplished, in such places, the common discourtesies you and i are such experts at!   but i'll stew over it, have asked harvey to tell me if he knows any characters in such places who might give credence to me on you, and shall do likewise to any suggestions from you
(the best idea i have, is on the reviewing of FLEA: you should make sure that Laughlin sends one of his first advanced copies to Stanley Edgar Hyman, in Westport, Connecticut   this guy bracketed you and I as the only successors to Lawrence's Studies [in Classic American Literature (1923)], in one of the literary reviews recently, and i Plan to be in touch with him by correspondence some time soon   if he should take to FLEA, he swings, at the moment, the kind of reviewer power than which there is no other (he is another of those bright yeshivas, but he is the only character about who is aware of mythography as you and i are now writing it, and who we must woo along, so long as possible, despite the lesions we may see or find in him: he is a tool, to be used ::::::: i say this to you for your ears alone, dearest friend—don't blow it, one day, if you should get sore!)

one idea writing to snow was, albers: where he is known, he is mighty but my major reason for thinking either you or i ought to get out of him a letter characterizing your power as teacher, is to offset what has already been used to murder me and undoubtedly would be so used against you colleges have a filthy way of asking questions of each other in the dark because you probably state that you taught at black mt, i should imagine that any place would write them   and who would be describing you?   natasha goldowski, david corkran [taught American history at BMC] or raymond trayer [on the Board of Directors at BMC after 1951, head of farm projects]!

(i anticipated it a little, by pointing out to bill [Albert W. Levi, taught philosophy at BMC], that it was these three who ousted you, albers and myself—accurate enough for our purposes)

well, ed, this for that   & the very best of fortune (i'm holding my stomach, and sending the little boke to homer icehouse [   ])

& let me know as soon as anything is interesting

love,
CHARLES

■══════════════════════════════════════■

[New York City]
April 19, 1950

My dear Charles,—

Thanks deeply for the letter and the kind notes and epistles you are sending out for my bread. I had hoped the Homage to you would be in the mail, but I doubt that I can get an extra set for you. I have not seen the original galleys of it yet, and wrote asking for it again. THE FLEA should be out, I imagine, in May. It was to appear this month, but I could not get what galleys were sent corrected because of sickness, and then I insisted on page-proofs, not wishing to see page 10 on page 27. If I do it, it is all right, or so I imagine. I am eager for you to see the BELLEROPHON; originally, it was a portrait of you, and then I got baited by my own vices, and now it is you and me, and may Heaven and the Dragon protect both of us from each other and ourselves. I hope the Homage will be good on the page and give you that pleasure that dogwood and April and the unavenging flowers afford us.

I go to Middletown Thursday evening to stay there much of Friday, anyway, and will call Cornelius Kruse. [Wilbert] Snow constantly asks that you join me. He wants you to come up. He thinks I have the power to pull you out of the Washington Tombs. O my good friend, I have some lines on Acheron solitude in Bellerophon! Yea, I have fevered Iliums, but who has the Boreal blasts to blow you out of the feral privacies.

Thanks very much for sending the charming little trade edition of the POEMS. There are some sweet chanting lines out of the honeycomb of your [vines? veins?]. Sing More, More.

My teaching ends this May, and I must get out of that college; there's nothing for me; but being the academic grammar charwoman, and on a part-time basis. I am really worried about the summer months. So far I can't get enough reviewing on the Times. And you see how puling and small I must be. O to get some crumbs from the anointed table of the American hack. But how stupid must I be? In my own right, and without the help of nature, I am capable of huge stupidities, but if some demand idiocy of me, then I go proud, and alone[.] Like you, my fine Bellerophontic solitary.

Why don't you come down; I am at the moment intellectually slack, and I promise not to be more vapid than you, but a little adhesive companionable relaxation, some good, lumpish inertia, this is my bread, my leaven that I offer you. I picked up the Book of the Dead the other day. When a man finishes a book he dies, and I have not come up yet out of the grave.

I have half a mind to do a play, half Elizabethan and half Restoration, before going into a Tragic Poem. I do not know. I know nothing these days, and I am no meek braggart when I say so. There is nothing wily or Phoenician about this remark. It is the only truth I have in my flesh. I leaf, I bud, but only as the animals do because it is the season to do so, and not because I have the Will from the Apocrypha or one of the apocalypses for it. I have no will, and that would be a horrible vice, were I in a loathsome mood.

Well, this isn't a letter or a confession. It is a budding April velleity, the grass leaps up in hidden places, the violets pulse at even-tide, and

when Sancho Panza trumpets to me from some vale or glad hill, I shall
bring him a russet leaf from last fall.

My love to you and Constanza
EDWARD DAHLBERG

[IN SCRIPT ON TORN NOTE PAPER, BOTH SIDES:]

Charles, The Homage on page iii is not set as I had wanted it to be. At
first the printer *omitted!* it. I was quite frantic to think the Homage to
you, should have been so put upon the page, so that it would be
apparent that the Bellerophon is dedicated to you. Please forgive me: it
is not my fault. Some day, & again pardon me for being the Braying
Ass, or let me Bray for a week or so, when this Book is reprinted, for
some young Skelton, or Smart or Olson, the correction can be made,
for I would not give you anything in penury————

Again my love
EDWARD

■ ══ ■

[RULED INDEX CARD, IN SCRIPT:]

saturday [April 29, 1950?]

Edward:

Your sumptuous words! Elizabeth!
"sea-boke" (beautiful), grammar-Castrato,
Eunuchal Comma   book-Barabbases!
thank you, Edward—I hasten it back—for England, a proper issuance!
And say: don't you owe me word of what happened [in] Middletown?

I am your Olson

■ ══ ■

[New York City]
May 17, 1950

Dearest Charles:

I am replying *at once* to your card. I, too, take joy in the marriage of
our names. THE FLEA, my dear Friend, is to be published in London

next month. How soon I shall have copies after that I do not know. But you will have a book as quickly as I can mercury one to you.

I continue till the end of this month to be the academic charwoman of syntax. The journey to Middletown was futile. All that depraved and pallid foliage of learning there sends me to Erebus. I saw little [Lionel] Trilling at a cafeteria table in the faculty club at Columbia. He has that yellow, sere face seasoned in hell, and the bulby, glazed eyes of the despicable ferryman, Charon. The Matthew Arnold man! I have done another hack review for the Times, and if I was not inadvertently intelligent, they may print it. I am trying to compromise, you see! I have always said that the reason I have never compromised is that no one ever tempted me. It is true, in a sense, and I am like that noisy Paul sold unto carnal lust. Aside from this, I have the most holy fervor of the heart to write, let Satan and Rahab point the finger at me, and each claim me as his orthodox devotee. I want to do a poem, a parable, on that obstreperous, and lusting and alienating Paul. I have also been rereading Blake, and bought a fine copy of THE BOOK OF THE DEAD, which Blake used for so many of his allusions.

I may have a job as an assistant professor for four weeks, lecturing on American Literature, and will have occasion to celebrate CALL ME ISHMAEL. I must read Parkman, and some muck-rakers. The other day I was looking at THE CONFIDENCE-MAN. So much bitterness, and so little upsoaring power to wing it. Poor Melville, I cannot believe that either Hawthorne or America balked him. There is some deeper, metaphysical devil of aridity in his soul. No man can either harm himself or be ruined by another. Baudelaire, for all of his orthodoxies of satanism, foolish man, he was not content with the vices nature had so lavishly provided him with, he had to labor for more sins, was no more evil than his original nature. What a hapless folly, for you cannot add one turpitude to your soul, nor subtract one from it. And so no matter what he did, he could not be less or more. That is not strictly speaking determinism, and Baudelaire thought there was some free will in man. It is a good creed to have. I sing of the Tree of Life, and chant vice and skin and error, and let the good and the evil, and not reason take care of the song.

It is incredible how little talent there is in the world. I am reading a very bad novel for review, and no matter how badly I should write, even as hurriedly as I am making these words, I would, maybe, be apt to make one living, upspringing, phrase. So long as I have my faculties, I shall go to Cana, to Joppa, to the wilderness of Beersheba to make the stones speak. I will walk in slain hills, and there find the wild honey in the carcase.

Write me soon, will you?

I send my loving friendship, and bless your Muse.
EDWARD DAHLBERG

■ ═══ ■

[Washington, D.C.]

wed. june 7 '50

edward, my friend,

the howling way i was, i have continued to be, roaring from a storm which heaves up from the hidden places   (are they forever sexual?)
Lear, even Lear, stayed obsessed.

And so a man
better, eh?
(Is it all we do, to recreate parenthoods?   to bring back into existence he was our Adam, she who was Goddess?)
To prove, prove, that we are born?

)o,
smell the blood, fellow(
And so i kept on, carrying you, thinking,
remembering
yr voice
And awaiting THE FLEA.

(what, in the world, shall i
say, eh?
"what is narrative?"

& exactly in what way does
dahlberg's return to old resonators, project
eh?

Myself, the last thing was, a attempt to do a story which was not, to make verse come rasslin out of prose, as tho it was difficult, had to swim for its life, the prose returning, and giving way
some lines perhaps

124   ■   IN LOVE, IN SORROW

(((This is a new 2nd machine (my own just broke down) and I have trouble with it, as you see,—and which you will, please, excuse)))

I am very happy. How are you, Edward? And where will you take yrself out of, the heat? (It is just here, the last two days, and both satisfies me, and gives me a headache. Washington is a swamp. There is some chance I may be along yr way soon. It is time I went on, for a bit. Will let you know.

& it pleaseth me, that Paul is to feel yr sting. For he has long deserved it, noisy Paul, Paul who does not have rosy flesh, who was the 1st one on the wire, to make the Trilling.

I treasure, fr yr letter, "no man can either harm himself or be ruined by another." It is beautiful, and is to be added to such other dahlberg aphorisms, as I am collector of! You use the simplest sort of statement hugely, my friend. (You once praised my short sentence, alas!)

And yes, it is not form but chant you are,—how shall I say that, to those who do not know *either*? "let the good and the evil, and not reason, take care of the song": hic fecit.

(hah, my friend: either you steal, or, again, we make doublet, for you talk like the KINGFISHERS concludes itself: did you ever see it?)

I do not read, these days. But I am full of reference. Was surprised, doing a long verse ["I, Maximus of Gloucester, to You," first poem of *Maximus*, Volume I], for the first issue of a magazine which was to have been born in Gloucester, Massachusetts [*Four Winds*, I-IV (Summer 1952–Winter 1953, ed. Vincent Ferrini], (think of it!), to have Anthony of Padua flying over the roofs where the gulls shit! and blessing my city for me!

It was called

I, MAXIMUS

(and it was he, of another sea-city, who was, of course, in my mind

(((whom, by the way, I have not yet had a copy of, fr that hunter of mine, edward the Sharp: here, here)))

O, yes, one thing which would please you, is, that I am now (by my wits) the owner of a water color of Lawrence's, one of the very few outside the collections of them that he left to Vence

it is of a man pissing into
daffodils, and retains DHL's whole sense of the cycle of nature

(And all I did to get it, was to sell a Lawrence collection I stumbled on in a bookstore, to the Lib. of Congress.)

It is a very nice fetish to have. (I lost—to, of all the possible creatures, Mark [Van Doren] Some-No-Body—the chance to do, for Viking, the preface to a new collected poems of L: it was a thing I wanted very much to do, for he is still fertile to me.)

here I am swetting into my eyebrows, and hungry, and quite, quite silly, and so i shall stop, asking you to receive this more, as a token of love than of intelligence.

> Fr yr friend, and
> who invokes on you,
> all, all
> > benificences, particul
> arly, rosy flesh
>
> OLSON, CHARLES

■ ══ ■

[New York City]

june 17, 1950

dearest Charles,—

you should have a quick reply to your budding summer letter. i thank you for the sun, the grass and the june you emit. i know the pollen of flowers and the savory sweet of stalks, and all that equatorial sexual love you have, which warm days and cool, blowy evenings, yes i know this furioso season of the flesh, but at this long moment of ennui i am in a desperado misery, and for that reason did not write you at once to praise your letter and to thank you for the balm and the gilead of it.

the book, you say, should be a comfort; you're a writer, my friend, a very fine and noble one, tell me, what is it to make a book, ay, fine and quick for the soul to make, and when it is made, a sin, and a folly and a disgrace, for how can you make a book out of virtue, which no one possesses but liars and soup and money hacks. so we've made a book, why then miserable toad, adder, and summer croaking frog, go and make another folly, sin and disgrace for another book. i have no solace in books, nor can i say with aughte else but tombstone laughter that a book finished is just a cold ague, to be printed, and misread, o let us not be fancy, just by three or four or seven to get to hyperbole, why seven that's a planet of people. you might, charles, if you've the mind to, write to harvey breit and ask whether you can do a times review of the flea; otherwise i shall of a certainty have that m[o]cking fleabite of a fate; you know the little dagger silence.

do you believe the universe has moral ears; that sounds droll and rather assish; or let us so phrase it, do you think the earth hears our cries, and that when the heart bleeds herbs and mallow and rush spring up along some woodland mushroomed marge? or that we carry in us our fates, and it requires the greatest faith in absolutes we break at night or in midday boredom and dead affliction, to sharpen a constellation of a fate for ourselves.

the book, i mean the littlefleabite of verse and prose and parable, should be out in london the last part of july, and here on the 28th of the same july, six days after my fiftieth birthday. does that sound eerie or decayed or mummied, fifty years old, that's hardly an achievement in itself. and shall i say, now that i am close upon the fiftieth year, i have learning, and books, and shall we use that cute little word, genius, the philistines have preempted, shall we say it, no we guess we better not. this is quite irrelevant, but baudelaire says that sexuality is just the lyricism of the masses. that'll make you laugh, whether you agree or not, and he also says that pederasts require intelligent women for conversation. give me the intelligence of the soft breasts, the learned feminine fingers, the erudition of her lips, but that's banal too. i mean particularly that erudition of her lips.

two little yogi artists may come to see you, one you know, [Janice] biala [wife of Ford Maddox Ford, painter, book illustrator]'s brother. he once came to me and said, "i have wanted to talk to you for fifteen years, but i always feared to approach you." "alright that[']s fine," i said, "let's talk," and he did, for fifteen years, but when i saw that i was as wretched as ulysses on the barren sea and that the twentieth year was about to revolve, i got up, and went back to my room.

i've been reading kierkegaard; youd probably be very vexed with him;

he writes about dialectics of history, and finitude and infinity, but he had great sickness of soul, and he was not a philistine. consider the lilies, charles, they toil nor spin not, nor make deceitful books; why a book is an infernal lie, spun out of vanity and out of the raiment of solomon and many winds.

now when will i hear from you?

how is constanza? i cannot find up till now your maximus of tyre, save in the original language at daubar and pine. youre a latinist? i have no languages, only sometime deceiving myself into imagining that i write a little english, but write it when i can not in the holy cave but by the devil's tombs.

you have my love and my friendship; but consider the lilies that toil not, and when you are so bored that you can sup upon it, why then make a book. i know no other relief from this unrelieved monotony men call the world or the planet or that strange little thing of skin and malice that is called man, or the foolishness of trees, flowers and streams and the ways of a maid.

EDWARD DAHLBERG

[Washington, D.C.]

sunday june 25 1950

edward, my lad, that was a sweet awakening, my scoundrel, only, you got my brains in their best but least wary mood, and so i add this note to our talk, to be precise about some certain things, mostly

Jas. [James Laughlin, editor of New Directions] (pronounced jazz, as his intimates call 'im!). For he is an important instrument, and I want one day, in my own rhythm, to "have him". But the time has not yet come, and the little incidents-accidents which have happened I like, just as they have happened, which I want you to know, so that you have the record, and will, I think, see the plot this "stage manager" (please, in Goethe's sense, please, not in—o High Critick!—any too shrewd a sense!)

((in fact it is quite simply,
rhythmic, and, because,
of the way it got off so

> bad, with Jas., there, so
> long ago, in Mary's Kitchen,
> there, in cambritch,
I am having some sort of a delightful
playwriting with him, (unknown to him,
of course,) which I want to let work out,
as it works out, without any push on 'im,
because, actually, the whole thing is sort
of a game of innocents (for he is, literally,
an innocent. And I?), and, whatever the issue
> (the reason why it is delightful, just as
> it is, is, that, in the end, Jas. is going
> to have to do my will, so long as he is
> the publisher he is))
this stage manager is
managing!

The two recent developments are, (1), *The Praises*, a long verse, which
he will, as i told you, issue in ND#12, next December; and (2) the
Melville iconograph, which he offered me, himself, right out of the
blue (the blue of St Moritz, and, of —o, snow, at eventide), all, ALL,
by himself (ain't it, bee-yoot-i-ful! fellow
> artificer?)

(1) first: it happened this way: [Ray] West, editor of the Western
Review, took the pome on receipt of it, but then, in the dark, one of
my enemies (I have 'em, too, Edoard!) put the knife into me, one Paul
Engle ("The Continent Screams", En-geld), and by god if West the
pitiful creature, doesn't go and welch on himself, turning the pome
back to me with the suggestion, it is too long, and, mebbe, a publisher
like Laughlin, would be interested. So, to my own amazement (to
allieve the anger, even after I had tore off a two page letter to West,—
a straight Dahlbergism, givin' same the LESSONS of, life!), I up and
ship it to Jas., who, also to my amazement, TAKES IT (1st time, Jas.
has taken; and I, pleased, in a way, pleased, yes, sure, I, too, would
very much like to be,—o, well, not so much now, but once—a ND
"writer," one of those . . . .

(2) the other was quite different, was, as I say, HIS initiation, based, I

suppose, on ISH, which he was quite gentle about, when it appeared,
(had, in fact, before Reynal had took it, suggested he have a look at it,
and I, not doing, because I was, even then, going along this same path
of timing with Jas., what I have described above)

> (he was at the time, spring, 1947, on the Coast, and it was
> gratifying, the way he up, and from the talk there—I
> imagine it was mostly the review that the S.F. Chronicle had
> carried, thO, perhaps, it was a little [Kenneth] Rexroth,
> whom I did not then know. Anyhow, he did, up, and write a
> letter, which, for Jas., was something!)

date (now)

> ((((interruption: add one other detail: I had, Jan., 1949, sent him,
> for NDAnnual last year, AHAB, A DANCE (the thing done for
> the Graham Company, prose and verse))))

date April 20, 1949, letter, fr. Jas., asking, wld you do iconograph
(photos etc., with intro by O on HM)

> > ((Attractive to me, a twin to
> > ISH:
> > I blocked it out, have, still,
> > 5 page plan))

May 20, same (more on same)
June 13, same: saying, "I'm afraid you will think I am an Indian giver,
or someone who cries "wolf! worlf!" (O No!) but since I wrote you,
things have taken a very bad turn in the book business in general, and
I think that we ought to delay this Melville project until we get into
the next economic upsurge."

So that's that. And it's okay with me, that it is, though it is only in this
sense of letting the things come out of Jas., at the moment, as I have
indicated it has come out, not any unwillingness either to do the
Melville book, or, to have him publish verse of mine. (As I sd to you
on the telephone, about a year from now I sort of figure I shall be
wanting to move in a little more on him, that's all.))

> As a matter of fact, between
you and me, what I am reaching for, with no one's knowledge,
certainly, not Jas., is, a book of verse by O issued by ND, say, 1952. (It
looks now as though a chapbook of verse will come out, Golden Goose
Press, about spring, 1951 ["Anthology: The Praises," *Golden Goose*, 3,

no. 1 (1951), pp. 31–42, including "The Dry Ode," "In Cold Hell, [In Thicket]," "Move Over," "Other Than"]—and there has been, for a year now, another slated, called THE PRAISES, from a printer in San Francisco; but I guess that's a dead duck, no word from him in a year). So, Jas.—well, you see, I have plans for him!
[ADDED IN SCRIPT ALONG LEFT MARGIN TO BOTTOM OF PAGE:]
I sort of think I push "Melville jobs" off, ahead, simply to get "olsons" out there, sufficiently, to make more "Melvilles" sit, properly, where they belong, on me, not on me as—a sort of H M Son: though you, perhaps exclusively, see ISH as Olson-act, remember "the World", & how lazy, how stupid, how automatick, it is!

That took altogether too long, but I wanted you, Edward to see the whole picture, have the whole record, and understand my way of working along with Jas. (You see, I am gratified, that you tell me, he is well-disposed my way. That's fine, and, if it stays that way, a year from now, or so, it will be really usable. Thanks.

As a matter of fact, who the hell else is there, beside him, in the publishing business? He has damned well done the one continuing job, of them all. And he deserved our applause. (It was one proof, wasn't it, that FLEA . . .

I await it eagerly, and I shall drop a note to Harvey soon (better to be cool, with that fellow, he is so scared of, us HAMMERERS!)—and though I am scared to death about the doing of the review, (it is not my form whatsoever, nor my way of putting my sense of you forward: you are too close to me for those public places: too close, for critique— for critique as I imagine critique, that is)

but, for you, I'll do, do, do, do

This is no answer whatsoever to
the magic of that special of yrs,
which was as rich and sharp (yr
wisdom has now a hardness (of the
surface of water from which,—I
steal from a friend, in quite other
relevance—stones skip before

they plunge) so fine, the ironic,
the sort of lying like a Saturn
overthrown . . . .
but is just a note, to fill you out,
and, also, to send you

love,
CHARLES

---

55 morton street
Apartment 7 L
new york city, n.y.

july 21, 1950

dear charles,—

   i have moved to 55 morton street, apartment 7 L, and my phone
number, not listed, is algonquin 5-3368. please, charles, give no one
my address or number. i have had mail forwarded to you, and pray it is
not too much bother for you to send any letters that may come to you
to me. sheets were sent out july 6th, and though laughlin is anxious to
publish book soon, i wonder whether august would not be a poor
month for that. tell me what you think.

   got word from herbert read; he said a professor had asked him to
suggest candidates for the nobel award. read mentioned me, and the
professor took this as a coarse jest. read was quite vexed with the
academic epigone.

   have been reading kierkegaarde, blake; the eye ailment has given me
great trouble. hope to go into poetry and parables soon, but not
without more books in me. i mean more reading. have done some hack
reviews; the baudelaire will be out in august in the times. all that can
bring me is perhaps some notice at the churl's academies of learning,
and maybe some one may yield up a decent job at an indecent college.
you will have, of course, charles, the flea soon as i receive copies. i
think the books have been bound in england.

   this is, alas, a slack epistle, and i apologize to you; my energies this
morning are scant. i need the ocean salt, but fear that no such tonical
poseidon will be mine this summer.

meanwhile, what do you? this matter of making a book, a whore's book with angelical visions, with the aid of theuth, lucifer's foot, and heaven, is a hard enigma. i am still looking for maximus of tyre. have you stumbled upon any new reading? routledge has brought out the complete smart, and i have asked them to send it. i have made no mention of you to laughlin, but then, my wily nautical mariner, it seems to me my past efforts for you were never bootless. the mistakes i have made i have committed in my own behalf! don't worry, you are as skittish as the foal, the ass's colt that entered the gates of jerusalem. i happen on admirers of yours often. so don't drop into any evil pits or snares of despondency. ishmael is in my mind, and when the time comes, [nod? knock?] at new directions, so don't bridle your chimera, i[']ll fathom that possibility, unless you rather i would not, and i don't say that slyly at all, for i just don't know what plans in sheol or in earth or in the seas you are devising at some far end of no time.

my blessings upon you, and my love to you and constance. let me have your word, for i am not only hungry for the barley loaves and the fishes, but also for the miracles.

your devoted friend,
EDWARD

[ADDED TO MARGIN OF FIRST PAGE:]
Just got word the Flea to be published July 24th

■ ══ ■

wash

monday july 24 50

my dear friend Edward:

Nor shall I, apparently, go to the seas this summer. So if you too cannot watch yr kine of Poseidon play by it, in case it is any alleviation to share your city imprisonment, we share.

And so yr mail will be handled by yr postman, & readily, my friend, as readily as when he was a lettercarrier, and you met him.

(Strange drops & syntax this morning, Edward! It is always so, when one meets that stranger, the blood, again, after a night's sleep, at least when one is tired, and needs salt sea to spine & sponge the rote of same—is it not so?)

is a friend here who has a car, and we have been using Sundays
(Constanza's only day off) to make quick trips to the extraordinary
meadows and rivers on which the Civil War was fought: a week ago
Harper's Ferry & Antietam, or, what I prefer the Rebel name of
Sharpsburg; before that Manassas. And yesterday, four of the fields of
the terror, Fredericksburg, Chancellorsville, Wilderness, Spottsylvania
Court House. It is very weird, how much it was Anderson's blueberry
America that was the time & people of these frightful places of
slaughter. And how they sit now, as they did, 100 years ago, a few
monuments, but crops, fishing rivers, the same stone bridges, &
wilderness roads, even such churches as Salem Church, Wilderness
Church, standing where they were, white as the bones of the men
were, the bones you do not now see. But wood outlasts men, and there
at Spottsylvania, at the Bloody Angle, on the edge of the woods, I
stumbled on an abatis, with the sticks still sharpened and raised like
snakes to impale a Fed coming in from the forest. (The past is
prologue)

And so, in my
reading, where am I? Not here, but in Sumeria, Cappadocia,
Baluchistan, and, farther back, against the melting ice, what my friend
Sauer calls Mankata Substage! [cf. Carl O. Sauer, "Environment and
Culture in the Last Deglaciation," *Proceedings of the American
Philosophical Society*, 92, 1 (1948): 65–77.] For my old obsession of
space works in to time, by time's back door. (I finished last week an
argument on the problem of verse now, which, in perhaps too muscular
a way, brings all this speculation together. ["Projective Verse," *Poetry
New York* 3 (1950): 13–22.] And I succeeded so in intimidating the
editors of Poetry New York by it, that you shall see it soon. They are
bringing it out in their issue August-September.

But it is nothing. I do not care for critique unless it is made parable
as you have made it, and I do not seem to. I more and more take it,
that, so far as I am concerned, critique, like argument, properly
belongs previous to the act of composition. And so I go, daily, on,
from one verse, to another, trying in each, to make each obey that
form it seems to my slow growing eye and ear it demands.

I wrote to Harvey to suggest I do a critique of FLEA, however. And
when you say, the 24th July, TODAY!, does that mean the American
FLEA or the English? It is most exciting news. Do keep me posted on

reviews. For is it not a measure of our contemporaries, how they put their hand to one Edward Dahlberg? But this is nothing. What is something, is, that it is out, for those who *can* find it. Keep me fully posted, my friend.

So write me soon, and, if you are of a mind to share my curiosities, look at some cylinder seals of those Sumerians!

All love,
CHARLES OLSON

■ ══ ■

[Washington, D.C.]

Tuesday, August 1, 1950

Edward! Edward!

[Paragraphs 1–4, 8–9, 14 and the handwritten conclusion have been bracketed in soft pencil, probably by Dahlberg.]

It is as Bellerophon, of Bellerophon that I will write you today. For you have so made the Sign of me, and I am so atremble to be inscribed to in such a Connection, that this is enough for the first day of the life of this extraordinary Book which you have so quickly put into my hands and which, in its Enigma and its Beauty, already enlarges me. But. I have suffered too much, Edward, to speak easily of the sage & parable you have put forth here.

I thank you, thank you, deeply, to be made a part of it—and to have the beautiful words of Rhodope who knew what a fablist is, and of— how deeply correct you are—the Amorite Whore, instead of all present dirtiness, put there by you as the gate Prouti through which I entered, bending the head, of this temple of your bones.

And that an Error has put my name as well in Beliar as in Bellerophon, is to double the Honor, for, having read it too today ((I have had to struggle to get beyond that "Author's Note" which now, in print, seems even more remarkable to me than it did in mss., as deep & gifted & engaging a two pages as I can think of: so rich is it, so, to use your lovely word, as lovely a word almost as, of woman, that she pleasure us, is your word, replenishing))   I put it with my first love for the story of the Flea: it is another scimitar into the rotten belly (how you urge the Wheel, press it in on . . .

But who is Bellerophon? You wondrously say, he is a sea-nature of the Muses. He is. For he is the son of my Glaucus, half fish, half man, he who was my father, the father of all Phoenicians, Barat or Panch, who was the king of the Flood, and surviving, found fire again and thus was also Prometheus, whom we have heard of, in the Caucasus.

The first of the curious things, however, is that Bellerophon's grandfather was Sisyphus. This is surprising because Sisyphus was the unknown father of Odysseus! (He waylaid Odysseus' mother on her way to marry Laertes, the story goes.) But then you've sd it, you've sd, Bellerophon is Odysseus the artist—or do you know what you've sd, when you've made it conceivable that an Odysseus should be an artist? (Is it at all possible that the Bear's Son—for so Sisyphus is, the Bear, the cunning one, Homer calls him, most cunning, "much-knowing" says Alcman, two poets who are not moralists (two that are, Hesiod & Pindar, put it differently, the first saying Sisyphus is a man "of shifty plans," the other, the State or Grandpa Poet, saying "Shrewdest in devices." (We know now, how Odysseus was marked!)

Which gets us ahead. For, in the light of that peculiar melancholy which settled down on Bellerophon when he was getting old, it is also Sisyphus who throws some possible clue—, though I should mislead you, if you thought I thought this was the answer. Why was Sisyphus compelled to push a rock? That he might not, a SECOND TIME, escape from death! For he did, the first time, and revealed god-plans. (We shall want to remember this, later, as of third figure in this puzzle of who was Bellerophon-Odysseus-Hercules? For Gilgamesh, older than any of them, in search for an end to this ache of death, went to Utanapistim (another Barat or Noah) and through him found out that the seed of life was buried at the bottom of the sea, where he went, and found it, only, in his joy, to have a snake steal it out of his fingertips.) (With this in our minds, with the Cave of the Sea added to the Cave of the Bear, shall we wonder that Bellerophon and Odysseus are of the same line?

The second of the curious things is, that it is not at all in Greece, not even in Ionia, that the events of Bellerophon's life take place. We are told he was driven from Arkadia because a Potiphar's wife (this Peloponnesus of exile) paid him off this way, drove him off. But this, if we will believe Apollodorus, was a decadent story. Apollodorus asks us to see in Bellerophon a deeper "cause" (it is the cause, it is, the cause). But more of that, later.

Or should we delay, any further, the real gloss to the text of Edward Dahlberg? It is true, that in his "Bellerophon" Dahlberg does not speak of death as the dying of the mortal touch, but only of the dying of knowledge, the danger of the instrument of knowledge, the mind, which, in this extraordinary interpretation, he identifies with, as, go low, he says, Bellerophon, come down, O learned Dust! But elsewhere in the enigmas and single-sentenced parables of this clay tablet which he has called the Flea of Sodom, he does disclose how, that the Earth bleeds back the blood of the murdered, especially of a man's kin, is a cause, is a cause that man is restless, nomad, hunter, Beliar, for ever in unrest, unable, as the Seer demands of man, that he sit, if he would humble, his head, go low.

Now Bellerophon, the myth-mongering Greek poets had it, successfully attacked, in this order, the Chimera (sez Dahlberg, Pride, thinking, perhaps of Perseus mirror, by which he did not have to look upon the face, the beloved face, of his "mother"); then those mountain giants, those Cyclops, the Solymi ("lawless heart-rock" Dahlberg calls these Pelasgians, these crude first people, these eaters, "extinct Centauric crags" of dead knowledge, Dahlberg also says, wise as he is about knowledge); the third of his tasks, this peculiar horse-riding Herakles, was to slay the Amazons, an incident Dahlberg leaves entirely untouched, it is curious to note, perhaps because he sees, in the Chimera, a female of the man himself, sufficient to include these other exaggerated women; and last, before he gets—I sd these decadent Greek poets—the girl, & the kingdom, he slays the finest of all the warriors of her people, the Lukki or the Lycians.

There is much blood that Bellerophon spills, though none of this blood, apparently, is the kind of blood to become a curse, for even, as I have sd, though he kills the Lycians themselves as well as such monsters as the Chimera, the Solymi, the Amazons, yet, he is rewarded with half the kingdom of his father-in-law, begets three children, and, you'd think, would be left alone—would be, that is, if this whole tale of Homer were not some late and degenerate lie. (It is as though Homer proved Dahlberg right, his Bellerophon is such a piece of the mind, is such a bad mural by Polygnotus, is, a faery tale, even to the horse Pegasus, who has been so run into the ground by poets, even to the sword of Mercury. I honor Dahlberg, that he has, in one ambiguous sentence, saved the whole business from collapse:

Bellerophon, astride Pegasus, he says, addressed his Furies, the raging, Iambic hoofbeats, each regards the perfect wisdom of high Zeus, 'Only he who is alone can be wise without being double'

I said, we should not delay any longer, the older & the deeper story. Best start with this queer horse. Is it not very strange that this horse was born out of the earth at the place on the earth where the blood from the neck of Medusa poured out when Perseus, that twin of Bellerophon, cut off her head?

I insert at this point a story from Pausanias, the story of another of these brother "heros", Alcmaeon. Pausanias tells us that when Alcmaeon had slain his mother Eriphyle, he came to Psophis in Arkadia (again, Arkadia, the home of the Cave of the Bear, the second home of the Lycians), but there the infection he had acquired on the death of his mother would not abate. He then went to Delphi, and the Pythia taught him that the only land where the avenger of Eriphyle could not dog him was the newest land which the sea had laid bare subsequently to the pollution of his mother's blood. And he found out the deposit of the river Achelous, and there, by that new and unpolluted land, he could be nourished, he could live.

Now we can unravel the ambiguity Homer offers us—and in offering us, saves his tale. Says he, suddenly, when all seems settled, when he is familied and landed, without warning, without cause, Bellerophon comes to be

"Hated of all the gods. And in the Aleian plain apart
He strayed, shunning men's footprints, consuming his own heart."

((What is very beautiful, in Mr. Dahlberg's Wheel of Sheol, is, that Beliar, even, is made to suffer in the very opposite way, is made, because his wanton and drunken knowledge separated him from men, to cry out for a piece of human flesh, and in his loneliness so fierce, he falls down wherever he can just to lie in a fresh human footprint, like some poor crazed modern Sodomite, who, in this manner only, can cause the swollen seed to be spent.))

This Aleian plain. We are back to the sea. We are back to—now at the end of Bellerophon's life—to the reverse of all, to, the origin point. For what is this Aleian plain? It self a delta, and possibly the first important delta of civilized man, the delta of Cydnus, where Alexander got an infection, where the Caliph Mamum died of a chill, where the

emperor Tacitus died, where, like the Emperor Julian, he was buried.
TARSUS.

Is it not a curious place, Cilicia, for Bellerophon to end in? Why?
Why he too must end in a DELTA, in a rich stoneless loam? stoneless
Mesopotamian place? stoneless, my dear Dahlberg? where river & sea
are joined, where men who are of water and of land are born, split
men, perhaps, by concept as dangerous as race theory, but men who
are civilizers, men who in delta bottoms begin towns, begin,
Mohenjadaros, or such ports as Barat came from, LAGASH? (or Uruk
(Erech)

WHY DOES BELLEROPHON END WHERE PHOENICIANS
MADE A PORT?

Apollodorus, as I sd has one answer. He says, what no one else hints:
that Bellerophon has murdered in Arkadia, not his mother, but,
unwittingly, his brother. And only on this NEW LAND, the Aleian
plain, could he find a place to rest, could he find an absolution from
the Earth, herself polluted, poisoned by the shed blood of kin.

I add one last curious thing, that Tarsus, this end point of
Bellerophon, who, riding a horse born of the blood of one woman, slew
another, is also the city which is said to have been founded by (1)
SANDAN who is local of Hercules; (2) by Hercules himself; (3) by
PERSEUS. And that it was Iapetus or Japhet, the father of JAVAN or
the Ionians, who named the river of that city "Cydnus".
[ADDED IN SCRIPT:]
Edward: this is token, TOKEN, of how you have *aroused* me! I enclose
it, merely to TELL YOU. This has been a DAY.

Love, & astonishment, before the door of, yr WORK OF THE DAYS

love,
CHARLES

■ ══ ■

[Washington, D.C.]

tuesday, july   *august 2 50*

edward:

i was broken off last night by the coming in from Mexico of a friend
of Connie's /   i mention it, because it revealed you have a BELIEVER

there, in Mexico City, a man—35, Billie [   ] says—who thinks you
are the *onlie makyr*, who, when he heard that Olson knew Dahlberg
(here! here!) was interested to know Olson! His name is Mike Rossene,
comes from Cleveland, has only just now got himself a GI education,
&, says Billie—it is how the whole thing came out—has ALL your
books! (my only regret is, that, says same, he has a fine sense of
humor, & his stuff is bought by the Atlantic Monthly!)

Now Constanza wants to have three copies of FLEA for friends, one
of them a "poet" whose work she likes—as a matter of fact he is a
"poet" in the old frenzy sense, the "personal" or lyrick mode (you will
have a chance around Sept 1st to hear me on this mode—Poetry New
York, at that time, brings out a long statement on PROjective Verse vs.
the NON-projective (in which, by the way, you are acknowledged as
the transmitter to this citizen of first principle necessary to OPEN or
FIELD COMPOSITION). Will you, therefore, let us know where we
can buy copies? Does it mean waiting on Laughlin's edition? Or is
Dauber & Pine handling Nevill copies?

I'll be honest, and hope I do not have to raise myself up soon and do
a critique of you, my dear wise friend. For it is an overwhelming
experience to have this book in my hand. You see, you are most close
to me, I am here present, and, beyond all else, your images are some of
the very same images I have taken up for myself. And you may judge by
the fluid state of that "essay" you got back on Bellerophon yesterday,
that I am only now in mid-place, in this whole disposing of the more
ancient past.

But if I should, it will be easier than I think, simply because one day
has told me why it is I preferred the story of "Flea" to the "Tree", say,
why I prefer now "The Wheel" to yr "Bellerophon". It is FORM. Even
in "Wheel" you have personages, "I"s, who fold the wisdom back into
the vessel from which it came, it comes, you, the human, and,
therefore, give the truths an energy and place in which they express
themselves, a meditation, an intercession which creates the very thing
you elsewhere (conspicuously in "B") make a statement of: in the
"stories" and the "parables" the MORTAL TOUCH is present, is able
to work directly on me, instead, as in the "essays", on the mind. IT is a
wonderful thing, Edward, to do such INVOLUTIONS now.

Which brings me to the beauty of the PARABLES. (I should also
congratulate you on the shape the book has been given, the fineness of
its organization, opening on the FLEA, the WHEEL   after TREE, and

140   •   IN LOVE, IN SORROW

the PARABLES returning to yr FORM, the FORM which makes this
book ADVANCE.)

Parable I is absolute, intimate, done, perfect in its image and its
ambiguousness, all poured back into a thing self-made, self-existent:
and such phrasing as "The birds are hurt, and the branches have slept"
is the purest verse, the way they recur, as do the Griefless Cliffs
(someone shall one day examine your imagery of STONE), in that rear
of it all, "the branches and the birds are dry", and, suddenly, "the
Wind blowing."

One thing, Edward. When, either fr Nevill or Laughlin, you have press
copies, there are two or three places where—if the publishers send
them as of Olson—the book ought to be noticed:
(1) Robert Creeley, Editor, *Move*, Littleton, New Hampshire
(2) Richard Emerson, Editor, *The Golden Goose*, 1927 Northwest 34
Blvd, Columbus, Ohio
(3) A. Wilberg Stevens (and Kenneth O. Hanson), Editor, *Interim*,
Box 24, Parrington Hall, University of Washington, Seattle 5, Wash.

Others, where I don't think my connection is strong enough to make a
difference, but where the book ought to go, are:

Imagi, Editor Thomas Cole, Muhlenburg College, Allentown, PA
((Oh, yes, above (4) Rolf Fjelde, Editor, *Poetry New York*, 14 Avenue
A, NYC
The Western Review, Editor, Ray West, the Univ. of Iowa, Iowa City,
Iowa
Wake, Editor Seymour Lawrence, 18 East 198th Street, NYC
The Montevallo Review, Editor Robert Payne, Montevallo, Alabama
The Voyager, Editor Vincent Ferrini, 3 Liberty Street, Gloucester,
Mass.
The Little Review Digest, Editor Rudd Fleming, 211 Elm Street, Chevy
Chase, Maryland
The Quarterly Review of Literature, Editor T. Weiss, Bard College,
Annadale-on-Hudson, NY

And let me know if such a mailing list is possible, and when it goes
out, so that I can be aware it is there, for pushing.

Oh, yes, it occurs to me. He praised you ambiguously, but he is aware of yr work (in the HUDSON REVIEW this winter bracketed you, DHL, and myself), and he is the bright boy, the new [Alfred] Kazin, with a particular knowledge of "myth". Laughlin, at least, should spare him a copy: Stanley Edgar Hyman, whose address I do not have but I believe Westport, Connecticut, is sufficient.

So add to above (2nd list: they have had their chance at me, and rejected it, mit violence!) THE HUDSON REVIEW, P.O. Box 45, Village Station, NY 14, NY

My love, and the fullest sort of excitement, that FLEA is here!

Yr friend & companion,
OLSON

[ADDED IN SCRIPT:]

P.S. By the way, I think it the best READ I have seen! I only demur he confines you with CHRYSTAL—& Joyce!

[ADDED IN SCRIPT AT TOP OF LETTER:]

P.S.: tell me in "B", on p. 114, 2nd para. what happens at "each regards the . . .", each of the IAMBS? or B & P? what, precisely, do you mean? And is the quote yrs? or can you give me its previous context? I should like very much to understand THIS!

■ ══════════════════════════════════ ■

[New York City]

August 4, 1950

Dearest Charles:

I have your two epistles from Zeus, and any thanks even from the deity of the heart cannot be nourished enough by mountain and river and tree roots. Take, then, My friend, my Thanks, and though they must be poor and pithless and lazar-wormed, for I have no grace or goodness or some legend to meal you with at this instant, to put into Themis's Scales that has any weight in justice or in heaven to equal your LETTERS. Then, God be kind, and let not Charles be vexed, I am sending this to you in a hurry, or as you said to me in a letter delivered to you by sacred Theuth, many years ago, I must *mercury* this to you. This is not at all an answer, but just the bow of the eyelids closed of dust. Let it be, just for the moment, and with your pardon and mercy upon me, for I shall soon write you. I do not wait, Charles, to answer you as the gods would reply, or even as the meager footprint of Vulcan, for it is said also that he is the Father of all mankind, is some dim tracery in sand or earth or in pebble, of the first brazier. But I should be more ashamed not to reply now, though it be the niggard word of a caitiff than to wait, having you in the meanwhile, regard me as something even worse in the morbose bottoms of the earth. I am asking you please to forgive me, for though I love your two LETTERS, I cannot just for a depraved moment study them, as I wish to, and send you again the homage and maybe even a dim perception, borne to me from Hermes or even some oracle pouched in the wings of Attica's OWL'd Athene.

'Only he who is alone can be wise without being double.' which you care for, and the gratitude of the angels to you for so caring, is, I blush to say, mine; I was not borrowing from Pindar or Hesiod or furtively inclining my ear over the tripod. I was simply considering you, Bellerophon, and what you are so tempted by the AEOLIAN WINDS, or the ALEIAN PLAINS, which is, as the scholiasts say, which one? Charles? Apollodorus, perhaps the lute-head Pindar, is new found land. Jane Harrison too has some matter on Bellerophon, but you know it, I am sure, and then there is the lost fragment from Euripides. What I was attempting to write was that each man, having you and me in mind, me and you, regards his jovean wisdom, which is really the raging iambic hoofbeat in his distempered, and dionysiac soul (for it was Archilochus' Rage that made his Iambic). as something other than that kind of priapic or heart-fit, we are always mistaking the ugly cucumber head of the garden variety of phallus for the soul anyway, for Mount Horeb. But I am not writing at all what I want to, and I shall, if you please, return to this, when I have reread the letters.

So far, Charles, I have received four copies, one went to you and Constanza, a very frugal kind of singleness I own I made out of this, but I shall make amends to her, and one I gave to RLene, lately returned from nice and firenze, and so the Cana waterpots are filled with the wine again, and of course, I phoned her at once to tell her your feeling about the Parables, and I do hope Lady Constanza believes as you do. Of course, you were as much of an augur as Calchas in one of your fine, ear-quickened moods, for when one reads or writes one should listen to the stream on the bed-rock, or to the hamadryad in the tree, or to some deep ravined earth-root which has so many miracles in it, which we do not know if our ear is not mythologic. Deukalion heard the Flood, and Charon oars the desolate boat to Styx, for the voices of the dead are infinitely more doleful than their aspect or visage. To have you or Constanza buy copies would be to send me to some merchant's Tartarus; I could not endure such ignominy from hostile Esaus, how then could I bear the wound, much more piercing and blood-pronging from one's friends, for who can hurt like a friend, or a lover, and how blunt is Galba's butchery, or Domitian's bodkin, or Caesar's assassins!

I shall send copies soon as I can for Constanza, and one to Cernovich, and to the names listed. If you do not do then the critique, what asps, toads, moles, osprey, kites, infected bats, taxidermist pards and hollywood lions am I a prey to.

I send again the thanks of a miserable wight, a gnat, a flea, and say to you no less in lamentation for any inadequacies what David wept in the presence of tall, august Saul; he had rare majesties, he who sat beneath the tamarisk, although in some scholia it is said the tamarisk is not tall enough so to umbrella him, and maybe the tamarisk is much of a pauper as the terebinth which abraham took for his canopy for the Angels at Mamre, and is an almshouse and bewighted ash, or a balkan or levantine bush, just as the burning Tree was no more, perhaps than a little sumach, the desert tamarisk at Gibeah is no less than the temple at Ammon, and as for the terebinth, i take it more quickly to my bosom than the Oaks of Dodona.

My deep, deep apologies, Charles, and Constanza, and soon, I pray to the hills, and shall go to Ur, to Baal-Peor, to write you some words not so uncivil as these. After your letters I do not dare ask you to forgive me. You send Pauline Messages to the Corinthians and the Ephesians and the Romans, and all these three damned, banal, Christless [Churches?] return salutations. O the dryness, the devout vascular idiocy and baboonish head-grimace of man, I am now speaking in particular of edward dahlberg of kerioth, forgive him, O Giant of the Word, and in the name of our Mythic Friendship and Love, please, now, do not send Epistles to the Churches of Gaza, Gath and Ashkelon, and I bend my brass-neck, and unhinge my proud,

stubborn, fatuous knee, do not now in Giant Wrath Mercury an Epistle
to the Laodiceans!

You have, my love, my total friendship, and my FAITH, grounded as
it is in this letter from homunculus dahlberg, and please tell your sweet
Constance that she shall have her 3 copies soon as I can get copies. I
spit upon myself, and drink the gall and the hyssop, and this I do in
monkish haircloth. if you wish to abash me the more, really humble
me, and cast me a helpless, hapless, hirsute beggar among the nettles
of aristophanes and adam, and the potsherds of job, write me, then,
another magnificent letter, and so shame me as no man has been
disgraced since the first sin. were i whitman i should throat it out, i
cannot suffer enough for the venerealee, but i already see you in
leviathan strength roaring, who's venereal may not you, blessed virgin
mary charles, or were i edward dahlberg i should roar out a mighty
noise through a mole-hill, what is the difference betwixt an evil-doer
and a hypocrite, and let the fool answer, i mean me, not you, MAN.

Your very fond and loving friend,
EDWARD

[Washington, D.C.]

sunday august 6 1950

you may cry "sheep", edward, but your three pages of protest are of
such charm and beauty, wilyness; and disclose so much of mythologem
and so little of perturbation, that I am led al-ong, Constanza and I
have been led along, this whole Mediterranean day;

though i should immediately say, to be honest with you, that the
picture your letter gives of you   Zeus-Zeusing down the street (to be
pronounced sashaying down Morton street) struck us both as being
not at all slack, as you would have us believe, so much as indolent, as
though you had risen, or been pushed out of, like Zeus, some
lady's bed.

As a matter of
fact, my friend it did not need your subtle commentary (to
Bellerophon, back, shall we call it) on the tamarisk tree to see your
whole letter as something lying out at ease under a tamarind or
whatever tree it was Abraham chose to shade the Angels at Mamre by

In fact it is the loveliest sort of proof of what you pray for, this letter—and that, despite the knots it gets its syntax in—the very sort of knots one can imagine Zeus did find himself in, whether he had just been a shower, a bull or a cloud!

So we send back, I reject, your Nilus' tears, protest, in turn, you need not, when you float so idly, think you are, or try to snare us into thinking you are, homunculus, or so caitiff as you cry you are, my flesh-fattened and replenishing "liar," my Proteus who has just lain down, this noon, with his herds, on some Manhattan beach. The truth is, my truth-dissembler, your pleasure pleasures us— or what are these sides of many-sided myths good for, my allusionary?

But I also tell you, Edward Dahlberg of Hazor, Hadattah or of Kerioth, that though you propose, in answer to my simplest question of where Constanza might possess herself of three copies of your sweet, savage, sage book, to bring into this house, it will then be four copies, for three transgressions of this man of Kerioth, and for four, I will not turn away the punishment thereof, however I shall manage, she will manage, thus to thank him for his money-folly, this edward dahlberg, who so Jove-like offers his generosities, in this amplitude of August mood and noon. I shall punish him, I shall, I now decree, by not doing, then, this sharp critique, and leave him, for his too-rich and substantive acts, his David largeness, a plague to the very catalogue of terrors he is hosted by, by asps, toads, ospreys, infected bats, 3rd Avenue leopards and White Spot lions out of that Gaza on which his people gaze.

Or shall I suspend my double-axe & sign of anger until he has another chance to write, when he is less melon-like and delta'd and can so use his intellect, of which he once was as full of as Hebron was of vales, that such barbarisms as mercuried some wild & ignorant savage has poisoned the wells of his language with, or such neologisms as he himself has invented to umbrella him, are set aside   And he is able, all by himself, single you might say, not mixed and doubleted or hose down-gived, to make clear what he means about cucumbers, or diseases?

I shall.

With double love,
C–C

55 Morton Street
Apartment 7
New York, New York

August 15, 1950

Dearest Charles,—

I shall make up a list, as you suggest, to see whether we can make some Noise in the tops of the Mulberry Trees. I do earnestly wish, Charles, you would write a critique on THE FLEA. Lucre we don't hope for, being men of Cush, it is enough to erect the Temple at Ammon, or as Cuthites to found Colchis, and the brazen rivers along osier banks. So, my fine nautical Tyrian, we who smart for the nymphs in the Euxine Sea, or go to Cadiz, and there cast up the obelisk graven with the dolphin, or settle in the mountains with Ham or Baal-Peor Cycklopes, we with the dove, and the serpent in our hearts—for what are our hearts but Ophite oracles, let me too not be without that food from Sidon, Damascus or Gihon, without which we cannot be fabulous.

A note came from Richard Aldington: I had asked the London publishers to send him a copy, and he writes, having read the first two parts, so far, "with much respect for your [l?]avish and prodigal writing," and being, as he says, weary unto death of modern ramshackle prose, that "Now you come along . . . with a fierce apocalyptic prose." He is in the south of France, at Var; there are so few left of that irascible, sage tribe of writers that it was good to have a note from him. What can I hope for from the newspaper Centaurs? Since we live in a day when man is too depraved to hear the word, and can only write himself money-changing phrases (do you know that Carl Van Doren, having worn out his heart on the radio, the television, and Benjamin Franklin) died a few days ago.

I am sending out this morning a letter to Nevill in London, asking whether the copies have been sea mailed to me. I think they have, and as soon as I have them, you and Constance, that summery reed by the warm Nile, shall have your four books.

Last week my baudelaire review appeared in the Times; you can learn nothing from these hack squibs save how I hope to get some cummin seed for my table. I am still hunting for Maximus of Tyre. I have a 1766 translation of Virgil, whom you disrelish; but the Georgics are sweet thyme, and do not avert your face from the wind that blows that sweetly; the pipes of Pan and Tammuz are in the secret groves as well as in the holy temple of Jerusalem. Do not scorn Virgil, nor Callimachus, a stout grammarian who knew some enigmas about the tutelary gods. One goodly line makes a learned heart, and Virgil has many; and even dour rhetor Milton can teach much to Keats and Olson and Dahlberg.

I shall be looking for your heady, Dionysiac line in Poetry, and thank you deeply for the acknowledgment. I thank you for not hiding me in the earth before my time.

Now, I've got to read an urchin volume for a little Mammon, ay very little, for the Georgics, for the anointed table, and for Rlene. And the last shall come first! And a note to Peter Owen in London to fetch you and Constanza the little osier volumes.

So if you will not do the critique, but insist on interring the book in some Sidonian mound near the marge of the Pillars, where mariners take their dories with lamentation and trembling, going first ashore to pour libations to the Nereids and to offer prayers to the Trident, the Serpent at Sais, and to Poseidon who blesses the oar, before passing through the Gates to noxious Lethe, then may you in a moment of blasphemous inattention write a lettuce eunuch adjective like Waldo Frank! But after this torment, may you then return to King Aeolus, to the source of the WINDS; for there the MUSES chant, as they sit on the purple kelp, and heed the lowing of the sea-calves, going to their oceanic stalls; and after you have composed a perfect quatrain, may you then admit that a friend buries his friend with the same myrtle, cypress, and Plutonian spade and implements as his enemies.

I am told that Eugene Debs was an affectionate man, and kissed his friends with prodigal soul, living then when the pederasty of Caligula and Ham and the Apuleius was not so rife, or at least was subterranean, and civilly hidden, and so I send you that same token of friendship, and love, notwithstanding the shoal of catamites that simper and fleer at the spirit and the healing fountains in the wilderness of Beersheeba.

I have the complete works of Smart now published by Routledge in London. When I lay hands on some money, and get, I pray, some fall teaching, I shall order it for you. Did those two visionary apes, [Jack] Tworkov [painter, summer visiting artist at BMC in 1953] and Ibram Lassaw, who does stalactite sculpture in some mystification material, come to see you. I send everybody to see you simply out of a bountiful and overflowing heart, jades, courtesans from Styx and Cocytus, dilapidated whores from Toledo, shipping clerk scribes from Memphis Tennessee Egypt, churls from the rivers and mudbanks of american pragmatism and knavish acquiesence, but what does it matter, who arrives; what is of greatest importance is he that receives them. We wait, my friend, for the Angels at Mamre in the sacred and private precincts of Pisa and the soul, and all other guests are rude intrusions jarring our cadences, and marring some form which we have wrenched from Vision at Peniel. O my Timon Misanthropus, I, too, know the wiles, and all the pulsant circumlocutions by which we eschew baboon, infidel, scurrile men for whom we pine, and smart, and bleed. For a maxim I will take unto my bosom Herod; for a gnome can so cure a man that he has the stomach for all the knavery in the world. A man then that can write some healing or curative or purgative line has sufficient energy and has that goodly, genial climate in his visage to receive him that cannot [   ] those high nullities, and I've got an East Wind in my belly, and some rough boreal blast in the head, and I had better come to a stop, and wait for the Harper, and the woodland lutist, and Silenus to give me the song, and the dulcimer, s[h]aking knees, and the Ass, lest I be the ass without the song and the dulcimer.

Your garrulous, fond friend,
EDWARD

■ ══ ■

[New York City]

August 17, 1950

Dearest Charles,—

I sent you a special delivery the day before yesterday, or earlier, and hope it got into your hands. I doubtless disturbed your deep Cyclopean sleep, and they say that though these men, with the wheel-eye in the front of their heads ate men, they were skilled at building memorial cenotaphs, temples, lighthouses, were as tuneful as the Sirens, and were probably the progeny of the men of Anak.

I gave your entire list to Laughlin; the book is supposed to come from the binders this coming Monday, and is to be published about the

12th of September [published September 6, 1950]. I put you on the list for another copy. Have not yet received the books from London, and have written to find out what has happened to them.

Don't misunderstand the tenor of my special to you. I should like very much to have you do the critique, no, not for lucre, that you know is just buffoonery, but for the pleasure I should receive from your yea. Then if the book should not have just a subterraneous audience, it might not be so hard for me to get another book published, whenever that will be. I am hoping out of the attention that might come from this book to get some sort of college post, so you see, Charles, I do need that kind of help from you. If I tell you there is not a single person to whom I could appeal, save yourself, to do this (outside of Herbert Read in London), you might believe this to be wily hyperbole. But it is the whole truth.

Got a letter from Elizabeth Sparhawk Jones [painter, "the original puritan artist," wrote Dahlberg in the "Homage" to Ford Maddox Ford, *ND7* (1942), p. 468]; she saw the Baudelaire review in the Times; have some fondness for her, but she has a tongue, laden not with myrrh or the hesiodic honey, but with gossip.

My warm love to you,
EDWARD

[POSTSCRIPT 1:] *over* [written on reverse] I shall send out 2 copies today to Constanza—a small parcel came just a half an hour ago—from London—then one [Airmail?] on to you Monday or Tuesday, & I still owe Constance one more! Is that right?

EDWARD

[POSTSCRIPT 2, WRITTEN ALONG THE MARGINS OF PAGE:]

Just spoke to Harvey Breit about getting [a book to review?];— [heard] you spoke very enthusiastically about the Flea. I told him that pleased me deeply. I think he likes very much hearing from you— [TOP OF LETTER] R'lene, an ardent admirer of Melville, had, of course, "Call Me Ishmael" in her library when we met at a party, & considers it, as I do, the *best* Melville of a maelstrom of the Melville rascals [who speak] in peals silenic than by their roars of praise.

Edward, my friend: Do forgive me. I was in a sort of hell, had
descended again, to try to speak with someone—and I think you know
how the living can disrupt such conversation, break off the appearance
and unanswerable speech of those whom you have tried to bring to the
other edge of the trough, there.

I'm sure it was that, rather than, that I
was troubled as to your request I try to box Breit in until he gives me
your book for review. ((Laughlin reinforced it, by the way, later in the
week, in a letter to me on another score, (on releasing, as he was most
willing, both the poem and the title of THE PRAISES for this book of
verse which will be published October 1st (Golden Goose Press)).))

You have me very troubled. If I were asked to do the Times review, I'd
do it, for the reasons you advanced, that, such a review might serve
your other necessities. Follow you here, absolutely. But it would be a
usurpation of my forces and my senses of you to do a "review", a form I
abhor. And that, plus my distaste for "using" Breit who left me myself
so exposed in the same place, leaves me still with a huge reluctance to
write him again. I would so much rather leave this thing to his doing,
on the base of that earlier letter, if he so chooses. And meanwhile go
ahead working on what is my own plan, to do a considerable critique,
without reference to the magazine where it might appear, and then,
when it is done, send it out ((this is the organic way in which I have
worked now so long, that any other conventional method—or arbitrary
one—especially where it is such a major thing as your work, and my
first real grappling with it, for critique—would be scattering, to me))

Well, don't be worried. I will go ahead keeping my attention on your
book. It is the imagery which I am now studying. (The major
statement, of the narrative by parable, as against all contemporary
narrative; and in distinction from the other "prophet"-parts of your
own book, is pretty clear in my mind, but the imagery, which comes so
thick and fast, it is a more difficult matter to get behind you in. And
there is this other possible solution to the Times matter, that I should
be going up to New England soon, and can make a call on Breit and

get the thing, if it is not settled, thus settled directly between us. For I know this lad, a little, and know how resistant he is on you. (He has never gone to the mat with you, Edward, and thus is routed by his own failures.)

I see that neither of these plans solves your immediate difficulty, that you want a big-time notice for leverage on the akademicicars, that time is important. But you know, in your heart, that I am no good where time is, & though you jibe me, that it is Anak or Tyrian or Celtic of me to go slow, you also know, in your head as well as your heart, that it is not so, that my practicalities exist, only in another relevance. For I should want to say nothing of Edward Dahlberg which did not stand in the same mortice as the thing I might say of Herman Melville. For Edward Dahlberg is more than my friend: he is of my own substance, a personage of my own fable, and I heave him out with the gravest torment, as if it were parts of my own flesh. I am not practical and realist at all, where such is of my concern. These are the sources of my being & my image, and I do not do things with such with the shamelessness I observe my contemporaries are so prone to.

Nor must you think, or say, Edward, that it is not at all mortal of me, that it is an "ideality", that it is a wretchedness in the face of my friend's needs. For it is. And I see that. And I will do what I can do to undo same. But do not impugn my innocence. It is my only gift.

One thing you did not do, that I want you to do, is to explain to me that sentence in "Bellerophon":

> Bellerophon, astride Pegasus, addressed his Furies, the raging, Iambic hoofbeats, each regards the perfect wisdom of high Zeus, 'Only he who is alone can be wise without being double'

> (it is not your incredibly fine ambiguity in the quotation, but the phrase "each regards the perfect wisdom of high Zeus": what is the meaning of your syntax, here? which does "each" refer to? just, please, for my understanding, fill in the syntax.)

((((I am so foolish to think that I, or anyone, can so extricate your meanings as to make a critique which will stand alongside the FLEA.

Yet, that is what I would try to do!)))) [IN SCRIPT:] IN CONTRAST
TO H. READ—look, an idea, & worth more than me: why shouldn't
the *Times*, by air mail, ask READ, for the review? He has a large
following here. And the *Times* might give *him* a full page! [TYPESCRIPT
RESUMES] (((((I find this out: that what one does with your "prophet"
pieces, your "revelations", as against your parables (which stay right in
place, in themselves, belong, are left alone) is, to make an anthology of
them, to pull out the "gnomes" and rejoin them, to each other—

it is the same thing one is led to do with the image))))

It is your "history" that bugs me, the suck of personages, events, images
into your own vortex, where they swirl as ps., es., ism., of the micro-
Ed, when Ed is there as "I"; but in the "revelations" the history goes off
a piece and stays somewhere in between Ed and—what?—the
historians or poets who previously used them, from where ED got 'em.
It raises up the whole question, of how, what form forces all such
things to their knees, and makes them servient to that emperor—how,
in fact, the god gets inside.

It can be sd another way: you may remember the 1st piece of my
work you saw. Anyhow, the curious thing is, it has come up again in
this way, in this opposition: the "heroic" vs the "ethic." One of first
reasons why your narratives are of first importance is, that you have
broken the lyric "I" and the egotist "I" and the rational "I" completely.
You have, therefore, made it possible for your own "I" to take on the
force of the "Hero". Thus ethic is disposed of—which has fed on the
mediocrity of life as it is. You allow in (fr the Ixion wheel image, on) a
multiple man (it is not so important as it may seem to those whom you
know daily, and who know you, that it is Edward Dahlberg!).

For such reason I should be tempted by the proposition to go too far,
to say that the "ethic" steals back in, in the "revelations", because, by
chiasma, that where Dahlberg is not folded in to this wonderful
multiple "I" the Dahlberg whom we know, who knows us, is, by the
very loss of the myth-force, allowed in, and ethic comes with him!

But this, of course, is not true enough to invalidate the very things
said that I, or anyone, would make an anthology of: the wisdom needs,
my friend, to receive the same shredding that Heraclitus' has. And
become 130 ultimate sentences!

Well, that for now. And do not be troubled. We shall do what has to be done. And it shall be done, if not in the big spread stupid place, in a small place where it can be properly done.

My love to you, and
my faith,
CHARLES OLSON

■ ══ ■

[55 Morton Street
Apartment 7L
New York, New York]

august 29, 1950

dearest charles:——

I should be at a coistrel review-mess at this instant; but there is a fine letter from charles arrived at 7:30 this morning, which was good, as it got to me the shower, and then to the bakery to be off to my rlene's apartment to coffee and sweetroll her. but then returning, i thought it better to reply and go to the reviewing public-stews later. i should tell you, and this is in darkest secret, because of ann hathway winifred, adder brach, that rlene (she is 25, with the dark, moist eyes that bettered those of lady fitton that slew shakspeare, and a very sharp reader of melville; she has read all the books of that poor, moaning troubled dust whom the rascals are now showing at the newstands), and i are to be married shortly. we are bound for detroit to visit her parents this week-end to fix a date.

of more tidings, i signed an american edition of the flea to you, which new directions should be sending out this morning, and i still owe constanza one more copy. does she want me to inscribe one to her, which i have not done up till now, because she wanted it for friends; but tell me, please, her pleasure. more english copies have not yet come, and i could send her another american one, and don't worry about that; i would rather have my book in her delicate, chaste hands than give it to some akademic stable-boy of american culture.

now you ask me, my good friend, to give you some appropriate explication of a passage in the bellerophon, and this essay really belongs to rlene and to you, and is dedicated to you, and about you and me. well, good friend, i, too, am one of the stupid, drowsy oxen, having fed on asphodels for some years in God's Meadowland, and now having nothing in me but mountain and bare tree stupidity; i am a sere trunk, not as tall as Anak, but more stolid and statuesquely clownish. i also have that blood-unwillingness to explain what you could misinterpret more profoundly. i am only laughing a little, but not really; remember that sokrates went to the poets to ask them to interpret their images and they did not know how. there is something in our river and glebe and sheep inceptions that forbids us to explain what we wrote, we [do] not know how. and, honestly, i would feel a little showy, gaudy, doing some balaam braying, feigning moloch soothsaying in the secret groves, were it in dead earnest (and the earnest in this manner are surely dead) to give you a scholia, a piece of fatuous exegetics; it would not be blood-sport as it is in making a book or a trull or a fine my lady the doxy, and you would be bored, and most uninstructed, and i should be by caitiff premeditation a fat oiled fool.

so now we come to the same point, saith friend ox, after the lordly spermaceti sac is emptied and the book is done, to friend anakim. now for the matter of the review in the times. let us be most plain, and even plainer than that, [a] spread in the merde-sheet, even from you[r] noble hand, would cocker my vanity, and be doves and lucre on the market-tables in the temple. some of me wants that, and urgently needs it, to get a post in some money-changing college, and to maintain a seemly, orchard-bearing wife, and even with you on the earth, without rlene, i walk alone on the planet more lonely and hurt and image-wounded than God. I should like to make a book or two more, if the Great Truth of all the apple earths and fish in the salty underswelling seas; if He that walks alone, from star to planet, being Space Himself, and what is more Alone than Pure Space, not even Time, which is another manner of speaking of Lord Space, seeking two or three Companions, also earth-hurt, and slain by the Image, will permit it. You should do all that your soul commands you to do, nor would I desire to encroach upon innocent Cordelian blood, asking of Her who is our Muse, our Fealty to the perplexed, bilingual heart, to give what the Alchemist Himself cannot yield for infertile, dunged skin hid in AEcus' Cave. I know, AEcus can be driven out by the club and lion's skin of Herackles, and not by you or me. I will probably get, and this is not nose-sniveling, flunky petition or so help me god local 12 waiter's union oath (for in my own heart, too, i don't care, knowing and believing that God will provide the lamb of Abraham, even after the times' tombstone either or 800 word review—either he should have written another book or better, not have written one at all. The critique you propose you suggest, coming slow and meditative like the ruminative thoughts in the hunkers of the cattle of seth and enos, would be an anointed table for my cup and my soul. so do as you please, and let harvey breit, the de luxe pederast with the low, murmurous voice of hairy esau, do as he will, or as he tongues, for the pederast cannot will and so must lie, and lie until the villainous world takes its ultimate breath. another word of news in the world; at the new direction office, barbara asch, who does the publicity, said it would be very fine if i could get a statement from mr. charles olson, who is a very Good Name. Despair not, the merchants of toledo, the clothiers from barcelona, and maritornes, of hair of glisteringest gold, trumpet your name, and everyone runs to the brothels to look again at the whores to see the metamorphoses; but we ride away from this whoring merchandise accolade to the glades and the fruits and the oxen-cribs, and make our orisons.

have i told you all? one of these days i shall so smart again for a beauteous apocrypha boke, by a man of tyre, or an obelisk-builder of the house of cush or ham, and then let us see what the furioso heart can spill, and i shall not ask you nor you me to explain what we wrote because that is what is so much the inexplicable fable and allegory, and the mazy, star-shod lodestone.

all my love for your Genius and your jubilant friendship; when the prophet bloweth into the ram's horn, the anointed shall sit beneath the tamarisk, and saul and david will reenact their texts, for there is no time save in the heart of nabal.

your loving friend,
EDWARD DAHLBERG

Let me know, i beg you, constanza's wish; for i am one to wish your lady's wishes.
[IN SCRIPT:] P.S. I am very happy about the book publication of your Poems, & also wait for the Sept. Poetry [i.e., *Poetry New York* issue containing Olson's "Projective Verse" essay].

EDWARD

tuesday [August 29, 1950]

my dear sweet wild tormented friend: i want to say this, to assuage
you, if,
what i said yesterday caused
you any Saul
that i had to have my innocence
to play to you in public!
Or that my trident had to be picked up
if i were to ease you, a little ease,
my child!
Look, my fellow Fish: do not worry—
there is a Wedding in that ocean called
the Stars

(One thing. I am terribly worried about another son, Cernovich. I
have just heard he is now dancing again, and walking twice a day up
that dangerous hill. It is clear, with his heart, he is toying with killing
himself. When I saw him this spring I knew he was eaten, badly. But
he is a proud man, cannot be spoken to direct. Nor does he write me,
or you, or anyone who could help him, perhaps. He wishes only,
immediately, to be in power. And so he asserts himself on boys and
fools, offsets himself to those who are less foolish, less boyish perhaps.

It occurs to me that something as simple as the receiving in the mails
your book from you might be of help, might be the act—which a letter
wouldn't—to remind him of, how not singular his pains are. Which he
knows, but doesn't know (because he is so young? but then, rimbaud.
(but then, american

Now there are only a very few days left before he will be gone. So do,
Edward, if you possibly can, get off a copy of this wondrous revelation
of yours THE FLEA to this poor bitten creature whom I also love.)

CHARLES
OLSON

[Washington, D.C.]

wednesday [August 30, 1950]

Edward!

Delight, Delight, to you and to Rlene!
The Vineyard, for YOU BOTH! the Quest!

And to tell you I have just joined—in two pages of a letter about you
to Ernest Brooks, of the Bollingen—your name, as Visionary, to that
other Discoverer of What Grapes There Are, H. Melville, saying,
exclusively, that you two men [IN SCRIPT:] *only* have made Fables &
Parables (you will accept, I hope, One Harbinger!)
    Your letter, in fact, is so Palpable—I almost said Giddy, in its
Delight—that I feel like Jacob's Best Friend, that night after Seven
Years (Fourteen, I correct myself) that Ancient Modesty!
                                            Go to Bed, Both of You, for Joy

                                                        love,
                                                        OLSON

■══■

                                                [Washington, D.C.]

                                                Wed Sept 20/ 50

Ed:

    Bad business. Had planned come visit you on way back. Instead, as
Con told you, came straight thru (by air, in fact! the urgency.)

    Real trouble is, the trip broke me off in mid-going on FLEA critique.
(Hell of a time for it to happen!) Will get back now. And push.
(Haven't the least idea where I'll come out: you are a tough one, to get
down, really to get down!

    Found ND copy here on return, with grand inscription, which we
both, cherish.

Write: you owe me for a couple of letters, and a note, before yr departure Detroitwards to give parents look at ED. (How is all? Yr move worries me. Anything go wrong? Is Rlene & you all right?

Am faced with difficult winter (another in this house seems too much). But there it is. Spent the day battening down, repairing frames, puttying windows, trying to make out—and the rent! O god, this reminds it. It is due, yesterday! (Haven't it).

And empty-headed. No wish to work. Want to go to some other place. But here is my Circle (with sides, down, and ice).

Enclose answer fr tidy Brooks, of Bolingen. (Tell me, Edward, what are these moneys—and their conditions? Any chance? Shall ask my Gods to favor you.)

Jas L is sure keeping on yr book. (Like his job with the sheets much more than Nevil, the cutting down of page real improvement. (Response on little mags copies beginning to come in. Shall urge reviews. Hope. Anything, a mercy, these times, eh?)

Well, write, when you can. And I shall be less cryptic, another day. This is merely to indicate I breathe.
> Anything else, like you say,
> would be an arrogation.

> love,
> CHARLES

━━━━━━━━━━━━━━━━━━━━━━━━━━━━━━━━━━━━

[Washington, D.C.]

Thurs [September 21, 1950]

Ed, that was a mess. For my part in it, sorry. God damn it. Mess. And no use beating over it. There it is. Sorry. A shame.

But just so you don't have to carry unnecessary parts of it, this: I could no more, at this stage, toss off, easily, any remarks on FLEA[.] As a matter of fact, it is in the nature of, the most difficult thing imaginable. My own work would be easier!

And for the very reasons that you should lead me naturally forward, to speak up, about it: that I am so close to you!

It comes to this: that I am now in grapple with—not one book—but the relevance of the whole of Dahlberg's vision.

(So, calendars, or New Directions, seems—and please, in this, nothing, flint-hearted, dear friend—very very small.

In saying that, I do not, of course, make it small *for you*. Am instantly ready to see how not small it is, your way.

So if I choose to go ahead very slowly, recognize, Edward, that it is purchased at cost.

Something of that, is what I meant, when I sd: I think about these things, too.

It is such a shame, we should get in a brawl. I was afraid of it, the moment you called. You were sore, and looking for trouble. Inevitably, I suppose. But don't feel too bad. As I say, I intend to deliver, solid, hard, straight (as I did, on the Bollingen: strong.)

If I were not determined to go on, I would ship you, with this letter, all the mss already written. Let me just look at it, to give you a count. (And all, mind you, written up to only the beginning of the Tree: that is as far, I am going in so, that I have yet progressed (my original racing thru Bellerophon, of course, excepted. And first reading of the whole book, for that matter.):

17 single spaced typed pages
PLUS
the Bollingen letter (2 s.s. typed solid)
PLUS
4 pages of analysis of the images, pp (of book) thru 24

And only—as I say—up to p. 68! (I abandoned total concordance of images simply because it gets dizzy, to do—and, the pattern is so readily reducible—it is isn't worth the scholarship)

Just to emphasize—to extricate you from your suspicions—that nothing privy is going on (except in so far as any rear of writing is privy, thank the Gods of the act, the Cool Ones). And that it is outside probity, as you put it, or Purity. (What probity or purity is there in public place except as there is privy preparations? Would you, of all men, have me careless, be,—what you made so much of—YOUR van doren or brooks? Nuts.

[ARROW, ADDED IN PENCIL:] I smelled this, you must admit
                                        It comes to this, ED:
I am f[l]unking on the practicals, clearly. But it is not because I am careless of them, thoughtless. It is because it happens that you and yr book come to hand at the moment that I am ready to engage them, not, as a passing act, not as another book, but, as, the vision of a man who has been my mentor.
            (In such circumstance, there is bound to be trouble.
            Only, abide, dear friend. You, your work, this life, is
            worth it.)

All sounds too god damn big & noble. And thus the hell of it, makes me sick of the whole business. And I shall have to hold, like mad, not to turn away. But do not, my [f]riend, blame me only, for this sort of feeling: you'd better have thought, then to have led in, on, why haven't you answered New Directions? Jeezus, Ed, who the hell is N D?
                                        Really, who?
                                        In such a
business, who, such marketeers?
            Are we in a serious business or not?
            ONE I take you very seriously TWO I take the art of writing very seriously THREE I take it, that books are men, and not to be toyed with, that there is value, which each man must go and find out. FOUR I am engaged with setting down what value you have.
                                        In such circumstance,
the question is, huge.

Anyhow, I wish the hell you'd sat on yr hands. But you didn't. So there it is. Let's carry it, lightly,

yr friend, &
fellow worker
OLSON

■ ══════════════════════════════════ ■

[Washington, D.C.]

thurs 9/29/50

Ed: I don't know. Last night, when I read yr letter, I was angry (at old charges). This morning, when I reread it, to write you, your own hurt—"stung", you say—comes with it, from beginning to end, and I am tormented, that you are so. For it does no good, that I might argue, the cause seems so ill-proportioned to your hurt. For there it is, you are stung, and I did it. [ADDED IN SCRIPT:] (Or did I?)

I say, I don't know, simply because it is much more intricate than this given event. That is, you do pitch writing into love (friendship). And so a "statement," as they call it, not done, becomes, for you, a denial of *you*—not, as it would appear to me, a denial of a "system" which I think it is of some moment to keep clear of. (You will imagine I have acted likewise, did, in fact, same publisher, like problem, same time as of FLEA.) But there we are: this does not seem to you either of any moment or but more proof of yr case against me: that I am inhuman and cold and unyielding and act without those Mediterranean parts of the human body which you feel you do possess. For you wld take it, as you so warmly put it—and I made happy by—I am yr first friend. [added in script:] And should act a way you declare.

Of course, of course. There we are. It is true. I am (And do you think— my friend—that I am so "pious" (or choose any number of other adjectives you toss at me, moral adjectives to describe my so-called moralism), that I do such a thing "coldly," confident I am at all right? that I am not all you say I am?

But you see, this is where I *am* deceived, I begin to think. I have been fool enough to believe, that, an examination of yr book, done—as I sd, some weeks ago—as roundly as I have tried to do things on Herman Melville's books, say—would be an act you'd value, that that "sodality" (you could not have chosen a more evil word, to one who was raised in the Catholic vulgarities) you talk abt twice, is not some New Phalanstery, but an older one, of men who look upon their work as undone, who want, from each other, to go ahead to make another work less undone.

But even here, I feel the helplessness of making such statements (and this, my friend, is what is so killing, that I do not find you *care*, here, where, to me, something—as I sd, last week—lives, which is worth *all* our care.)

  ((I must, here, vent my full rejection of yr whole notion, that the "privy" is what you are getting. (I completely abhor your indelicacy, in using such a word, as of myself, or anyone. Indelicacy, hell. Just straight on, known to yrself or otherwise, these adjectives— these moral adjectives: yr letter is loaded with em.) That I do not express my affection & friendship as you might, is *this* cause for you to sit in judgment of my whole nature? Was it "privy" of me to join you, in ISHMAEL, to my two other loves, to say, this man was the man who, by his friendship (belief) and his "critique" of my work, put an element, Fool, here, in this book, which I would wish *anyone* reading it, to recognize, as his doing?

It's crazy, straight crazy, the proportions you do not seem to be able to get yr mind around. But I cannot find it in myself to say, I'm right, you're wrong. I can only say, I see it differently—and this, to me, is of the heart of love & friendship—and art. That, difference is. This is, what we might call, the life of it. The difference. And it takes recognizing, is not at all easy, or eclectic, or "honest", in yr sense. And when I speak of "critique," I mean, in this business of writing, just such labor to make clear how, where, what is the fine essence of, this difference. After which, one may say—fr *his* different point of view— its relevance.

                 I

despair to say any of this, because you have forced me, more and more, to ask myself, does Ed care for anything or anyone except ED, does he want anything—when he cries, affection & friendship—but what he protests he does not want?

  You see, Ed, I have loved your person and I acknowledge, happily, I have learned from you, from all you taught me by taking such care with my earlier work. (It was such a joy, writing ISHMAEL—I have never told you this, I think—to have those mss. you had so incisively done a job on by me as I went ahead each day composing same, the clues they were, to me, and to what language had to do—in fact—and this, now, at this point, seems such irony—what clues they were to FORM. (Form, Edward—which, behind all this disturbance looms, so large, to me.)

I'm afraid I give it up. As I sd to you last week, some way, you involve me in pieties which I am *not* a party to, involve me in presenting you the very false faces you want to strike. (What *is* this anyway? what image do you want, that you so create it to your satisfaction—that is, the satisfaction to strike?)

Why do I feel any difference is in the nature of some crime, to you? That you really do not allow, admit—perhaps even see, any difference in another?

(Don't you see how impossible such a state is? who is, actually, being denied? who?

((God damn it, there you are again, it comes out, I am crying, I am denied. The hell I feel that at all, the hell I am that fatuous, or self-pious. I do not feel denied. The fact is, you say, *you* feel denied. Jeezus, what a squirrel cage. Christ. It's no good. Ed, no good—not life, no life in it, no breath, no space. Christ, give it over. There *are* others, no matter how fine you may take yrself to be. (For I do not buy yr doctrine, "we are all dirty", that we are "at best any more than clever worms with moral agonies." This is the deepest mis-engendering.)

This whole business comes out so crazy. You write a book. A year ago I read it, am very excited by what I take to be an advance in narrative. Say so, to you, direct, move on Black Mt, to publish it. (You see, right from the start, a difference: you see the act *only* in a total sphere of friendship. I see it as such, because it is true, what do we grow by, from, but love? But also, there is this other element: work, yr work, mine, anyone's,—or have you learned from another's work, even where you did not love—or, more pertinent, where the person was not yr friend?) Anyhow, to go ahead, a yr passes, I have, in that time, (due to the story "THE FLEA", shall we say), (as one cause—there are others, of course), for the first time, almost got involved in narrative . . . .

Aw, Christ, again,
it goes flat, to try, to tell you anything. (God damn it, that I shld come to think, that Dahlberg, honestly, isn't interested!)

Well, just this. I
propose, a yr later, to go right inside this man's work, to see what's there, at the heart, what it is that moved me, that leads me to say such things as I say abt this man, to, say, the Bollingen, to others. To do a thing I very rarely do. But that I also want very much to do—not for him, no, no. Nor for myself, wholly. But for that thing—to me, at least—which is outside us, that "sodality" of which, so often, he cries he is a part: men, writing, since when, since, men (those animals) got sounds, sounds, sounds. (as well as livers & kidneys, in fact, apparently, after they got these organs, which he insists (as, for that matter, he does sounds), in turning into a moral system, or a physiological philosophy, a personal humanism.

(awk, go down,
language)
I set out to do such a thing. Tell him so. And what, finally, do I find? Does he want this thing? Does he indicate it is of any importance [to] his book?

> (Nope. It won't work. Again, look: now I'm in the position of making a very fatuous statement: that a man's book means more to him than himself. O dear. o dear. odearie me. Just fuck it, my fine-feathered friend, fuck it. Of course I don't give a good goddamn whether you care for it or not. It doesn't matter. I'm not doing it for you, don't give a damn. I'm doing it because I believe that a book is a thing which has power, and has value, and that, if I can show what's in it better than another man, then I ought to do it, and that there is value, use, to someone that I do it. That, this, precisely, is why books come in to being (or, no—you are right, for you it is fame that is the spur, as it has been for so many great men. OK.) But once they are in being, those books, what shall we do with them? *Market them?*

What it comes to, then: all you want is a PUFF (a thing I do not

believe in, that, to my way of looking at writing, defeats the very thing
I am talking abt, when I say, how important a book is:

(gd it. Agn.

Nor, my friend,
is it *my* confusions. Do not, so easily, content yrself, so easily, assail
me. Stop a minute. Look around, at it—just for a dying friendship's
sake. Good god. You say, you value same. Don't kick it in the face,
then.) (Because it doesn't do the tricks you take it, it should.)

Who are you, really, Ed, to say, what is the well, what the water is, in
another man's soul? (I find yr use of that work as literary as yr use of
"privy"). (And don't, please, for friendship's sake, at this point quote
me (misquote me) Heraclitus, on the dry soul.)

My despair, is, it isn't any use, to talk about it. There is no advance.
You are set. There it is.

OK. OK. All right. What's wrong with that?
Nothing. Our sense of friendship differs, as does our notions of books.
All right. Difference. I make no more of it than that, cannot place
myself in such absolutism as you do,—and give yr game away, I take it,
my Jehovah—when you imagine that Court "in another life, and when
the parable is done . . . etc" and who is pure and who is impure (your
inversions are transparent, dear good warm-livered warm-hearted
warm-friended Edward).

Really, all this hierarchy! All this physiology! All these absolutes!
What do they say? Do they not say, "In this friendship, I am the Law, I
know how a friend *must* behave—and if he do not, he is damned."

All
right, I am damned. I do not feel so, but, that you say it—I have been
so willing—do you think I do not ask myself, is he not right, am I not?

The only trouble is, one gets tired of so many commitments to
another man's personally contrived (however absolutely assumed) Hell.
(O miserable earth, you say.)

One does go along, dragging one's
damnation after them, like some escaped criminal, who does like life,
who does, with his nose, smell and enjoy a northwestwind, likes a
friend, likes to do a day's work, enjoys it, that another does, and, if that
work is a book, and comes into his hands, will take it as something he
can enjoy, disagree with, but go on abt in his own fashion—as he finds
it, in his devices—to enjoy or do abt it, what he will, thinking, his

friend is, like the wind, or the walk, or another person he knows and enjoys, a part of things, things he does more or less about, things that ask more or less, depending upon his relation to them, things he likes—if he loves—to do what he is prompted, not, what some non-existent Law (this is not liberty, or love) is supposed to require of him, as a condition of, continuance.

Look, Ed, let's just not continue, at least on such levels that I am supposed to do something. For I am not, the life of it.

Love,
CHARLES

■══■

ed: I just guess I am a grrrrrreat pppeeeeeeeeeee—
cock, and all the other things you say. yes, i just guess.
and when you've sd it, what
have you sd?

(such, interests me more than, the tally-sheet, the score-card, the bills of lading, the storage charges, the butcher's scales, what was, what was, we do lament:
  you recognize, of course, you had more to give. I do. I dare
  say that's why i am, you might say, embarrassed that it is you
  who make the totals

I shall not swap hallowed remembrances, what was, what was. but i will, (must, it was so crucial) correct you, on your drama, of that night, you came to my door (Christopher Street): it strikes me, that Henry Huffam [   ], who had died, had figured—. look, again, even here, who am i to argue, which of us: that's the point, any such weighings—there is something deeply WRONG, in the whole procedure. (i walk off)

And that you again appeal to the court of us, dead, for decision on which, of us, is the more—look, it seems so unimportant, stacked against, that you, that i, must breathe   It is, (as above): when you've, what have you've . . . .

I think you have written me a beautiful letter. i think it is very straight, with tenderness in it, and it is a true proffer, as of you, an honest business, given your incredible sights. Even its absolutisms, are you.

But I don't know, that—where it is a portrait of me—that it is I. It may well be. I am so vulnerable. It may very well be. In any case, it is the way you see me, and that, surely, for you, is the fact. Well . . . I am not you. I have to put up with, myself. I have to continue to make the son the father of, himself. So. I have this, what you call, bad material. Too bad, too bad. We'll agree he won't go far, shall we. Shall we also agree he'll go as far as he'll go?

(Even such, as these immediate sentences, won't come straight—that is, they are straight, but—you are such—they echo wrong: ex., because you take me a grrrreat peeeecock, they sound back as tho my modesty were put on. Bah. Or sd to cajole. Bah two. HERE LIES, THE TROUBLE.)

I don't know. I am tempted to say, it is this simple, that, your friendship is,—as you imply it is—a greater thing, than mine. It very much may well be. Yet, I can't say that simply because I cannot clear the whole thing from the *ritual* you make of it. It is this that puts a strain in, which, so often, causes the bridge to come down. Now I love to throw parabolas as much as you do, believe, as you do, the absence of ends & projections in lives around us, is, why, there is so little life. Yet, I'm not sure your way of doing it, does it. That is, keeps all these things you talk abt, *in,* inside, as going, advancing, present realities: that we stay *current* to each other, that, in a very deep sense, you allow us to (the frame keeping so much backward to it.)

> (To hell with that, any more of it. I want, on my part, to try to insist upon present particulars, to stay inside what is, what is. So I go back, now, to read yr letter.)

(1)   I do not know that I sd, that I do not think you value, as you put it, my affections & friendship. To distinguish their way of

expressing themselves from yrs, is not—is it?—to say you do not receive them? It has always meant more than I have sd, that you *have* received them.

(2)   I stop over nothing, from that point to the end. There is nothing, *nothing*, my dear, dear friend—in all those swift & beautiful sentences to be gainsaid. Nothing. As I have sd, this, to me, is you, and I thank you, thank you that it is important that you say it all to me, even, (or the more), that your concern for me (as friend, you say) leads you to wonder if the path i am on as writer is not leading me further into what you call involved syntax values.

That I might wish, that, instead of this lumping, i should have each piece of work seen for itself, taken, for itself, as a part and yet as a separate thing from the whole of my life & nature;
                                        that, by this process, i might
feel motion, and air, and a going-ahead (that is, as i am going ahead), gain, from such a particularism (each of us, do we not, alas, have to carry *all* of ourselves at each instant; and it is precisely to be, for a moment, free of that bearing down and in, that we look to our friends or our loves, for replenishment?)

You see, I come back—this whole thing comes back—to, what we have been over before, what you put here, thus: that you think art, or literature, is, friendship. I think friendship is, friendship, has, its own laws & motions, which, because we are writers, but also because it is important for itself, it is—as you have made it—one beautiful and important substance to be expressed. But that it is all, that it is art? (I think it is the story, "The Flea of Sodom"; you say so yourself, when you make the epigraph, "My friend, there is no friend." I recognize, too, that "Bellerophon" is, a substance, from this particular friend, fr your concern over him, me. It is also true that, the whole of the book the FLEA, is, essentially, such a substance. You see, Edward, why I both say, yr letter is beautiful, straight, and also, why, I say, the trouble is, I do not agree. We are, at root.)

I have to take my risk. I remain astonished, that, what you call my friendship, has been to you,—I quote you, here, exact—"you want and

have given me a sepulchral bookish friendship." But there it is: it rests
on, yr notion, by paradox, that art is friendship, obviously. Thus it is,
that all acts or the absence of acts, are taken to be—that is, acts
toward yr writing—as, personal, as, towards you. Of course. It has to
be that way. (I am puzzled, if it also follows, that all acts toward you are
acts toward yr writing, and thus, is it this way, that my friendship has,
perforce, become, to you,—that is, looks that way to you—or, equally,
had to be that way, to me—bookish?)

I don't, like, at all, where all this examination leads. I don't like it.
But I also do not want you to put it off, as non-visceral, as not, the
"logic of the heart" (I question the phrase, but it is yours, and will
mean something, to you). Or not to shoulder, as well as i, the weight
of it. For these are your risks, as well.
   (I mean, you shall put it down, so. All right. And write me
   back, so. All right. Only, please, please, do not, in your "soul",
   not hear me. For, I deny Aristotle: there is, a friend.)

A friend,
CHARLRES
OLSON

■ ═══ ■

[New York City]

october 25, 1950

dear charles;

   the book has been out for close to two months, and i still sit in a
room like a pariah and wormy lazarus. i really don't see how you can
think i was ever sly about getting attention. you and i know the rotten
literature swill business, and if i wanted a statement from you to affirm
the book, i still feel you should have given it fast, because the book
stands for your belief and mine. the n.y. times bedlam continues; the
dudley fitts review has never come in, and petticoat breit is full of
double greasy tongue babble, and i cant depend on laughlin. [William
Carlos] williams wrote a twelve typewritten page critique; he was very
moved by the flea, particularly the rational tree, but he's off in oregon,
and he has asked me to place it! me, what can i place? i had one

gehenna experience to get the book published altogether. there have
been no reviews of the flea in london, although i am told the book is
having a good export sale! what does that mean? much as i need
procurator pilate's lucre, i don't care much about the money the book
might bring, very little, anyway.

i wish more for the sake of your own poems than for your refusal to
come out and defend the flea that you would dissipate some of these
cloistered preciosities; i don't think they are a benefit to your own
gifted muse; you say you don't like the word sodality or logic of the
heart, and maybe both are bad, but don't worry, i don't belong to any
sodality, since i detest the dirt and [evil of?] religion in the baptist or
baptist catholic american, and there is no difference between the two,
for art might make the distinction, but there is no [will?] in either;
there's got to be a leopardi or petrarch or a bocacio in religion to save it
from the forgeries, and there is none, and i have no use at all for it,
getting my religion about seth or enoch from smart. there is a complete
two volumes on smart that has just come out, and pretty soon all the
filthy slummy pederasts from uptown, the mademoisel elle chic
fornication group; the harper and flair magazine catamites and the
village dumpy denim fart homosexuals, will take up smart as they have
done melville. poor smart in bedlam got a catapult which is just the
thing for the dirty feminines in ny, and i'll wager we'll have a smart
'revival', which will be the burial of everything that was genius in kit
smart in three years.

tell me about the flea critique; have you finished it? i want you to
understand i don't mind sharp, nut-flavored criticism from you; but
you're wrong about my playing along with any clique, pray what? [th?]at
i hate to make moral announcements about myself; i think that bothers
me more than almost anything else; a man's got to be very dingy and
have a lot of the church mouse in him to tell other people how good he
is. i only say i am not the man for trade literature; ive got to write
bread and butter reviews now to support a wife, and just to get once in
a while some sun and air and fruit on my face and life. i wish to hell
you would get more human, i don't know how a man does it, but when
i ask you to defend what your bowels tell you is right and the earth-
truth for you that you wouldn't be affected and get ethical with me.
save your moral fervor for the lousy gimcrack celebrities im not one and
never will be; i'm too immoral for the american to be a trade literary
saint, you know that, and there is a lot in us that is just automatic, and

that simply takes care of our moral reasons for asking people to do things, without you and i bragging about our principles and what we should do and not do. when you have to get up a pragmatic formula for your deportment with another man, then it's time to take your leave of him, and say he's no good for your liver or for your paracelsus. what is important, charles, is that i'm not really fixed at all; the reason i never will be and will always be centuries ahead of the rotten, staid, mediocre blokes in this country is that i shall always be a devout and religious and earnest servant of homer, isaiah, strabo, longinus, and your maximus of tyre, if i can ever find him, for i love to distraction a great writer before i have read him, and attack on the hurt of my small finger a piebald louse of art without reading him. but for hell and art's sake, let us let our noses be our guide, and let us defend each other if the poem and the book is not an offence to erasmus, and better still, to the top blake, or to the highmost statius, and is some quaint addition to man, who is knowing dust when he is right and true and promethean-livered, and rotten and decayed and fart-arted otherwise.

each time i write a book i hope it won't be so lonely, and i just get more lonely, what with your help, my fine postage stamp and envelope friend; oh i know you would do me your services, but that is no good, and you, more than i, will suffer from this friendship in absentia; for i can still somehow or other teach you, i don't know quite how any more than i know how i can write a good line when i have a learned song in my diaphragm or navel or belly, but let's not go lower, and fall into our modern grecian habits. i read a great deal of plato, but not as a platonist, or for such trite reasons, but to come to some understanding of nature as an evil breathing animal. id like to do some more writing, like the wheel of sheol, and without plato, and i want to go to the gnostics, too, i couldn't have done it, and to your sumerians, and after i have found a form again, i'll write some new old world hieroglyph, and do you think i can be sly or odyssean writing that sort of egypt, abydos, mycenean literature, don't be foolish my friend. i did a piece on [Randolph] bourne for tomorrow, not very good, but i got 50 for it, and mentioned you along with three other books, as clean rebel vision ["My Favorite Forgotten Book," on Bourne's *The History of a Literary Radical* (1920), *Tomorrow,* X (December, 1950): 59–60]. i'm all for apostasy [when?] making [writing] learned and julian, and laurel it in ancient metre, and make it a dagger soldier phillipic, and if we do that, why we're vulcans in the bowels of aetna, for then we've got bowels and aetna in us, and so don't have to worry about right and wrong when we ask one another for a chanting, male yea to a book we say belongs to both of us. i've gotten so i hate anything that is not positively male in morals and art; the penis has to get back into a poem, and I am not crazy about fornication literature as such; but we've got to have a male penis literature, or everything will die out and all we will have left is allen tate, and ransom, who write about meanings and neatness, and call it metaphysics, and what they really mean using foetid feminine platonisms is ugly polonius-stooled meanness.

well i send you some straight-out love, and hope you get the straight, human diction out of your beloved iliad, and all those remarkable tarsian and tyrian scribes; you've got a lot of washington quagmire city to spew out; and please, remember, by way of exhortation, that a moral act is phoenician or theban or aeschylean, as we mean it, when it has also something of the birds and the turds of aristophanes in it; a moralist has got to be always a great bawd if he is not to gibber and squeak like some of our little dung saints who use adjectives like verbs; that kind of misuse of words belongs to a man in the public stews. what is most important than any word you might have given me for my little book is that somehow or other i pull out of you a leetle marrow boke that is even better than ishmael, and if i rebuke you, remember that i can see your faults better than mine own, for aside from a few rules i don't know how i write, but uneasily find out what shouldn't have been written at all. but let's get the ethic business clean and straight between us; when i do one of those lazar-house cash register books, you can throw all the hills and mountains and rivers at me, but until then lets try to be a mountain, hill and river pome; if we're that, why doll tearsheet, and our lousy, whoring novel were plainhead it[   ].

EDWARD DAHLBERG

[New York City]

November 6, 1950

[TS TORN AND WATER-DAMAGED]
Dear Charles: Would you please send this letter off at once. It's a bill, and I haven't the money to pay it. My former wife is very slyly trying to seize whatever I have on the cape, and so far has been very successful.

You have been on my mind a great deal, and I have thought about the whole literary purity dilemma, some of which is artistic virginity; and there is also a perplexity, and I must somehow believe that the animal in my nature that cares for Hermes Tresmegistus and the TIMAEUS, and the Book of the Dead has a moral nose that cannot be too corrupted. You know I hate to make protestations about my sanctity; I have seen too many trade saints in the country, including our erstwhile friend, hapless and pious-dunged Waldo, in this sort of role. No matter how you may feel, and I cannot feign any more than you that I relish being smitten, and you must recall that you were the first to put your heel upon my neck when I telephoned you, I want with what religious heart that is in me, to see you come out as a real poet. You must not believe that because I am no Nazarene, and that when you raise your voice against me, that I bother about who is more or less. I cannot measure myself against another gifted man. I only have some anamorphosis of my own soul when I hear a man lie to me, or some one praise me, and then offers me a wormy, la[zar] hand.

My Bourne piece in the magazine Tomorrow will be out in about seven weeks, and there is a good mention of you there. I am doing a long piece on naturalism, attacking that kind of scataphagous, merde fiction, and am putting rue in my own nostrils while valuing these, by refering to Ishmael, the American Grain, Rimbaud (Oh, I know there is a great deal in Rimbaud and in Baudelaire that is catamite verse, but the prose poems and the baudelaire journal are worth thinking about), Lawrence, I'd like to go back to our Greek, but there are very base and ugly limits to a magazine piece, and I have no way of earning money, Charles, save by [my] pen. I don't intend to dip my pen in Circe's swill. B[ut] so much for scruples.

Rlene and I were married a little over three weeks ago. She sent you and Constanza the announcement.

Meanwhile, you have my love and faith in your genius. I have done a couple of pieces on Pound, one for the Times which may be out this coming Sunday. He's been in many ways the good Socratic gadfly of poetry. I have done the Letters to[o] for Tomorrow to be out the end of this month ["*The Letters of Ezra Pound, 1907–1941*. Edited by D.D. Paige," *Tomorrow*, 10 (January, 1951): 54–55]. During the war I was very angered by his antisemitism, but now that the man is penned up in a dirty, lunatic hospital, I simply cannot be one to hurt him more. For years I was too busy with Attica and Uz and Joppa and that

wonderful temple at Sais, where Athene reigned to give any thinking
to Pound and the others, but I can see that you don't get baited by a
gen[　] outside, obsidian poetics, that he is very good in some ways.
My love again,

EDWARD DAHLBERG

■ ══ ■

[Washington, D.C.]

tues nov 7 50

my dear edward: it is the most terrible thing. so very much is involved.
i almost do not have the heart to speak. but your last letter was so
sweet & whole, i cannot let my failures amputate an answer i very
much wish to write.

　　there is nothing i can say, actually, where an act is all that is
called for. yet i put off, put off, that act, not even knowing its issue,
frightened of it, yet, looking forward to it (i am, of course, referring to
the examination of, the Flea: i was well into it, a while back, when it
got broken off, by two Black Mt characters coming in on me; and i
have not, again, picked it up)

it goes so to the heart of everything, for me, to examine your book,
that i avoid it　no question　But at the same time (why, i say, i look
forward) i shall do it, have to, will haul myself up to it, difficult as i
find it, to say all　That's the trouble, why, I am sure, this thing has
come to be a crisis　I *have* to say all　I cannot, at this point, be
partial, or party, or take—as i might want to—part instead of whole
(a part, anyhow, the way you have written it, is not a handle by which
it can be, said)

　　　　　　　　　　　　　　　　　　　　　　　　　((it is
weird, how difficult it is, for me to read you: i have to go in by the
sharpest sort of bearing down
I am sure this will sound very silly to you, but please do not let it: it is
merely the confusion of you as person with you as book that brings this
difficulty. You make values yourself, anyhow. And I dare say, you would
not put it, that it is you and me, here, in this place, or there is
nothing, without a recognition that, we are also, however alike, deeply
opposed　Or so I think the wall i break the jump at, is, the stating of,

my opposition: I am really quite a little rabbit, you know   That is, I
am always confounded, at how personal we all are   And dread it

It is stupid. But precisely that,   too, is of cause: that, for some time
now, i have been hugely involved in this very problem, of, how to take
up such strength, generally And am miserably worn down, as a
result.   It could not have been a worse time (or a better), actually.
For, that it   is to be done, is there to be done, is worth the doing, is
a joy
    Yr announcement of marriage, coming on top of yr letter, brought
quickly to my senses, your own pressures, and troubles. I do hope much
is better, much much better. (What did happen, on that Bollingen
bizness, anything? Did they stake you, or not? What did they say?)

Look. Let this be just a note, to greet you—and Rlene—and to tell
you you are much in my mind—*on* my mind. To stuff all silence, that
dirty thing. To send
his love,

CHARLES

■══■

My dear Charles:

    Your letter has just come, and I am in much distress over it. You
know that work is the only redemption for Adam and us; you had
better set your mind to the thistles and briars, and put some words
together to heal your distracted skin. Whether you go on with the
critique is not of great matter at the instant; you must write, or start
taking notations from all the marvelous Greek readings you have done;
get together all the gleanings from Boaz's Vineyard, and start at the
word-toil. For in the beginning was sloth, and it was a curse to man
greater than all other afflictions except his boredom which was really
his idleness.
    You must write the critique, should you go on with it, unmindful of
me; it will happen, for it is the abstraction that counts most for a poet;

the weak and the mediocre are concerned with events and nostalgia, and all that squalid detritus of wan and fatherless images.

You might look into Baudelaire's Intimate Journals. Of course, Baudelaire, is the ideal paradigm of the modern pederast, but he has some fine spleen, and a remarkable understanding of the nature of the velleities in us. He knows that the two contradictory characteristics about mortals, free will and destiny are identical, and that is great self-knowledge for the poet.

The Flea has been out two months, and two reviews have appeared, and *not one* in London. Maybe, you can understand now my appeal to you. I have heard nothing from the Bollingen Foundation; I took a chance, but I don't seem to be the sort of man who gets awards. You ought not to worry too much, Charles, about the morals of the artist. If he has the sign of Cain in his forehead, everybody will run away from him, anyway, and he won't be in any pinchbeck and warm sheepcote. There has never been a warm lazy cote for the poet. Remember, too, the patron is dead, and the mediocre man has his dagger pointed at our heart, and he has astounding nose for artistic smells which repel him more than nitre or lysol.

I am taking notes for the naturalism article for the Freeman. I did a piece on James, the cutpurse philosopher, a review, indicating that he had purloined his entire doctrine from Peirce, and got $17 for it ["Cutpurse Philosopher," rev. of *Williams James* by Lloyd Morris, *Freeman*, 1 (November 13, 1950): 124–125; rpt. in *Alms for Oblivion*]. Compromise, my good friend, and I get N.Y. Times reviews to do once in about two months. I am compromising my barest soul to be—crusty Lazarus!

I have a sea-island parable narrative in mind, with Poe and the Apochrypha, the Jewish pharisaical writings, which were marvellous, and which were the source and the river of Christ and the scribes and that mad-torn, carnal Paul from Phoenice Tarsus. Would have been better had he made sails like his father did, and left writing to Xenophanes and to Seneca, and Ovid, and Amos, and the Apocalyptic poet of Baruch, and to Charles Olson, and I pray by heaven and that God whose name was never mouthed in a dirty, scataphagous church, to Edward Dahlberg. But, go, go, and write, that is your pining; go, and with the will of guileless Daniel into the burning furnace, for your Ideal Forms and Jahweh and Sais Athene Abstractions.

My love, as always, and my great faith in your gehenna doubts; for only the artist really doubts—

EDWARD DAHLBERG

[ADDED IN SCRIPT TO RIGHT MARGIN OF PAGE:]
my wife Rlene has been reading aloud a lot of american history to me: that's her background. it's very helpful

■ ══ ■

[Washington, D.C.]

wed nov 8 50

oh my foolish Doll-Mountain, my big kid, how you go on, picking up stones and throwing puff-balls, and deciduous things. Now its "lies" & "virginity", my looker-only-at-himself, little Glass Hill, o antique Eighth St Mirror:

come off it, Reactionary, come into the air, o Auroral One: stop making such heaves/ without strikes

o Moral Nose, is it: pah, you. You Nose. Ha (or ho-ho). I can say one thing: it is true, I do not know that you ever "lied". (Ah, purity!). But having sd that, I ask myself what other non-virtue have you not practiced. So, for sums.

And as for "virginity", o Lecher—Lazar: try to regain a little ("virginity renews itself, like the moon," who sd). If you had a little less personalisms you might have a little more of the imaginative innocence, my Doll Burger.

(It strikes me, in these exchanges, who uses, the moral nouns, as euphemisms, for acts and facts, for sticks and other devices, to lay on another man's back.

There is a law, here: invert what the Doll sez, to find out, the stuffings.
(Ah, Corruption!)

A poem, sd Ecclesiastical, makes no more echo than a
   rose petal dropped
in the grand canyon:

      You cry, o, my loneliness. Ha. (I think of a hen man in New
Hampshire [Robert Creeley].)

And as for "our" Greeks. Please, separate me from them, and you,
please. I do not know that I open the door in the same direction at all.
I take it, it is a swinging door, opening both ways, and I, I prefer the
kitchen. I take it, Hermes Tresmegistus AND the timaeus, as well as
the Nazarene and the naturalists are broken down humanists.

                              The *virgin* fields, Sirrah,
are other places, other
times: e.g., downstairs

                       downstairs, get downstairs, Mister
                       dahlberg

I am mailing yr letter to the Clinic. I do not mind at all, my friend,
being "used".

                               The rime is, abused
                           OLSON   CHARLES

■ ════════════════════════════════════ ■

[New York City]

November 10, 1950

My dear Charles:

   I have your wild letter, and I had rather hoped my own letter to you
would quiet you and set you to work which you sorely need. I don't
know what the Black Mountain characters did to you, or what has
brought you to this achelian distraction. I think you are being very
roundabout in this whole matter. There is really very little to say more
about it. You deeply affirmed a book which you refused to do anything
about. You have claimed that I have been some sly Iago in literature,
and I protest that is not the truth, although I have told you many times
I abhor making saintly protestations about being the pascal lamb in
literary matters. I have seen too many stinking, lazy book people do

that, and I do not like being the overt moralist. I still do not see that it matters where the truth is spoken or written. Had you found my book bad or a lie, and I had asked you to affirm it, then you would have had all claim to abuse me. I think you are being very affected about purity and the loneliness of people in this land. I cannot speak for you, although I noticed that you were very put off when Rosenberg came to see you so seldom. You call me a reactionary, and you also say that I have practiced "other non-virtues for sum", and my plain and bleak reply to you is that you are a LIAR and that you have had much greater skill in cunning than I have ever had. However, I do not blame you for being nimble-tongued enough to get awards off of that ward heeler, of the seven Muses, Moe. But I do hold you culpable for feigning that you have not gotten money by lying for it, and by going [?] to disreputable and mercenary scribes, like the late Carl Van Doren, and the merchant, Van Wyck Brooks, for help. If this is not double-dealing in our corrupt literature business, then you are actively [?] mad and unwilling to perceive your own acts. You villify me for wanting some attention in the Times, so that I can somehow get bread, and yet you scurried down to see Breit so that you could secure attention for your book. It is a hideous, ghoulish thing, all of this, for you and for me; all I ask is that you stop lying about your own ACTS. Every poet, including Plato, and I imagine Dante, and Michaelangelo, has had in some sense or other to be a toady to a patron or to a united cigar store Medici, like Moe. The difference between you and me is that I told off Moe, and when Brooks had the effrontery to write me and say that he had used something from my book, a line out of Poe, which he had sordidly mutilated, and then put into a footnote, I told him what a miscreant he is. Now, I don't know how you or I are to get published, or shall let us say, printed, without being a little base and disgustingly humble, and I imagine you are quite the boulevardier flaneur as well as the skilled sycophant with the Van Dorens, the Brooks, and Moe. How you could act otherwise, I don't know, and I have had to dissimulate too to get a book published. But you're a great stupid pachyderm to accuse me of having written books for lucre, and if you are referring to my personal life, when you say I practice non-virtues for sums, the only reason you aren't more of a lecher than you call me is that you're a damn'd gawk at it, and that is why your poetry the result of so much extraordinary reading and real plain honest labor is for the most part esoterica syntax, and lacks bowels, shit, and fuck and sweat, in it, and

I'm awfully sick of that kind of cant. Talk about euphemisms, what do you think your conduct has been. By the time you grow up as a writer, and the man who has in the past stepped out because of his defence of your work, you haven't got enough marrow and integrity guts to come out to defend a book you believe in. You say you can't write the critique because of certain temperamental oppositions, despite the similarities between us. Do you think that bothers me? You're crazier than your fatuous letter. Go ahead, if you want to; do anything to be a poet yourself. That is what I have always wanted you to be. The way things are, I fight for you and you fight for you. Why, in simplest frankness, is it a truth to lecture about my books to a black mountain covey of catamites and slatterns, while it is perjury to make a clean, inward remark about a book you claim you deeply admire. Why this coarse and craven parody, O My Loneliness; maybe you have never been honest enough to admit you are desolate, and friendless; it's that kind of unashamed honesty that makes a man a poet. If you scoff at me when I tell you that I was miserable and alone for at least sixteen months, and that the man whose Muse I had lavishly befriended, was such a skinflint and so precious with his time, that he would not ask me once in all that time to come down for a visit. The last time I was there as a self-invited guest you said it was a deeply crucial [one] for your vision. You have said it in books you gave me, and so don't lie about it now. I have been very lonely, and am still so, though much less, because I have a wife and many men, like Aeschylus and Euripides and Nietzsche were wretched solitaries; so what is all this pinchbeck and very cheap laughter in your stupid and [morbid parody?] I do not mind a real masculine attack, something straight out.

The truth about you, Charles, is that any of the things you accuse me of are guilts in you; years [ago?] you called me a Kansas City merchant, which was just a [   ] remark, because I have never been able to make money, and now at 50, my situation is a real peril to me. How, liar Olson, did I ever make money as a KC merchant? How do I hide behind euphemisms; what lechery do I practice or malpractice that you shun? Why is that so many literature bastards will help you and not me. Why do you cry up a Brooks in a remarkable book, your Ishmael, and soil your page, while you deny me, your mentor, a word for a book you believe in; and why give a name to a Van Doren; of course, he helped you, and if you remember, when we were laboring for your first guggenheim, I said go ahead and use these literature turds, but don't pull a waldo frank or a horace gregory saint act with me. do you know I went to laughlin to ask him to print some of gregory's poems, and then marya told me she did not want horace to appear in such company. at the time, i said you were in it and so was I, and besides a poem is good or bad anywhere.

I don't mind being attacked for a low or vulgar act; but you are at fault in this whole matter, and not I. If you are so balefully pure, why did you not wish me to speak to Laughlin; you wrote me quite a letter, you were as skittish as a young colt about it, fearing, my fine 'maidenheaded writer', and in this business that is just what you are, that I might spoil your *strategy.* You say, come downstairs, Dahlberg, you have the effrontery to talk to me about being straight and outside about what I do, while you go on practicing these little circumlocutions, and braying like [LAST PAGE OF LETTER MISSING TOP LEFT QUARTER, REMAINDER HEAVILY WATER-DAMAGED AND SOILED, FOLD BROKEN WITH MISSING PARTS; MARGINALIA INDECIPHERABLE:]

/pure and simple small magazine Pisgah. Why
/and not me? Because you are very enterprising,
/iterature spotless lamb. Again, I do not blame
/printed; it's a gehenna to sit alone in
  /tudio of yours, somewhere in the untouchable
/quagmire tomb city, and even if you don't have
/my own life, and you fleer at loneliness,
  /on for you, and would do all that is in my

/attle of the wits, i'm ready for you; I'll
/yours, and we'll let Osiris who weighs
/world, determine whether you are more than
/honest as I am. I'll put my dagger words against
/n a number of letters, who can better the
/mastery of bastardy. I don't want it, and i
/ubtle gifts, but I don't like being falsely
/es I have not committed. We have both our
  /against your father and I against my mother,
    /You will also remark that in the FLEA that
    /and that is what I have always done for
    /and anywhere I could. Though I say that
    /love and friendship, I never said one ought
    /ise a vile book. I have been very straight about

/ould quit posing as the clean Angel at
/far as you are gifted, no more and no less
a dead language, and ancient past, to recover the [?] lives, and so feign
that we are really not dead; that is a very [?] great artistic hypocrisy,
but if you go beyond that, Charles Olson the crier for the Roosevelt
committee at $12,000 a year, and the choir-boy of Van Doren and
Brooks, you are simply saying that somehow or other I have been as
much of a sycophant as you. Maybe yes, maybe no. I have tried to keep
alive and not put my pen in swill; it's very hard, and I have said that
though I must write these reviews for the acorns and the masts, my
book whenever I write it, shall be of that desolate desert and rock in
Luke. Poe, too, had to live, and he did a lot of potboiler writing, but
only a scoundrel will deny that his Ligeia and Eleonore are not original
forms and abstractions for which a very poet pines.

If you want to co[ntin]ue this vendetta, I'm your servant; I'd just as
soon knock your head off when you get fancy Waldo Frankish with me,
as impugn some of the churls who are making it well-nigh impossible
for us to write and eat.

I send off my love and some of my wit, because I think you need
some of it, if you intend to get into an outrage with me; you're a very
inchoate and gabbling fool when you're splenetic, my friend; now, if you
want to get the better of me in a phrasebrawl, be as cool as the alps, as
dry as nantucket; and you ought to be able to do better than Doll-
Burger; get at some ideas, never mind the pothouse puns of the vulgus.
If you've got some lucid antagonisms toward the Flea, go at the book,
and not at me. We need some intellectual [fis?]ts in this doleful,
addleheaded land; you're an awful ninny not to be able to sit down and
write about a book that so kindles your mind. Write, write, and make it
frontal, direct.

I am the friend of your genius even though the monitor of some [of?]
your half-wit epistles.

[FRAGMENTARY MARGINALIA ALONG BOTH MARGINS AND AT TOP OF
PAGE:] Well, I send this letter to you with a woebegone heart; I am
concerned about the health of your spirit

■ ══════════════════════════════════════ ■

saturday nov 11 50

my dear edward:

yr most moving letter came last night. the odds of it, against my
second, which you must have had yesterday, leaves me chewing my
teeth. for i have found, when i go by sounds (as i did there) i cause
much pain (not even knowing; in a way, not knowing—or at least
permitting, as you say, freewill to be destiny: it is a beautiful concept
full of terror because it is cause of pain. and do be eased from it, a little
ease, anyway, my friend.

but as i remarked to you, as we walked away from that "trial" in New
Rochelle, you are in metempsychosis, and, since then, and remarkably,
in this letter of yrs, as well as that long previous one (not the one I
roared at, say), you continue to advance, powerfully and widely extend,
yr reach

it is pleasure,—and learning—to feel *that,* to hear you in yr
quietness phrase as, so: the squalid detritus of wan and fatherless
images. Or such a joining, as, nitre, lysol (the sounds, I mean, which
are as much the abstraction as there is, permitted, to poets: to bend
the will to them, and find out, in them, what more can be done. For
the thing is, they do contain, their own revelations, of which a man is
instrument.

I venture to think this is also true of,
parable-narrative, though, here, I am not acquainted, actively.

But the feeling you gave me (and it was not just yr mention, that you
have a sea-island story in yr air, for music) that you are open, and
wandering straight ahead, encourages me to go most ahead with the
critique. For all I should wish to do, in such a thing, would be, to get
to *you,* to dig, to make the run home into yr consciousness of yr work.
(I dare say, my cuts at you, have come from a sense, that—as i may
have sd—that you were closed).

I would woo you fr all generalization (god knows where you got the
idea I am moral abt the artist,—not at all, tho it must be this very
thing you play back to me, the abstraction as what counts, which is

form, that led you awry; for what i wd undo in you (what you undo more and more, out of wisdom) is, such, as (here), you put it, the sign of Cain in his forehead (the artist's forehead): I don't honestly think you need these positional devices one day more. I think all this is a part of a struggle you maintained against the 20s, 30s, arms for obliquity, but which you have already thrown aside, as used, and useless.

So are yr plaints, you are commercial, or compromised, in these reviews. I don't believe it, even tho, you have not clipped & sent me, and I have not read one, of these same. Yet, I doubt deeply you are whoring. For one thing, you are unable to: yr shot on Peirce as source, is the sort of use which these contemporaries are needing of. So much of yr perception is needed. And I note how much the reviewing Baudelaire fed you, in yr turn.

The abstract (form) versus the generalization (moralizings): for example, how impeccably you disclose yrself abstractly in one rising passage in FLEA (I think the finest you ever wrote, and one of the most moving passages—well, *who* has done, in yr order of literature, such pages as 18 (bottom, Cana's waterpots) to 22 (top, I put a cicada in my vest). Here you are yr poet, and abstract, abstract, diffident, and thus, entirely, by disclosure and conjecture, MORAL.

(And what form, what a form, implicit, in it (the same form which made me, rise to the story, the FLEA, tho, there, so often, yr generalizing, steals, eats away the cheese of, yr form).)
  You see, I delay, and study, for, to unwrap you from yourself, is most hard, because, to say what *is* yr order of form, is not at all easy. (Now don't take that as a feather. It is not so. Every line you write shld be—excuse me, it is not at all stiff of me, to say this—abstract, (not personal only in this sense of, the impersonal: yr own sense, of, this, as you say, go, go, and find, in yr innocence, in yr forms, your abstractions.

Let me be mischievous also, with the text of yr letter: I know that work is what we're here for, period, flatly true, not, "the only redemption for Adam and us" (that is what I mean by generalizing the experience or the truth: every allusion, of any sort, historical or otherwise, must *add* to the reach or spread of the gnome, or it eats, instead: to my most christian ears, this only perpetuates all the christian rot, thus diminishing, instead, as so often you do, increasing the gnome. And why? Because, basically it is a cliche you are pumping: the sweat of adam's brow. And with that comes that desperate false notion of original Sin, language is so fullsome, and its references so wide. Suddenly, instead of yr sentence pushing reality now, it (in this allusion) wearies us with the filthy pack on the back of all the moral errors Moses started and Paul and the rest of such churchmen have piled on pile.

Likewise, thistles & briars: Christ-talk (derogade, bankrupt—but of course I do not mean just such use of Christ as in above passage in Flea, noted, where you have gone in by dahlberg and by him come out with a christ as fresh as this frosty November morning.

((It suddenly strikes me! Who was it, that took his eye and pencil, and swiped olson good, for just such wrong-spreading biblicalisms! Oh, Maitre! Listen to yrself: For in the beginning
       NONO olson: you are wrong. It is not here, that edward, errs. As a matter of fact, the irony of this use of the biblicals—"sloth . . . boredom, . . . idleness" is perfect, perfect mockery, & force, fresh.

It is Adam's sweat, or Daniel and the burning furnace, I am calling you on, not, on this or, gehenna doubts, say, where, yr adjective, adds push to the noun, as a matter fact, saves the noun, from contemporary cliche.

Well, just, that you are so fine I, because I feel so close to you & yr imagination, want you to be, as they say abt sugar, superfine!

Hello, Edward, and best, best, best. You are coming along fine, Maitre! Sd the Pupil!

                                                      Ho: CHARLES

P.S.
    I had closed this letter, and was walking out to post it, when I did think to take this liberty to tell you, that, I am somewhat disturbed

(like *you* say!), have been, since, in yr long letter, you mentioned the WHEEL OF SHEOL as the paradigm of what you want to do next—of the sea-island parable, i suppose.

Now you will know, certainly, that of all yr friends, I shall surely say least of all, you could be wrong. For I say, a man knows best what *he* is up to. Yet of course it is also true i know how what a friend says, is, helpful.

All i wanted to say is, to remind you that, not so long—or maybe almost after the WHEEL—you added the passage I speak of (18–21). And that that thread for you to wind unwind yr labyrinth is as good, or better, than SHEOL.

Nor to say don't do both, of course. It is only, that, yr bull-whacking of society (the "World") stings when the whip is tight in yr own hand (when yr own back is under it), most. Or when yr own hand is whipless, utterly open, a palm, for fragrant gesture, & love. (I am thinking, now, of that fascinating para, near the beginning of WHEOL, when you base yr metaphysic in a physiology of the head: this animating of the organs is a precise & precious source of fable, more proper, I take it, to yr singular senses than a lot of the "history" which WHEOL also has

What I am dumpishly going towards, is, that, every sentence in those 4 pages (18–21), is clewed tight to *you*, to yr nature & mystery, the disclosure of same, the conjecture of, by, on same, that, by such a grip, by staying inside your own air so insistent—so intensive-ly, you let any one else all, all, all *their* air

But the world riles you so, you usually, beat the hell out of it, and out of everyone else but yrself.

Yet, there is this other gate, through which you enter & demolish the world: and the curious thing is, that it, too, is clew to you. (I am referring to that paragraph in WIIEEL (it is page 100, "the horse's ears" to the "slyest of vanity".)

These two GATES: they can't be beat. BUT, they must dominate, or . . .

And I'd hazard the guess, that, what joins them, what keeps the air in, is, YOUR SENSES. When the HEAD follows after your SENSES, especially your nose (now I mean in the writing as well as the thinking, in the act of the writing, the control) you are truly imaginative: yr page *invites.*

Let me toss this at you: the physiology of that para, 100, and the geo-physical base of another para (102, "Mortal learning . . . eat and know") are the TRUE CONTRARY of the OTHER METHOD (18–21) and simply because they are the true extension of THE INDIVIDUAL & HIS SENSES, EDWARD DAHLBERG

You prove again, that, no matter how much a man exposes himself, the more, he is, ambiguous. And the less he has to do with the world, the more he exposes SAME.

Okay. I'll shut up. Charles

[PARAGRAPHS 1, 3, 6, 7, 8, 12, 16, 21, 22, 27 AND 29 ABOVE MARKED (PROBABLY BY DAHLBERG) IN PENCIL.]

■ ══════════════════════════════════ ■

[New York City]

November 12, 1950

My dear Charles:

What skulking gnome or rotten mad genius keeps our letters not enough in the rear of our acts so that each of us sends a cannon ball letter or a pot of honey always at the wrong time. Your previous letter so enraged me, all that pother, Charles about practising non-virtues for sums, and virus-guffaw of yours about o my loneliness, as though you were more virtuous than I, my noble Cato on the page, and cynic rhetor of bile in the deed, yea, you and I. By the time this balm of Gilead has dropped into your treeless and ravined solitude, you will have already sent me, by the special dispatch of Mercury who is no better sandaled than your spleen, another enchante conceit and hotspur anger missive, for which I will then thank you in kind. And all of this may be allright, provided we are each garnering some jott of good beer and tankard and hard latin learning from it. But you decide, my fine writer, for I have just been looking over the ISHMAEL again, taking some notes for my naturalism piece, and I must say that it is a marvellous book; i make some small, niggard objections to a dropping of an article here and there which does not give the line that obsidian thrust and curtness which the verb ought to have, also, and now and then you omit at the opening sentence a thee or an a, and that gives the sentence a little too much of the soft, adjectival feminine pomegranate mood, and I think you sometimes turn an adjective into a verb, which is not at all good. But let anybody say that ISHMAEL is not a remarkable work of genius, and he is as much of a liar as you are when you fall down into your buffoonery bathos about solitude and my dollar-whoring for dollars nobody even offers me; so brother olson, if I am doing all this literature courtesanship for nothing, well, let us just settle it, and admit we are the literature whores of Gaza, and that genius is cultivated belles lettres lechery, as Chaucer and Olson know, only there is damn'd piece of perversity in that man, Olson, who has the Gold of Ophir in his mind, and if he had it in his pockets, pauper Dahlberg, would sure be reaching into them, call it non-virtue practice or pandarism, or beggarism; but you aint got it, save in your astounding spermaceti intellect, when it is at work, and writing, and not just spilling seedless clots of rancour, and so to repeat, in some quaint amerikan way, you're a rahab of amerik lietature, and no one can get into Canaan without your spying, and so am I.

I wish in the name of heaven's hell's earth, you'd pack up, and make a quick Israelitish exodus from that sodden solipsism town, and take your Constanza along, and get to where you can on occasion hear some human talk, or at least be near city art fakes, and those pederastic streets, where everything is teeming and dying, but all for art, and that is something for us, even though it is foetid and offends the skin. There is something about some of your letters, and the way they eat into you, that I mislike; despite all your troglodytic travail over words and ideas, you're too idle, and bored; maybe you need some lysol and nitre humanities, to rouse you to forms. Now you said some very fine things about the FLEA, and you should not think for an instant that I would try to get in the way of your oppositions to anything you said or wrote about the FLEA. I think, and I said before, that we are much too automatic to be bothered about morals in art, when we have to get a little bread. A man is gifted and he fathoms himself whether he toils in a dollar drudge office or for our late brother, the lump vulgus Imago, Roosevelt, or not. Otherwise, we get into emasculate and epicene metaphysics, the kind that seems to kindle your intestines, when I mention Hermes Tresmegistus; but you ought to know by this time that like you I'm a quarry-hunter, an analect, who'll look everywhere for his amethysts and Eden stones. I admire very much your fine, original obsessions with SPACE, in the opening [of] ISHMAEL.

Well, brother friend Olson, I'll try to get this, special, into your furnaced hands; but since you are a man interested in the Genesis, whether Cain struck Abel first, just remember you showed me the insolence of a wild horse; you are the horse alligator, as you speak in the Melville SPACE boke, that REAL GENIUS, no doubt about it, and I'm damned glad that I homaged you in the FLEA despite the fact that you're a great purity and virginity ass of a Balaam, and this ought to prong you, but you can't persuade me into believing that denying your Canapot yea to the FLEA, is not just circumlocution dirt and that you are not the foolish virgin who has no oil for the lamp she adores.

Well, I guess, I am your Father-Image, and either you've got to assume that I am ready for my senilia, or that I am likely to die without further ripening, and get staled in some frozen parable sea moral or first cause, and I thank you deeply for worrying so, even though a part of that is the groundwork for your own artistic egoism, and that is all right, too; for we murder everybody, and call it literature, and so much of amerikan literature is the dry guillotine to which we send those young, green novices of writing and feeling. I still maintain that though literature is Space and the wounded western man's longing for distance, and when a man says that God is close to him, it fills us with the greatest disgust, or that the Word is near to him, we know he is perfidious,—still for all that, if we are to get free from cold, Gothic Amerika, literature has to be friendship and affection, or else we all perish in an utterly homeless and dead hieroglyphic art that will be extraordinary and fatal. Go, if you must to dry, arid, mountain latin gods, and refuse the Mosaic wells, the soft feminine hills of hermaphroditic Nazarene, and both are mare's nests, but we die, as medieval fascists, with the inquisition rope of Loyola around the necks of each one we embrace, if we exclude for all the damage it has to us, I mean your gushing, liquid, Christianity, we are not men, warm, hot, fierce men with fire and daggers for our closest friends; we are just frozen homosapiens who starve everybody to death by the miserable congealed climate of our own resolutions and hermetica[l] distances, very valuable for art, and a great danger to any kind of Inca, Mayan, Mediterranean civilization.

I salute Ishmael again, but if you send me another of your damn'd froward brazen necked epistles, I shall in turn give you back fine sword and bodkin words, although I think much of this is foolery, and that if you have an ounce of outside, unchristian, hard pebble and Numa rock goodness in you, you would be damn'd grateful for the chance to say a real, flaming spear word in the defence of the Flea which is just perched and closeted in your ear.

EDWARD DAHLBERG

■ ══ ■

wednesday nov 15 50

brer edward: You are a kerekter! (out of yr own "Tales") (All thracian & coonskin)(And sometimes, fr the Red-Eye you've drunk, can't even read: example, a whole abusive letter, resting on, mistaking this sentence. Or, rather, what you did not see was sentence, separate, reading "So, for sums," having nought to do with ought to do with moneys, but, with (many references back), the making of sums, the summing up of, you-me, relationships, the ledger of, friends.

(Just to extricate you from your own confusions! confusions! To save me, from yr notion that, I think you are commercial, that is, on an economic level. Hell, I've seen you blow too many such dangling apples, ever to . . . . . And if you be a Merchant, of Toledo or Kansas City, you be a mighty poor one, where, geld is)

No, lad, or papa, this whole scream, this male shrew what descended on me bitin and tossin fur . . . . . Ah, me, suntax—oh, Solipse (shit, Edward, abt Washington, and the advantages of 8th Street, and all such preachins, and interferences: aw jes don bite such bait, Brother American Orpheus

And if you be senile, you is the dad blemdest wittiest old coot that ever drew a phrase from the hump on his back, you Quiver you, you Mississippi Hoot

I can't take you that seriously, Sad-Eyes. Come off that 2 inch stool, Cavalry Man, I seez you, ah knowz you, under all those hoots, War-Face. (You see, I'm crazy, too, fellow hunter, been on the trace too long: take a look at that country we been over, all the skins we've clothed ourselves in, Bro-Butternut!)

I'm campin, in this duck-shoot.

The eye-deer! that you all can squat thar, and make up yure tremblin singlin mind, on what ah's up to here in my clutch (try to bring me down out of that blue into the swamp by shootin at me with my own weapon, I who once took on to call myself a Biblical name!

Now you look hyar Mister Bumblin Boone, ah don take kindly to such back-fartin shootin gallery bee-hay-via. What ah did, ah did. What ah'm doing, I'se also, doin.

'Course ah'm mighty obliged for yr special interest, reckonin, as ah always have, how special a shootin iron you all carry. But ah jest think, these days, these fine fall huntin days, you ought to wad that thar gun of yrs, and try these new-fangled 38 longs they tell me you can get back at the settlement, Brer Wit.

This is just a shot, over the shoulder (look
ma, no hands), no mirror either, pa, just
for the hell of it, now, it's frozen, the sun is,
hyar in these woods

BRO CHARLES

■ ══════════════════════════════════════ ■

Washington *Wed Dec 19 51*

My dear Edward:

by god. by god. that is something! (i have just now read it/ it having been held here for my return—came into my hand an hour ago—and i am tremendously moved.

Here is an act of mnemonics & exactness, all Flaccids & Easies! (And I have no way of knowing whether you knew how particularly I did take offense at this [Newton] Arvin's robberries [Dahlberg's review, "Laurels for Borrowers," re Newton Arvin's *Herman Melville, Freeman,* 2 (December 17, 1951): 187–190]. And that you have exposed him on the public thoroughfare—that it shld be you, who only could do it—this is beautiful

It is a
beautiful thing, looking at it as though I am only the materials for your
wit & corrections
such sentences as, the institute priests are Goya foxes
with pens in their paws
knowledge has become an abstruse fact
the perverse
is now so dominant evil is often called good
It's polemic as that art is needed to
be restored: firm, & inside: inside, both of you and of the texts—that
is so very sure, the care with which you have disposed yrself and these
texts, the firmness of your management of both—the delicacy—the
delicacies
And in that swelling paragraph about the two of us—
(which does seem to me the loveliest of all)—I witness to you that you
are exact, exact & magnanimous. (The pain, too, I can also reinforce.)

It is a huge act, Edward, an act of your own size (a size all of us need
cultivate ((you see, I suffer under a restraint, that yr last word to me
was, Ingrate, the biggest this hyar cuntry might raise
(and i shall
forever suffer under such, from you or anyone, because i was born with
the damndest obsession of all, justice, that ugliest virtue, the
impossible one
(((i have yet to turn the corner of it, to slip out from these
balances, and engage myself, engage myself

So I blush, almost happily blush, with the pleasure & dimensions of
your act, so to praise me in the public domain—not to praise (it comes
to me so, it is close) but to point thus, and say, look: here is this man's
labors, once.

I was full of chagrin these days, peculiarly troubled, bottomwise, and
to have this wine poured straight into my hampered blood stream
makes me giddier than this strange machine's type & drop. It makes me
more dizzy than wild, and you must excuse it if this letter comes out
like quiet ravings. For I am to this degree mad, and you have
straightened it (straightened it like, say, De Quincey says opium made
harmonies where there had only been pains from a wet hair worn
straight to bed in a cold night for 21 days!)

Wld you accept, with this a swipe I took, this fall, at some such same monsters? (in fact, arvin is—as you will quickly note—one of the three I was the most after [*Letter for Melville,* privately published at BMC August, 1951 rpt. in *The Distances* (New York: Grove Press, 1960), pp. 46–64]. And surely, from malice,—not so wide & great as riders like yrself who go on [M?]apple's back, who are capable of living in the large and enlarging same ((my trial is still particulars!

(((and whether this is what joins to my bitch goddess, justice, i do not yet know—i rather imagine this is the connection, this is the foolish search to use oneself as balance

And what does move me) as I say (in this LAURLES FOR BROOWERS is how firm your own value system is (and certainly arrived at by yr own large way, and its endurancies carried out, carried out, worn for so long

((my friend

Another way: it is just such plain pleasure to see such pigs stuck! God damn them (and again i am wry, with so much you and I have experienced—or fr yr point of view, you have experienced—better, not experienced—from the likes of, me)

It comes out all wry.
(((One thing, there, is grand—& peculiar: Bill [Williams?]—I just never cld figure out his story, how much he was responsible for Van Doren & so, [Raymond] Weaver [critic and editor of Melville]

In any case,
I take it as a correction (still bitter, that, Bill could not see me for the Kouwenhovens, of course—which ate then, and eats now, like the whore in Koln,—same time

((You must excuse all the boners this machine has made—& they seem so significant I leave them, like the black back of the Soapine whale only dutch cleansers can do anything with,—not me, who is neither white nor black, nor knows his best scouring powder

Signed, Schliemeihl))

Crazy, nobong, bongo: by god, i say, to be there, in the public print, pt there by you so tellingly: thank you, Edward, for the long arm of your mind & its attentions!

For I feel also this: that what makes it so large an act, is, that I am materials—I am used for others, that, others may also be misued, eh? For surely these must always be fought, must be stuck.

And yr distinction is, that you have stuck em in our time as that like man & yr hero Poe did his work (Melville, like myself, are such who make it all in the margins of their minds, & are too reluctant to be of public good

no, I cannot so enlarge myself—strike it off. Leave it, simply, I do not do as well.

> With old & new love, & new thanks
> that you are more alert than others

> yr
> Olson

◼══════════════════════════════◼

[39½ Washington Square, So.
Apt. 1 W
New York, New York]

December 31, 1951

My dear Charles:

I telephoned you from Florida. A former student of mine took R'lene and me to Sarasota. The piece for the Freeman was too months labor and vexation. One glance at the sodomite book was enough, but to nail him on a thieve's cross at Calvary was another matter. It is done, and now your work cannot be gainsaid or garbled or pilfered. i took pains to see that no less than twenty copies went to Smith College. I know the little academic gnome was bitterly stung; everybody who has read it has said that there was no doubt that I proved that he was a robber. Charles Angoff [critic and literary historian] was very taken with the piece, and so was James Rorty [journalist and Socialist historian]. Well, can you believe any more that the American writer is not some Gadarene devil? But the fight, who else has bothered but me?

I have had a years' battle against Mark Van Doren, the canary Trilling up at Columbia, the albino Fizgerald beadles, the herd academic deacons of grammar [over Dahlberg's reviews in the *Freeman*], and for what purpose? If a few would use a pen as a whip they would go [to] their riggish kennels, but no one will help me.

Now there is the bitter iron agony of bread. Remember, you wrote me that I practice virtues for sums; if so, then I had better seek me a vice. Now, how about your Pound and Williams. Is your nose rough enough for the swill autobiography [*The Autobiography of William Carlos Williams* (New York: New Directions, 1951), containing excerpts from Olson's "Projective Verse" essay in the chapter of that title]? He is for himself, pater pediatrician Williams, that's the great infamy in the Cyclopes of Euripides.

I write you a little this time, Charles, but do not believe this reply is meant to be low-hearted. I wish you would do one thing, go back over the scroll of your life as a writer, and ask your own heart whether anybody has ever been so steadfast to your nature as one Edward Dahlberg, and ask what he has reaped in return, save the only knowledge that keeps him alive, and that he has always tried to tell the truth which people nowadays miscall by the name of slander or malice. Granville Hicks wrote in a letter to [John] Chamberlain [editor of *The Freeman* (1950–1953)] at the Freeman, saying that he should not print Edward Dahlberg, for he was vicious and sick and that the so-called stealths from your book were coincidental, fine word, coincidental, it is so useful and marginal another word for sneaking.

Well, I too send you my love and friendship; if you know of any college that would like a composition handyman around, let me know.

EDWARD DAHLBERG

■ ═══════════════════════════════════════ ■

Black Mt

January 22 [,1952]

My dear Edward:

A man shld show an enormous reluctance to making metaphors out of other men's facts—if one's own are not enough,—or if one's own are only the subjects of one's own sentimentalities—or dedications, then, maybe one would have to extend oneself, and start turning other's children into whales, or equally sleazy parodies.

—how peculiarly you outrage another, and how repeatedly it is by way of the things intimate to them:
                                   how gross this is, you, who wails whenever anything is directed home to yrself, one wld think you wld know. But patently you don't—patently, you do not know that the injuries practiced on you are the injuries you practice:

so you find fit company, find yrself now tallying such creatures as [Lewis] Mumford Angoff & who else
                                   and don't say it is because the company of your naturals is refused you: you refuse yrself their love, & interests, by outrages or rigidities

you shld be so heavy as to be so jocular to a boy like [Mark] Hedden [student at BMC], making metaphors & mock of me, mine, to such a public person, in such a public way:
                                   it doesn't matter, simply, that, you do it, do not feel these immaculatenesses: yes, i'll take the word & wear it, for they are as much my cloth as the same things you have chosen to praise in my one work you do praise, in public (& surely, as i know, in private)

i stand on my thanks to you, for the LAURELS—yet i stayed silent to yr letter from Florida (rec'd last week), simply because i do not know what to do when you count coups
                                   the trouble is, i know & grant you the reasons of yr demarches: i know the same craving for engagement of one's force. Yet this is the double gate which won't go down. And you know the obstruction.
    My sense is, you think the gate is to be tumbled, roared or outraged away.
    I think it is what we are.

It is such a welter, these businesses between us. My silences (which you paw at) are solely I do not know what to do when the skin is the gate, when you put your amour propre on your sleeve—as though mine too were worn there. It ain't.

I made this prayer, today: that you would wear your troubles once again as Lorrie Lewis [Dahlberg's autobiographical protagonist in *Bottom Dogs* and *From Flushing to Calvary*] hath, instead of thinking they could be thrust out on any other body, the society, a friend, a love, any place but where they are, where any of us has em.

I don't believe in wisdoms [cf. Olson's "Against Wisdom As Such" in response to Robert Duncan's conception of the artist, *Black Mountain Review* 1, (Spring, 1954): 35–39; rpt. *Human Universe*, pp. 67–71]. Ultimately, they, too, are slogans—and for this reason, that, staying with one's own particulars, one inhabits, and discloses, all there is to disclose. The sufferings are not to be put off, like an environment. They are not caused.

I believe in laws—and one of them, surely, is that each man does know the state of his own soul. And who's wise—that is, wise enough to get to the other side of despair? The humpty-dumpty of it is each man's: & one either knows & deals with that—one has respect for one's own life—or one doesn't.

I regret to sound like a toothed portcullis. I am not. Yet you do such things you make me so, to keep what I hath.

[ON BACK OF ENVELOPE:] In the midst of this damned Shakespeare go— & hate to break off, to copy! But will, etc.

CHARLES OLSON

■ ═══ ■

[*NIMBUS* LETTERHEAD:]   Nimbus
The Westminster Press. 411a Harrow Road
Editors Tristram Hull • Ivo Jarosy
Business Manager John Scott

October 10, 1954

Dear Charles,—

Do you have any prose or verse you might care to submit. I heard you had done a small treatise on the Donner Tragedy; maybe that might be suitable, as we could reprint it in England. You might have some other work on the early American narratives you are doing. We want something strong. The pay is not very much, a guinea for a thousand words of prose, and something more for verse. Nimbus has a circulation of about two thousand readers, here and abroad, and gets the sort of readers that should entice a writer. We are not interested in publishing well-known nonentities. You may know of some other gifted person. Any suggestions you care to make will be a help. I hope we can serve poets and talented natures, and I shan't mind running after a rare obscurian.

EDWARD DAHLBERG

Black Mountain College
Black Mountain, N.C.

[November 19, 1954?]

My dear Ed:

Your letter, & Nimbus, both in, and deepest thanks for asking me to submit something, as well that I hear from you. (At the time Creeley was starting to edit the Black Mt Review I heard, through Sauer, that you were around there, and asked him to ask you if you cared to send something to Creeley. I repeat. And his address is:

Rbt Creeley
Casa Martina
Bononova, Palma
Mallorca, Spain

. . .

Issue #3 is just in air mail from Mallorca (where we get printing of 750 with 64 pages for less than 250 bucks).

I shall enclose at least a poem (*David Ingram,* one of the Maximus "Letters"). And if anything of a present book on Shakespeare [unfinished; portion of study may include the essay "Quantity in Verse, and Shakespeare's Late Plays" published in *Human Universe*]—just now stumbling—should seem usable, I shall send it. (Such narratives as you speak of are either absorbed in the Maximus, or still shoot out in reviews, rather than in any use from myself, I mean with my own spit put on it).

It's great to submit them to you, but I despair of Nimbus using them [none of Olson's work appeared in *Nimbus*], unless you work a change there. I have read this issue (and noted the contributors to earlier ones), and, except for the [Paul] Eluard poem, take it there is a confusion of the simple with the obvious (or, the obvious with the simple, whichever way it reads right). And a real miss on what is "Old-fashioned".—I guess you are there, and think of me as of it, because there are currents in the position which make sense, viz—the fact of the piece on beans, as well that Jung . . . as well this import of the simple, and the old, in both verse & prose attack & form. But really, Ed! All here is soft, and I mean easy:

the whole problem of the art of artifice, of the restoration of the six other sorts of song (instead of the stupid lyric), the heart of affection, the rediscovery of Afghanistan: not [George] Barker, [   ] Whiting, [Hugh] Macdiarmid, that rotten [Jean] Cocteau.

Christ, I shld bother you with this! You change it. And I can suggest, in addition to Creeley, three others you might care to ask:

Irving Layton	
8035 Kildare Avenue	verse
Cote St Luc, Quebec	
Robt Hellman	
Writing Workshop	stories
Univ of Iowa	
Iowa City, Iowa	
Larry Eigner	
23 Bates Road	both
Swampscott, Mass	

(over)

And two others, Robt Duncan, whom you probably know (address: 1724 Baker Street, San Francisco) who I am "soft" about; and funny open if inefficient verse maker Raymond Souster, 28 Mayfield Avenue, Toronto 3, Ontario, Canada.

(None of these, by the way, with the exception of Creeley, are that conscious of what is going on, but each of them is quite clean about

how he does his own thing. And Layton, I'd say, is the *one* classical
English poet alive, a cross of Donne & Blake, & driving rhyme and
metric straight out from now. Makes the *Nine* gang [London review
edited by Peter Russell], & this splinter group Nimbus is—with the old
exception of Ia[i]n Fletcher, was it (in *Nine*), that most gifted user of
the old discourse system? Ian somebody, who, at last sight, was all
done, was diddling with Maryolatry (like you'd say!), or making
exercise books out of Medieval pictures!

Ok. Excuse me. It's just that the "republic of letters" . . . And the
English, in London, strike me as such journalists, as "arriviste"
(whatever that means!—i mean, late-comers . . .

Pick me this way: like Lawrence
said, the Americans were extreme in 1850! Now they are post-same.
Which is one hell of a way farther along the road than reaction. And
discourse has moved so far off that base of the explicit, without, by
now, being anything but sharply straight

what do those boys think it all is, a either-or? all
epater Pound, Eliot, Empson, back to academicism like Bonamy
Dobree (who once was of use on one of those English "centuries"

The crossing of what's been done with what was done in order to do
what now patently has to be done—it's a matter of feathers and steel,
not one or the odor

La-la! Just a pleasure to write to you. Will shut up, and go about my
bisness, at least copy you the Ingram. And let me know the worst:

surely
the title of your sheet is "a cloud, as of romance, about a person or
thing" (at least that's what I'm saying isn't so easy, and why I wish I
had this job on Shakespeare's late verse & *therefore* dramaturgy ready to
send you, for it would be a fair test run of Jarosy:

romance
ain't easy,
Jarosy

the cloud
ain't rosy,
it is

"uniformly gray and extending

over the entire sky (hey!
JAROSY, calling Herr Professor Doktor
JAROSY! Drop that
nimbus

All love, CHARLES O

PS [IN SCRIPT ON TOP MARGIN OF FIRST PAGE] Robt's letter just in—so will fire this, to get us on   And get to the poem soon. CRAZY the *Wheel!*

[Palma de Mallorca, Spain]

November 24, 1954

Dear Charles,—

Your letter just came, and Creeley whom I like very much should be here in about an hour and a half. The plain truth is, Charles, that I never read Nimbus. I told the two editors it was bad without looking at it. However, I said, if they would let me print real people in strength I would act as editor for America. I told them I was not interested in a magazine that was no more than a torpid anthology, a piddling verse or two by one man, a short story by another, then an essay on Eliot, Pound, Tate or Lionel canary Trilling. Well, I don't know how far they will let me go, but if I can't go all the way, I won't waste my time.

I sent out letters at once, not to every celebrated nonentity in the States, but to people who try as best they can to call A A, a chair a chair, an alley an alley.

Thanks, too, Charles, for suggesting names; everybody except, the knaves of letters, seem to get printed, and those who are having great difficulties, and are in one way or another in limbo, are hard to reach.

I got a fine letter from Josephine Herbst. She can't get a passport to Europe, and asked me whether I would run an essay on her hardships with the state department. I wrote her at once to go ahead with it, only beseeching her to employ early colonial references to show that from the start America was a refuge of bigots, like that scurrile author of the *Simple Cobbler of Aggawam* [Nathaniel Ward].

Now, I am very anxious to get the Shakespeare essay; send the poem or verses too, and if they are as good as you are, you know it will be my delight to print them.

I stayed three days in Paris, and after meeting several fornication prosemen, I quit. It was, besides, very expensive solitude.

Of course, Jarosy has no sense; actually you know more about him than I do. I met him three times, enough to tell him he knew nothing, and wondering how long he was going to pursue it.

Don't worry about the length of the Shakespeare essay; if it is very good, and it ought to be, the longer the better. Besides, we will be able to get some pounds into your pocket.

Don't despair; if I care for the Shakespeare essay, and there is any objection, I'll quit. You know how changeless man is. I am always the same, only more of it.

At this moment, I shall also write to Tristram Hull; he is the son of the Jung translator; he is half-jew, the english in him you can throw away; he is by no means unintelligent, but maybe too shrewd to have a development. Actually, there is also David Wright, an English poet from South Africa, who is also an associate editor. He is a charming weakling, not without talent, but I don't write to anybody but Hull.

After finishing a book which Laughlin says he will do [*The Sorrows of Priapus* (New York: New Directions, 1957)], I found I had two books, and so I may have to expand one, and use the other on the New World, for another volume.

Nimbus has a long piece by me in the forthcoming issue, on Brazil, Peru, the rivers, which are our veins and myths, in South America ["Myth of Discovery: The Americas," *Nimbus*, 2 (Winter, 1954): 38-48, rpt. in *The Sorrows of Priapus*].

If Hull will go along with me, we can somehow or other be a small, compact group, and I'll print ten poems by one versifier in an issue, and not one, so that a reader has a sense of the nature and the physiognomy of the man.

I move, Charles, from the ancients to the New Continent. I don't know how long I shall stay here, the usual flaneurs of the Muses at Palma and Robert Graves who writes for Punch and Jesus.

I read your letter fast, and will have to reread it, but I wanted to get a reply to you quickly, and also to Hull. Even if I go back to America, which I don't want to do, but wherever you go you walk around by yourself, and I am a dirty fragment by myself, I'll still be the American editor.

Meantime, my dear Charles, let me hear from you soon. You have my love and friendship, and if I can get you printed I am not altogether vile dust.

EDWARD

I'm giving you Cook's as an address, for I may move—

E.D.

■ ══ ■

[Santa Monica, California]

December 28, 1954

Dear Charles:—

I wrote to you in reply to your good letter. I fear, however, that my own words were lifeless, and hardly a savory answer to your epistle. But do not think you have not been in my mind. Now, I found that young Hull was quite rapacious, and that he was far more interested in owning a magazine than in bringing out a strong truth. I did not say anything about your kind invitation to appear in the Black Mountain periodical. For one thing, I forgot, and then I have other feelings, which I hope you will understand. We are the lost people of the arts in America. What good will it do us to print our work in a very small clandestine magazine which we have to hand about to indifferent persons to get it read altogether. If you give the mediocre nonentity, (and there are many sensitive, empty people in the world), a book for nothing, he does not read it. He only prizes what he buys, for that is almost the sole recreation in the States. So that by giving a book to a nobody you deprive him of amusement, and he detests you for it. Then what is the average magazine? a laodicean anthology containing one poem, a short story, an essay attacking Eliot or praising Pound. Were there a way of printing a vision, and printing a writer in strength, that would be different. It is necessary to get three or four gifted people together, and they have to have literary scholarship, by which I mean nothing academic. I abhor the subhuman professor of letters.

But to return to your Shakespeare essay. I had been contributing to [P]oetry for over three years. I don't have to tell you that it is pansy punctuation verse. [Karl] Shapiro had taken a long poem of mine, *The*

Garment of Ra, and then rejected it because it was gnomic and not
dramatic [published in *Big Table,* 1 (Spring, 1959): 63–78; rpt. *The
Leafless American*]. Anyway, I saw him in Chicago. I had had a long
altercation with him, telling him I did not care to appear in [P]oetry.
We were quite friendly when I saw him, and I talked about your piece
on Shakespeare. He said he had heard of it, and that it was too long. I
ridiculed him by telling him that he was always refusing good work
because it was too short or too wide, or too broad, or that the sleeves
of the chapters or stanzas bulged, insisting that he take a real interest
in your Shakespeare. Now, he is leaving [P]oetry in a very short time,
going to teach at Berkeley. The plan is this, if it is agreeable to you:
please send the Shakespeare essay to me, even if it is not done. He
won't publish all of it anyway. Let me, if you will, make suggestions,
and then if it has the alchemic ore that I suspect it has, mail it to
Shapiro with my own feelings[.] If we do this, I believe we have a good
chance of getting some portion of it printed. I shall do my very best for
you, as you know, though you have been irked with me in the past, and
imagine, for what reasons, I know not, that I have ever had any base
motives in doing something for you. That there is abundant affection
between us we should both know, and that in some way we are
unalterable kin our very intellectual travels amply indicate. You are
remarkable as speculative granite or water; you are yourself one of the
elements of the Cosmos. You can do nothing that is secret from my
own identity. Without knowledge of your own purposes or reading I
have been reading the Quiche Maya Scripture and diverse other works
on the Incas, the Chicchimecas. I took but a quick glance at the
MAYAN LETTERS and smiled.

There is one other matter: once I said that literature is a gospel of
love, and you took it to mean that I expected you because we are
friends to care for everything I wrote. You must be just, Charles; in all
the years I have known you, and labored for your gifts, I only once
asked you to defend a book of mine, and one which you had already
lauded. Whatever my defects are, I am not Waldo frank; I write the
best I can, and do not think I am modest, unambitious. I am droll
rather than virtuous, and the only reason that I do not make stupid or
gross compromises is that I do not know how. I am not in the habit of
it, and would only be a greater simpleton than I am were I to try.

I have a book done which Laughlin is supposed to do. He has had
the MS for sixteen months, and he won't give me a contract. He is

looking about for an artist to do drawings. He says the book will be a commercial disaster and so he has to get a well-known artist [Ben Shawn], to attract people to look at the drawings and pay no heed to the writing. Should he publish it the artist will do very well and gain more lookers; for this is a picture book century, and the most vacuous people look at paintings because they are too indolent to read.

Laughlin has had a long poem of mine for 2 years for the Annual which now comes out every three years.

What are we to do? Greed and absolute hatred of the mind have eaten up all values. You can alter the state, but not the customs of the people, so politics is not the solution. Everybody on all sides is killing the grass, the rivers, the poems, and demolishing a grange and putting up in its place the garage. No screed will be of help; the sickness is very deep, and the wheel is in the head.

My dear Charles, let me hear from you quickly, and I shall do my very best. Maybe, you have some suggestions. You know how predatory Williams is. We have to form some small cohesive group or each die on top apart.

You have my love and friendship.

EDWARD

Edward Dahlberg
General Delivery
Santa Monica, California
Mail comes to the apartment about two in the afternoon, and for that reason I use general delivery.

■ ═══════════════════════════════ ■

[Santa Monica, California]

August 20, 1955

Dear Charles:—

I am starting a small press [with the writer Richard Newman (pen name Hillel Frimet), published in *Black Mountain Review*; persuaded Dahlberg to join him on Bornholm, Danish island; friendship quickly deteriorated without producing a publishing venture], and am bringing out a book of verse and prose of no more than six to eight writers. I am not interested in anthologies, a poem of six lines by one versifier, a short tale by another, then an essay, all not making a vision, or a truth, giving you perhaps no more than the chaps of one author, knees of another, the jowls of a third.

What happened to the Shakespeare essay? I had hoped to make a magazine of strength of Nimbus. But I cannot do anything with punctuation pathics, rabble aesthetes, and the self-loving Ham of modern letters. You know my experience with Dorothy Norman on TWICE A YEAR, and that for all my labors I could scarce rake out some moiety of the dung of the Augean stables. I had no profit whatsoever from my labors except the publication of Lear and MOBY-DICK. The rest was stubble and hyssop, and I have eaten and drunk both until I reel at Gethsemane which is thinking, feeling, and writing, well, badly, and not at all. What boots it all, and does the Kosmos care one jot one way or the other, and it may be that our cadavers are of more worth to the energy of the Universe than all our scribblings.

I have only looked into the MAYAN LETTERS, but intend shortly to read them. Herbert Read and I are contemplating a book together on modern literature [*Truth Is More Sacred* (New York: Horizon Press, 1961)]. I shall, I pray, be Vulcan's Fire in this, but what with the conclusion of a book, I am now wasted and charred, and this may be a huge brag. But I will try again.

I expect to print some work by Read in this first book. I have already placed an advertisement in the paper, and expect to run notice of the press elsewhere.

It has been my intention to write to Bob Creeley; but again I was glutted with such inertia that to lift my arm some mornings was the burden of Sisyphus, nor have I been able to reach those fruits of Erebus (where else are they, since I cannot find them in the sun), denied to Tantalus.

You may have some suggestions. I hope through Read to have some distribution in London as well as in the United States. The purpose is to bring out work unacceptable to venal publishers, are there any others, a query to the buffoon.

I was appalled to hear that Ann Rita [Frank, intimate with Dahlberg and then Olson in late 1930s] had written to you in my behalf. When I want to relate myself to you in some way or other, and all cleavages between persons is Cain and murder and injustice, I shall do it myself, as I am now doing. I require no vicar either for my gall, or adders, or affections.

You are a part of my memory and experiences, and I can brew nothing in that poor limbeck called the heart, without in some way including you, nor can you do otherwise. There is no gimcrack pride, or Hubris, as the fraudulent academic names it, proving their erudition to the illiteraters on Mt. Ida, which stinks worse today than the brackish waters of Styx, between friends. I can throw a woman away, and be glad to rid myself of this tribe of sots and sins, and look for other Poppaeas to ransack my pores and dreams, but not a friend. Well, let it be as I have said; nothing can be changed.

I should tell you my own relations with Shapiro on poetry was a battle of the books for three years. I could not stomach the empurpled pathics of verse he printed; I never read the magazines to which I contribute; I know better ways to go to bedlam. If I finally was driven by the dingiest political dunciads to do a colum[n] for the fetid New Freeman, I had to appear somewhere, for I grow weary of putting all my work away for rust and moths and epitaphs. Let those who have lied about me know, that one who is not a marxist is not for that simple reason a blackguard, a vassal and ninny of the state. I have published five different articles on Randolph Bourne, but those on the left are as pusillanimous as those on the right. No one will gather up the words and the glyphs from the papyrus and the dust of the sepulchre.

I send you my love, for I have nothing to hoard.

EDWARD

EDWARD DAHLBERG
General Delivery
Santa Monica, California

Wed Oct 19/55

[IN PENCIL SCRIPT:]

My dear Ed

It comes out this way: what is *your* experience of these things, *any* of them, the slightest (the *nasal* I know is keen, & I always heard, the Carmine Street stable or the Rockport fields)—or the largest (say, Indians *you don't know*

And because I don't *hear* you registering *your* queer unique peculiar [dug?] done thing—because I miss that labor—

(and get, instead, these arrogations—what, I take it, have to happen if the scrupulous isn't: you must forgive me my most impolite failure to answer your letter

(my last letter to you some years ago was intercepted by your wife, from whom I received a pious screed in return)

Experience is, isn't it, a lot more guick & unknown to the best of us, than such phrasing & dicta as you give

(& so often *generously* give:

you *are* generous, Ed, that's not at all where you ought to suffer anything I say or do, I am not really I ain't the most ingrate in American letters

I aint in ["]American letters". That's it. That 's what I'm talking about. I'm incapable of a *literary relation*

I can only hear the quietest things—or at least only care for them. And I seem to find you address me too big in a voice. I think that may be fine. In fact, I read everything you write —either to me, or that I see published. That I don't answer—don't make anything of it other than this explanation.

Or attempt at same: that to undo what you yourself don't do takes more than I've got to give. I don't like war between men. Or even believe in it.

So please forgive me.
(Excuse pencil.
Suddenly felt able to say this. And have.)

CHARLES

■ ══ ■

[Black Mountain College
Black Mountain, North Carolina]

November 12, 1955

Look, Ed:

This "portrait" of Olson to Creeley is exactly what I mean, and more of same (as previously to [Mark] Hedden, some form of abuse of Ann Rita, etc): leave me out of it, dig your nose into what *I do,* [in script:] (not am) but if you have a right to talk about—and surely you have—make sure it's me. I repeat: to undo what you don't do is what makes you impossible. And several times outrageous.

I say this impersonally, and would reach it over to you (as my previous note sought to). But I throw up my hands at any chance you'll "hear it" when you take the easy way out and call it incoherent. And something else. As one said: he can't hear you if he don't hear hisself. And how.

I don't give a damn. But I do when you intrude via persons and details which are a part of another man's paradox of experience. Or rather: the "right" to use another man's details depends upon a formal virtue you won't practice; or a fluency I don't find your "portraits" earn. One or the other. And at heart form, and some actuality are both what any of us who are really busy are involved with at this point of the 20th century.

And I would write to you about these matters, to take this occasion to prepare for any examination of you in print which occasion may present. I think you play hob with too many important things in this letter to Creeley to make it any longer excusable to go by it. It was what I meant by not understanding a "literary" relationship. It belongs in print, brother. Let's go there. I believe you ought to, instead of this back-of-my-back traffic. Dig the work, and say you will; but leave my fate to me. It's that intrusion, that back-stairs chattering . . .

For example, your concept of a person: it is taxonomic, and retrograde at a time when context and relevance—motion—is palpably the advantage, and the care, not relationships. You think you can pin me up? But have you asked yourself first questions about the physiology and the psychology of Edward Dahlberg?

Have you?

In any case, I am not a specimen. Or is any man. His quandary is more examinable. And a dumpheap—man's dumpheaps—are more relevant than you seem to wish or dare nasally to allow. A man picks his way, he doesn't launch phrases—or rather, in your case, adjectives and sentences. You don't slam a cortex on a coelenterate and get a sentence, Mister Prose Man. And yet just such sentences are what you make so much of.—Brother, be less memorable! having looked at a basic-basic!

My beef here is your slamming around about vernacular—my "abstract" vernacular, Pound's "glacial"—and who else's what vernacular (?) What's your fear, Mister Man?

Obviously it isn't. It's that you have misled yourself about the nature of language: you think it's vocabulary. The rest of us guess it's for real.

You think it's words. The rest of [us] think it's force. Thus you are drawn up into the head (?) (and talk so much of the viscera?) Again, I burn that you should propose some slackening of my intelligence due to some Marxian ghost which leads me to seek commerce with the people???? wot People???

Baloney, Dahlberg. Look at it. Rub your nose in it. Find out,   Take a look. Lend an ear. Give it a once over—*it,* not you. Try it on, for size.

It's so dull, these prepared fixatives you reach up for to dip the latest in: i think it's you, really, Ed, who ought to ask himself what ambient "laws" you are suffering from, out of the last century—

and don't cry back the mire of veins, or whatever, prurience of any man, etc.: that's what I mean, the Weltschmerz, or whatever Oyrapeenische concept of fate etc

Look. I don't mean to be a drab. Honest I don't. Cross my heart and all that vernacular. But, you know—your counters are such one can only do two things, let em go. Or bite back. And either

doesn't lead to much gain. You are too intelligent. But not serious
enough.

The idea, that you should talk about the "serious" people, and
what they say about Olson.

Wow. How they miss my Swiss who wrote Ish-swish—o, and what a
moral disappointment serious people feel . . .
Blah blah
reawlly, ewward

It's just too damn bad I can't take you seriously
[ADDED IN SCRIPT:] (I can—2½ pages: see
later on in letter)
For another example, Indians (he repeated —my lawd,
Sahagun!

I just won't be able to write it, to write the exegesis and examination

a putting of the clock back to Lord Kingsborough at least, ought
to get,

in the public domain, so that . . . .
do you understand what *damage*
that Nimbus piece on Indians *does* ["Myth of Discovery: The
Americas"]
duz duz duz?
Stand up, Edward, and let's
take some shots at you, you great big white man you

Retrograde: no
wonder you yell the young, you say (i'm glad to hear!) read me. By god,
am I pleased.

Let me try to be serious. Otherwise, this only is no
good. There are two prongs for any man of intelligence who reads to

write (so far as I know there are you and Pound and me, who else?)
Ok. (The others
have better sense.) Bill [Williams], e.g., And Creeley, say).

But if you
are foolish (and so am I) the double prong is scholarship and
vernacular, that combo. And solely for one reason:
the discrete, and the
continuous.
Now
I'll be damned that I can see that you are discrete, either way, either in
hearing yourself or what certainly establishes continuity—others.

Ach: I'll rush to conclusion. It's appetitive words versus
language as precise.

You should ask yourself if a sentence is a
completed/ If so, there ought to be fewer. Otherwise, is a sentence?
I leave you/
in my coherence/
And do leave it—to me. You got your own troubles.
The last thing I want to do is add to them. And I regret, I can't relieve
them—but isn't that the whole thing, that we can't?
So we give each other
something else.
Ok. I'll sign off.

Yrs, with no offence intended. On
the contrary
OLSON

You really murder me, Ed—of course I'd try to break the tablets of
Choreb if you came down with them off the mountain, you Moses you,
you old Moses. My god the last thing we need today is more of those
ritual formularies of dead peoples—you'll be taken up by this newest
religious floating, (you watch out, you'll get that canonization now that
the English milker of anything, that friend of yours [Herbert Read], is a
knight, isn't it?)

You're so foolish, not to come down off the mountain and figure that
some of us can be concerned without wanting a large stiff language of
stones, and self-canonization. —And that just me, and I'm sure some
others, can hear you when you talk sense, as you do in those last two

columns and a half in Nimbus on La Salle.—Or me only that hapless
friend of yours, Charles Olson, is a luminous reader enough to feel
rewarded by those columns for having undone all the glutted sentences
from page 38 to that point—and capable of knowing that those two
columns and a half are worth calling to anybody's attention (like he
fought his way through the mss of BONES and set some order there—
like he was the first who tried to publish SODOM, here, with Nick
Cernovich——you ingrate, you!)

it's absurd: i thank you and I'll tell anybody read Dahlberg on La Salle
and the French to see the only drawing of a picture of the condition of
the white man as he entered the condition of the North American
continent

and there's a thickness to this seizing which I'm too sensitive not to see
you have accomplished—had to accomplish—by all that *wrong* loaded
weighing of Indians versus Jews-Greeks-Egyptians, and, in two
instances, Europeans, in the previous 9 pages BUT

                                        are we or are we not in a free
and paradoxical enough *passage* for such a discrimination to be made,
and to be used????
        I mean, can you see that you do load the continent as Indian
        versus man as ancient, and wrong the former by scoriation—
        and man with him—; and wrong the latter by sentimentality
        about how human life was then??
        don't you see how it is your own *selection*, which loads, and
        weighs in so that there's a cancellation, both the Aztec-Incan
        people (all you do use of the Indian), and a selection of the
        ancient which is as stereo as just those "classical" people, and
        not any others—and not even them in their density???

To hell with that. That is, I don't hope to argue you. Nor do I care, just
because if you have to do it that way, It's ok with me if, finally, you give
me this La Salle passage
                        —plus, by the way, the little lovely undone
moment of the humans and the saurians each on a side trying to rifle
the tortoise of either his eggs or his flesh on one of those South
American rivers

(If it's ok with me, I don't think it follows that it's—or ought to be—ok with Edward Dahlberg. He, too, shares responsibility for the government of words and the exercise of the forms of language. And if they aren't in his care, then there is loss the rest of us feel

It's crazy how, in those last two columns and a half, suddenly because you aren't *claiming* anything (what burns me up about the way you write letters about me to others, or, for that matter, to myself—claiming fate . . . . which is also what you are doing about both the Indians and the Ancients from page 38 to that point, page 47)—suddenly that deadly scale (which cancels everything, and immobilizes your sentences—makes them stones

    —god's arm is a stone separating the sheeps from the gooks—)

thank god suddenly that scale is down and dimensions of actuality return, the time is not a fraudulent copulative present but *the* time that North America (note, specifically, *North* America, the actual America you know, Lorrie Dahlia [   ] and Edward Dahlberg) N. America, was a *new* place—to a white man, mind you, and specifically a Northern European white man (a Frenchman, or, John Smith—even you throw De Soto and Cortes into a Florida sphere);

                        and space, that is, that precise but limited moment of space, when the land was unpeopled and pussley hadn't yet started to come back from San Francisco where it had been carried by the earliest Spanish ships—and from, interestingly enough, Phoenicia (pussley is a Semitic plant!)

                well, in that thickness, for the first time, what I think you must take to be your Cherubic (pardon, I mean, Chorebic truths, work:

            viz, who the hell has said anything as good on a crucial involvement of anyone of us right now than you, via La Salle, that

CHARACTER, FREE WILL AND DESTINY ARE THE SAME
                     Put that on stone.

And 2nd: NEED IS A GOD WILL GIVE MAN SOMETHING TOILING WITH CHANCE
                That will make a hieroglyph too

These are apothegms a man of the present can use. To me your question has to be, that all the others—I count 23—from page 38 to 47—don't. That's loss.

And I damn well think that the young, or your ungrateful friends, will know that loss. I won't, myself, for one, let them miss, however, the last two columns and a half—he said, boastfully—ah, boastful man

Oh Ed, really, in our vulgar speech, come off it
and glad to have had these words
with you!

ta—ta
CHARLES

■ ══ ■

[P.O. Box 138
Santa Monica, California]

November 16, '55

Dear Charles:

Thanks very much for your remarks about the La Salle and also for your prodigal misgivings regarding the other parts of that segment in Nimbus. I am not a maudlin primitive as you think. [SENTENCE UNDERLINED BY OLSON, WITH PENCILED REMARK, "What, possibly, could lead him to think I think this?"] Moreover, I do not claim to know the Indian. I imagine Sahagun knew more about him than you or I. Again, many of the monks did not profess to perceive the Indian. Diego de Landa is concerned with ritual, and that is my principal involvement. All this extra-human knowledge of other people seems to me very sentimental. What I want to do is go To Beginnings. It is preposterous to believe that Quetzalcoatl is not in part Phoenician, Basque, or a Syrian Atlas. Do I know? No.

I have found great fault with your vernacular because I do not believe it nourishes either the faculties or the fingers, the foot, the arm, or the belly. I thought your poem in the Black Mountain Review disgraceful. [OLSON NOTES: "O'Ryan, obviously"] Why you throw off something of that sort I cannot tell, except that you must have some wanton appetite to *shit* upon yourself. Now, your reference to my responsibility for the government of words is exceedingly good. I have such a burden, and do not pretend that I can always fulfill it. How often I fail I do not know either. [OLSON NOTES: "Can you ever? Boastful man!"]

As you know, and I, my work always requires excisions; I should be grateful to you if you would tell me, in a way that will lead me to particular transgressions of this kind, what sentences you find either bad, or worthless, or overburdened. Some other writers, who have seen the entire MS. feel quite differently from you. That I hardly offer as a reasonable claim for their value. Anyway, as always, I find nothing so hard as to write one good sentence. How much skill can one ever acquire. If you write very plainly you may be empty, or if you take the hazards that I do, foolish, bathetic, tumid. Longinus is far more satisfied with those writers who take great chances than with those who avoid all risks.

Since I had a great deal to do with your beginnings as an author I am naturally concerned with your own intellect. What I said to Creeley is the truth; you may not like it, and neither do I. When I became the friend of a remarkable young obscurian and did all within my powers to teach him to be a writer, I had no thought that I would ever call upon you to defend my work. As I did so only on one occasion, and since you refused, giving me sophisms instead of plain human answers, I had cause to name you a huge ingrate. I had given you lavish homage in two books only to receive in return perversity, and a great reluctance to protect the man who had been your buckler for many years. Were the book bad, and had it for that cause brought embarrassment to you, then that would have been a difficulty you could not expel. But on the contrary, you had written me numerous letters about it, giving me exceptional credit for many many pages. How was I to understand that. Yes, I accused you as a marxist of betraying me, and shooting my book to death, as so many of that infernal sect have done. I had fallen into infamy among these mad laborites of Union Square, and they had persecuted me, had seen to it that no book of mine would be reviewed, had offered free legal aid to my former wife, and you stood by, and observed the spectacle, pretending that what I wanted was to be in the big business of literature. I never will, Charles; I kindle too many antagonisms for my literary and human beliefs. As for being old Moses on the mountain, I care not a straw for such foolish talk. I am too often on the ground; either when I study, or write, or after I have finished a book, or a poem, not knowing whether it is good or bad. One of the most crass and unlearned books I have ever read is Pound's Guide to Kulchur. Now I lament that sort of street barbarism. I don't go to a book to find out what I already know. I know more about the language of the gamin than you, and if you doubt it, read your butchered syntax, which you imagine is the speech of the people, and then go to Bottom Dogs. But do not think I am speaking boastfully of that novel. I will take Piers Ploughman or Chaucer for my speech, because I don't think that the scrabbled gutterals of an auto mechanic are as savory or have the same moral or human weight as the words of a rustic or any bumpkin living before the machine, the cartel, and the big inhuman cities came as the black angel to every nation.

The desire to degrade music, sounds, English, rites, art is a scatological one. I believe you share in this malady. You may deny it, and I have no particular joy in charging you with it, but it is your burden. I don't think you are serious enough in the Mayan LETTERS. I think all those prattling references to Connie which are all right in your familial household but of no worth to a reader or to your line, are self-spoliation. Now, I have not by any means read the book, but intend to; I saw some fine speculative ore in passages here and there, and then that fossilized jargon which Pound so fatuously uses. He knows even less about the streets than you do.

Yes, I go back to Babylon, Egypt, to the Indus, always searching for the beginnings; it will bring me much woe, and maybe, mutilate sentences. At times, I look at an improper adjective and expire in a blush. I have said many times that the writer cannot be wildly alone, and not make mistakes that a simple proof-reader could correct. The trouble is we don't even have the proof-readers any more. What with the dying out of artisanship the sentence is ill-made, or amateurish.

I don't care for literary relations. I am a friend or I don't bother with people, and that includes you. You take on airs telling the man who reared you as a writer about having an artistic correspondence with him. That's all right for pederasts and self-seekers, but not for me. I still think, which is quite naive when I do it, but realistic when you do so, that we write books to create a polity grounded in affection. I am a portable tomb out here, and I don't need your epistles, often half-crazy, and on occasion shot through with some burning truth, to kindle the cold hearth in my soul. If I brought you into the world to be a writer now to prate to me about literary relationship, then I committed another grievous error. When you needed me, I did not say to you, you are ambitious, vain, self-loving and turn my back upon your petition. No, I said to you, Charles, you are fancy, precious, a peevish Narcissus, but I will help you. This difference between us makes for literature; you imagine you are coming down to the multitude by your use of jargon which they know better than you. I am not so pretentious or mad. You feign to write for yourself alone; I say simply, but forlornly, I write, and I am alone.

You imagine that being gross is an assertion of your vitality; my reply is that it is gross to accept a kindness from a man who has been your friend for so many years without even troubling to write him even a few words of thanks. I see, you hanker after friends, too, but the young are your fancy, because they cannot find out your faults as readily as I can. It is my duty to be of help to any gifted man in this terrible voiceless wilderness. Don't make a mistake about me. I'm not on my way toward that ugliest of all bournes, success. I fly from that word as I do from styx, perfidy, the lust of money, and from those who pretend that they have been friends when they have been enemies. You have been my enemy, Charles, all the while that I was your friend. In your earliest days you could not bear to have me say something true before you had said it. I had warned you about that. It may be that there is genuine understanding of flaws in what I write about the Indian. I do not know; but I think there is the same fligitious jealousy. We are always happening upon the same material, together or apart, the loadstone draws us.

I don't think, either you have to be a marxist or a political blackguard. Again, as I told Bob, your friend, and I want you to understand here, that if necessary, I shall leave off writing to him, if that interferes with your literary relationship with him? I should, myself, rather call it a friendship for I think that is a much more wonderful word for it.

I don't think you have much self-knowledge. When I suffer from the pangs of solitude I do not say what I need is a literary or an artistic connection. I say I should like very much to talk to a man who cares for conversation.

Let me ask you, and can you reply truthfully, and without evasion, why did you refuse to defend THE FLEA OF SODOM? Do you believe that after your bitterness over the mistreatment of CALL ME ISHMAEL, and my own generous words about it in my book, that your disavowal was just, decent, or friendly. Was it not the act of a foe, perhaps a man who did not know it, or might have been horrified had he realized it. As a result of the interment of my books which goes back as far as 1940 I have known all the hurts by the river Cocytus. What bread, little as it is, was stolen from me by those assassin book-Cains, the communists, and with your help! You can't deny it, because your acts prove it. You were always furtive with me, and I was always open with [you?]. You could not tell me you were a marxist, as though that would have mattered to me, had you been my steadfast friend. Yes, I have known all the hells of ostracism, but don't think I shall be dormant, or a supine antagonist. Speak of guilt by association, do you know Joshua Kunitz [critic, translator, Russian historian], a person who was once second in my heart after you, was told that he would be expelled by the party if he were seen talking to me. Take heed, Olson, the prudential Celt. Yea, he and others, I mean Kunitz, could review books in the Herald Tribune, and when a book of mine was published, the marxian myrmidons saw to it that my book was thrown into Limbo. You saw to it too; for you were one of them. Do you imagine that I would take bread out of the mouth of Kunitz who had been my friend. Nay, but you took it out of mine, not only the crust we cast upon the waters, but something far more valuable, the justice in our marrow, something that drives us on to other planets, and into inward spaces we believe may lead us to ALPHA, LOGOS OR GOD. Bah, sentimentality, mysticism, primitivism, but I stand by it, and when the day of reckoning cometh, let us see who has observed that "government of words" more obediently, you or I. The books already written are the reply. You can do it, if you will throw down your affectations, all those prissy verbalisms about being literary. The reason you want a literary relation with me is that you are furtive; you want only intimacy with some one who gives you big physiological ease; that's what everybody wants in this false polity. So long as there are no friendships, and people refuse to call love by the plain name that it is, we will be doomed as a nation, and our literature won't be worth more than that infamous poem of yours, or all the XYZ nonsense, or all that kind of congealed alphabet strutting. Go back, I tell you, to your speculations, & write about them as well as you can, never mind the people, or marx, or antimarx, use the books you have ransacked. You tell me I am not serious, are you droll? You damage your lines repeatedly because you want to be the vernacular clown or to be the jolly outhouse versifier, it gives you, you think, the common Touch. Ay, Touch, could you have but understood it, why you might have made some of my mistakes which appeared in that miscreant magazine, called Nimbus. Ay, fox, did you get into that periodical?

My principal charge against you as a human being is that you are a self-lover, my complaint about you as a writer is that you deliberately refuse to find out what element is yours and to work in it. Sure, you will make as many errors as I do, but you will come out with a truthful book, and not with a page and a half poem every year or so. Now, you know I hate the cult of size, but it is time to reveal your nature. It's no good going down to Guatemala, and I don't care who you went down for, and then after imaging that you are a pristine Quiche Maya, and that Kingsborough is just too niggling for you, you do another little diary. What makes you think that John Lloyd Stephens [wrote *Incidents of Travel in Central America, Chiapas, and Yucatan*, 2 vols. (New York: Harper & Brothers, 1841); and *Incidents of Travel in Yucatan* (New York: Harper & Brothers, 1843), both listed in bibliography of *Mayan Letters*] is better than Kingsborough or Sahagun. I found him a great bore; sure the drawings by [Frederick] Catherwood are very good, but what do I mine? Are you sure you have a better understanding of the Inca than Garcilasso? If so, produce the book, and stop prattling.

Well, Charles I'll take your corrections when you cease being arty with me? I said all this comes out your craft; you know you are very surreptitious. That is why you made acknowledgements to me on page 87 or 89. You can't be forthright; that is why you never told me you had a child; you like to have secrets; for some reason you feel they enlarge your nature, dilate your life which is as pathetic and as monstrous as my own. [IN OLSON'S HAND IN MARGIN: "the *Bastard:* no thanks."] You also want to sting a man whose greatest blemish was that he spent all of his time trying to help you.

Now, it is my right, even in a land where liberty is the word in black mouths, the marxist as well as the reactionary orifice, which has confounded a whole people, and made every body either suspect or an informer. I did not complete that sentence, but I say I shall talk about you if I feel so minded, and it really is none of your business. If you want to pillory me for making wrong assertions about our friendship that is your affair. What you do with your wife, or your child (I am glad that of the two of us, you at least have not been deprived of your son, and here again the communists entered into my private life), or with other women, I do not talk about. But what you did to me is quite another matter, Charles. I know you as you were to me; I do not know what you are to Bob. I am sure you are his friend just as you were not mine. We were involved with one another for too many years for either of us to pretend that it has not weighed upon us very heavily. The reason I did not reply to your first letter is that I could not understand it; besides, I had great doubts that you could ever be sincere with me, and avow the many wrongs you had done to a man who had been your benefactor. Who can pardon the man who has conferred as many benefits as I did upon you, o my quondam friend.

You also have a word here, gooks, which I do not know. Is there such a word? Or are you again being your own gull. Why help nature; you'll be a fool enough without mimicing an ass, you or I.

At least there is Black Mountain, one of my most paltry gifts to you; still you were in my heart, and your plight, when I even bedevilled you to spare you all the ills and wrack of your commonwealth. Tell me, simple man, what do you have to do for a man to make him hate you; give him gold, shirts, ducats, boats; 'tis dangerous. Be aloof, assume the stony visage; he might freeze, go screaming shirtless. Suppose you wound him, wound him in a mortar, tear out his tongue; will that fetch him? Is it true that if we clothe and feed a man we sow dragon's teeth?

One last word: have the greatest reverence for your own GIFT; don't meddle with it, let it come through; are you water, be it, as I think you are; the deluge is your Sin, work in it, in a good, clear language, do not be empty, or slyly plain.

EDWARD

■ ═══════════════════════════════════════ ■

Black Mt *Nov 18 / 55*

My dear Edward:

It's a very great relief to know that it was my failure to do anything about THE FLEA which lies behind that word ingrate you have thrown at me now so many years. And for the simplest reason: that that was the moment, that it was my time to speak, and that I spent—was it six weeks, in any case I have the pages and pages of it—doing exactly what I took it I was beholden to do, do a review.

I honestly cannot follow how you see me a part of a Marxian conspiracy against you over that book—or over your separation from Winifred. If you recall, as of the latter, I appeared in court on your behalf in New Rochelle—in other words acted according to my own lights. I mention it solely that I did not—found myself unable—to finish and publish any review of THE FLEA by the same process: my own lights. (My letters to Creeley at the time fully corroborate the effort I made to deal with THE FLEA in the way I took it I was the one to do it.)

I know now, from the Nimbus piece, where I was stuck on THE FLEA. (Yet if I hadn't gone at THE FLEA sentence by sentence, taking each one apart, as well as I might, in all the ways a sentence is composed of all the things it is made up of—including the unknown language each of us, any of us, is an agent of, willy-nilly;—I'd not have been able to find out how to find the LA SALLE passage, and how to see that it exists despite the total rest of the Nimbus pages.) It was this difficulty—*and no other*—which prevented me.

And if you weren't seeking some more suspect reason, like conspiracy, you might, Edward, have asked or found out that my reason was my own—as, for example, you so easily throw down the O'RYAN thing in BMR without asking yourself why a man of an order you do respect might so patently say shit!

It's either this rush, Pell-Mell, or some pre- which is such a missing of another person, Ed, that the other person says, come/ off/ it. Literally.

You ought very quietly to ask yourself, how right are you—at least about those whom you do have a considerable notion they are serious.

I wish one could exchange perceptions with you on the vernacular. Like I say, with scholarship, it's the pincer one wants today to get at matters. But if you mistake the O'RYAN, it's hopeless: of course you'll think I share a "desire to degrade music, sounds, English, rites, art," and that sd desire is a scatological one: who could stay with *the substantive* of the present and not appear so—*substantively?*

But to leap off the substance to whatever you do (Egypt, Judea, etc.) *is* that the greater risk? Longinus' "greatest chances"?

Paul Christensen　　■　　223

Ask yrself some *first* questions in your search for
beginnings

That is, I can not be so interested in what you do
there on La Salle without recognizing that there is attention, and
achievement on your part, on "beginnings"

And of course you and I often
come to the same things and places, because I am also interested in
beginnings

But do I need to stress to you that there [are] several sorts of
beginnings? And that the question of *origin* is as subtle as the
morphological one? I could write an essay on you on La Salle just in
terms of what Alpha of what "great waters"

The discrepancy is great between us if, as you write
in this letter, it does square away that "I have been your enemy all the
while you have been my friend".

I guess you are in an all or nothing
proposition.

Here, for me, it's the same as I found it in THE FLEA and
have said it to you as of the Nimbus: I can love the La Salle part, and
desire to say why; and I can find you so wrong in all the rest of it, so
importantly wrong that, like I say, because I think these are important
matters, find that if I had to say anything in print about you I'd have to
try to say why and how I think you are wrong.

And I *don't want to.* Can't
you see that?

In other words, just making it black and white, you
stiffen it against any one else. You begin, & also end up, Edward, with
a whole system, an applied and appliable system. And it's too much: a
man has got to do more than you do, in the *first* instance, than
throwing up your hands *afterward:*

I am referring to a knot about you which one does have to
undo because you haven't. I mean these declarations that *after* the
writing, for example, that you don't "know whether it's good or bad",
that you have been "foolish, bathetic, tumid", that you are "wildly
alone". They are the most devilish sort of dodgings behind which you
throw yourself because they are *true* for any man. But your use of them,
as a black against a previously stated white, makes you right for a

wrong reason. Or something. I'm not trying hard enough to say it. But it's there.

And it's there when you call me your enemy while you call yourself my friend. I'm sure we are both.

But the fact that you will have it this way puts stones up. For it isn't an either or.

Or at least my own vision of experience don't find it that way.

That's what I mean by the discrepancy.

And as a result of this discrepancy I find all you reply about "literary relationship" rant. I don't want to. For inside it is much that is true, and feeling, evident, honest feeling.

But it's *loaded*, Edward. As wrong as it's right. And the wrong you won't ask yourself. So the right can't be dealt with [ADDED IN SCRIPT WITH ARROW:], can't be *used*, by the person—honest it can't.

You got me set up a certain way. I ain't that way. But I'm not not that way because of the reasons you then go on, by the same stone and black-white, sticks, and system-premises, to apply   That is, you set it up, Edward. And then you deal with it as you've set it up.

Or if suddenly the difference—the discrepancy—from how you'd have it confronts you, you wash yourself out by cries of "of course I fail", or, I am "wildly alone".

And of course you damn well don't wash yourself out. What washes out is the very thing you've removed in the first instance—a little of the life of the thing, whether it's *what you are writing about* or *to whom you are writing*

Of course they are *one thing*. Friendship is one thing. Etc. But if it doesn't go the way you, Edward, want it, it isn't therefore only two things. Or one of the two explanations. Only choice is binary. The rest has a good chance of being *multiple*.

"Pangs of solitude". And how. Plural. And for each man *many*.

You ask me, why did I not "defend" THE FLEA. It wasn't, for me, defense. I didn't know it had to be defended. I don't think I ever have seen, to this day, anybody anywhere saying anything in print about it.—My sense was, one person, Charles Olson, ought to speak of this book in print.

Do you have, now, the truthful reply you ask for, and without evasion, why I did not finish and publish just such a piece on it?

Please tell me where I "disavowed" the book?

Please tell me exactly how it turns out that I am a Marxist?

Please tell me by what act I kept FLEA—"saw to it", is your word from being reviewed?

Please tell me, Edward, what you are talking about—how I "took" bread out of your mouth"?

The facts here just have to be facts [ADDED IN PENCIL SCRIPT:] For god knows if there are facts—& I suddenly remember some letter from a New Directions secretary (!)—then the more I should want you *directly* to know all I did do, & why I didn't finish.

God damn you really. You make it such a shame that I ever accepted anything from you. Why do you have to do this, sad man? Why do you have to paw over everything until the other person can't even retain what they valued? What a destruction.—I don't really want my life if it is to be confused by you as as pathetic and monstrous as your own. If it is to you, I say go aside, go aside. Leave what was.

It is so *indiscrete*, what you do and say with *everything* which has happened between you and another person—everything. It is a *dirtying*, Edward, which I wish you knew was so, and knew to stop it.

And it is for this reason that I say you don't have the right that you so grossly say "you shall talk about me and it is none of my business". It is, when you use what you know because you were my friend; and because you use it now for frustrate purposes. You ought to get yourself clear here. You ought to. Mind me, Edward, get clear about what is my business, and what's yours. It's possible. And it's important. I know when you are hysterical, Edward. We both do. And what happens. Things you say here are of that order. Don't say them. Really, don't. To me, or to others. Remind yourself.

I respect your distinction that it is what I am supposed to have done to you. Of course you must speak of that.// But let it be clear *what I did do*. These are facts which better be accurate, what you claim I did, to Creeley or to anybody else.   //but stick to
it. I want my
fate out of it:
yours, is your
business. Mine—
well . . .

It just comes out such a *shame* that you must prate and orate when there is so much can happen, and to be done, and there is such little time in which to do it. And because you have to have it *large* you make even what does or has happened *waste, straight loss*

  your *words*, Edward, your words: consider them
  It is such a *shame* not to be able—because you won't let it—to stay *interested* in you. That's *a loss.*

                              Make what you will of it,
  [signed] CHARLES OLSON   but I don't want to sign my name

[POSTSCRIPT:]
       Yes I damn well do because I intend you shall not get your hands on it nor demand any more than I wish now—you make me wish—you didn't in praise of anything I did or was.
  In the same year as *Flea*—1950—in a piece of my own in *Poetry New York* I acknowledged you as what you gave me as of writing. And that piece today has increasing circulation. And WC Williams reprinted part of it (including you) in his *Autobiography*. If I was engaged in some conspiracy to be silent about you, why did I do that?

                              [Santa Monica, California]
                                    November 24 '55

Dear Charles:

  Most of your letter is very quiet, and I read that portion with sympathy. You find it hard, Charles, to comprehend very simple words, although you are much given to the vernacular. When a man tells you he is hungry, don't ask him whether he wants a rock, a piece of water, or a bivalve? Give him bread, and if you have more, a pair of gudgeons. When I wrote to you that I was wildly alone, I am saying that I had at one period, when you forsook the man who had conferred more benefactions upon you than any one in the earth, I had in my sorrow not a soul to turn to. You are poor, but you only relished my companionship when I could give you benefits, my table which was yours at any hour.
  If you want to forget my multifarious kindnesses to you, you can, but

the furies will pursue you, and it is my own feeling that there is no stone for you to rest upon just as there was none for Orestes.

You are my great champion in one line in those two pages of yours reprinted in Williams' Autobiography. Do you expect me to be overcome. There are many loaves, and getting our work printed is a bread you and I sorely need. The Flea of Sodom was buried by marxists and homosexuals. You are an advocate of communism, as you have proclaimed in your writing, and I never knew one stalinist to defend my work. A weak friend is far worse than a stalwart foe, and though you could write me many letters on the Flea of Sodom, you found it impossible to print your feelings. Why not? If you think that the mangled people in Guatemala have no other hope save in communism, you say it quite clearly, and not in a private letter which no one is likely to see.

When I was one of the co-editors of TWICE A YEAR who profited by it, you or I? Was i forthright in your defense. Did I not throw away any advantage I had, and which I needed so urgently, to see to it that LEAR AND MOBY-DICK was printed, and not just furtively admired by me. You have to be plain about simple acts, otherwise you won't amount to much as a writer. I was *never* your adversary, although I am glad that you acknowledge that you were mine. I am not happy to know what apostasies you are guilty of; I am only *glad* to know the suffering truth. When you were in severe trouble in your relationship with Joanne [   ] my apartment and table were yours, and also these rocks at Engeddi to which David fled from Saul. Do I tell the truth? When you wanted a Guggenheim fellowship, I did all in my power to get one essay you had done into the hands of authors whom you respected, and the strategy worked. Did it occur to you that it was a rueful irony that though I could succeed for you, that no foundation will give me a pence for my labors. I am older than you, deeper seasoned in books and at least a journeyman in tribulations, but I cannot achieve the advantages I could make available for you. Despite my fracas with Dorothy Norman, and on your account, you continued your connection with her. I regard that as low and shrewd. I broke with her over you, but you were clever enough to go on because she was useful to you, although by then she abhorred me. I was such a fool in my friendship for you that when you told me that she had practiced an outrage upon you by making you pay a $2.50 taxi fare, even for such a small matter I fell into a passion with her, and was told by Stieglitz and her that I was trying to blackmail her! You know what was the blackmail; when I resigned I asked her in return for a year's service, without pay or publication, to print your work and three essays by Marsden Hartley.

When Do These Bones Live appeared, you were regarded as too green and callow by the ruffians of the Muses to do a review of my book? and I never asked you to do anything of that sort? Only once, when I saw that my very life as a writer was imperilled by the communistic roustabouts and the pathics did I appeal to you to come to the defense of a book you said you fervently admired. What happened? You were bold enough in your epistles to me, and wrote me eight to ten typewritten paged letters about that volume, but precious and too pusillanimous to be my buckler. [ADDED IN SCRIPT IN MARGIN:] Laughlin asked for a statement for the bookjacket, & my *friend refused!* Were you Iago, the jackdaw! Be plain; what were you. It is you, not I, who stand before Minos, in all my life, I know no one to be so base.

So few reviews of the volume appeared that ever since it has been a great travail for me to get published. Williams had done a prodigal encomium on the Flea of Sodom, and when it was sent to Margaret Marshall, a marxist, who ran a graveyard bookreview section in the Nation, she said that I was not important enough to receive such attention. As I told you, Harvey Breit was another burial-croaker. He [STRUCK OVER: ALSO] even said that he admired certain reviews I was doing then for the New York Times, that is, he admired them, but did not publish them. Would you call him a deceiver and a poltroon? Or can you only understand your own pains, and shun such words when it applies to others and may make you uncomfortable. If you really believe you were my friend, when I had fallen into the gutters, then, my quondam friend, you are doomed. So long as you adhere to this falsehood you will never do another book to equal some of the very lovely pages in CALL ME ISHMAEL. It cannot be, Charles; there is retribution; this I know, and have come to such poor understanding by having my flesh and soul torn out each day. Is this humble speaking, or would you like to believe that I mean something else. You see I do not fall into the short-hand orthography of the grossest businessman, and call this lettering artistic, original, or the people's language. How can you invent words with which to betray and gull the populace and say it is their tongue. What a cloven tongue it is? I abhor Ezra Pound, and look upon those miscreant books of his as more degenerate and reactionary than any tyrant can be. I am not a marxist, but I do not consort with Jew-baiters, or Hitlerite journalists of Hippocrene. No sir; I do all that I can to make my words and acts equal to one another, and if what I write is at odds with what I am, then both are lies.

You say you do not want to sign your name to the letter to me. Are you so foolish as to believe that your epistle is not your signature. And why this species of insolence with the man who has always been your friend and teacher. Even up to a few months ago I was doing what I could to relieve your plight. Now, that you do not care to acknowledge, that, and see in my reminding a man whom I have served that he has been perfidious, and not say that I pile shame upon an affection which you took when it served you, and threw away, when you imagined that I was no longer useable. The truth is you have some real vulpine blood; your properties are mixed, and betraying is a kind of artistic cunning that appeals to you. You thought, perhaps, that I was done for as a writer. Ay, many mistakes I may make (I remind you that I mean just that, put the words together as they are said, and they mean, [I wr]ite, and commit more errors than I can surmise); but don't depend upon my being a torpid failure, unable to be of use to you or any other man. Only nature will be my final defeat, and that, too, may be my triumph; then, without all this alloy of youth, you can say the words about some book of mine, you may happen to care for, without really imagining that I ever gave you a shame that you had not brought for yourself.

[IN SCRIPT:] Thought to include this [ARROW]

Now, I take no exception to any criticism you may want to make of anything I do. I should like to be able to understand what you are saying, which I must tell you very strongly that I don't. I can read the masters but cannot comprehend you. I don't think, either, you should make much of a very bad poem in the Black Mt. Review; just don't print that species of foolishness again if you can help it. When you want to write on the Quiche Maya, do a very earnest job on it, and don't bring out as a book ill-assorted thoughts, and uncreated ideas you hurried into the hands of a sensitive young man as a serious labor of your intellect. If you can write better on the Indians than I can, let the earth bless you, for the ground is very corrupt, and the dust we call books is an evil vine.

I could be lofty with you when you threaten me that you might lose interest in me and my work. But why should I? Since you are not my friend, why should I hanker after you as a reader? Will a man, who cannot give you his affections, ever be a friend of your thoughts? Books are wondrous pythian oracles when they are loved, and parched prophecies, when they are read by those who secretly hate us. Now, Charles, do as you like. That is your life. Again, you must forgive me, but I will not write about your intimacies with women, or whether you have done this or that nonsense with some doxy; that is your comedy and woe, and I hope you are lucky. My relation with you, and how ill you guerdoned me for a heart plagued by your every mishap, that, Charles, is my hyssop and should I choose to drink the bitter herbs or water alone or with another, is my own portion and right.

As for a literary relationship with you, or anybody else, I prefer the passions of a Horatio for Hamlet than some ice-cold and epicene epistles from a man who watched me suffer on the curbstones of New York, disavowed by the hacks of Grub Street and the diseased politicals; instead of honoring the man who had been his father by asking him to be his guest for a week-end now and then, gave me for a hearth, a table, & warm, loving talk, a letter; ay, the letter killeth the spirit, and the friend.

Do I speak sense, or would you be so ridiculous as to call this ranting, or how, pray, does one say to you, I am hungry, feed me, I am alone, give me your hand, I am derided, do not pretend that this is an abstruse phrase. Yea, yea, I know a little about the heart, but enough that I can never know it; just enough to understand when it is open and when shut, when good and kind, when clandestine.

I sign my name as I always do in a rebuke, in love, in sorrow.

EDWARD DAHLBERG